PRAISE FOR
A Full Cup

"The world's first businessman-celebrity—a showman-entrepreneur . . . like Donald Trump, although Lipton's appeal was far greater. The book's most compelling passages explore the origins of Lipton's genius as a marketer, not just of products but also of himself. . . . Nicely crafted."

—*The Wall Street Journal*

"It is clear from this account that there never was a more passionate competitor, but equally never a more gracious loser. And his failed quest drew great admiration and sympathy. . . . *A Full Cup* celebrates a remarkable man: a great philanthropist and entrepreneurial tradesman, blessed with style, flair and, most of all, great spirit." —*The Washington Times*

"Just as *Seabiscuit* captured the imaginations of many readers who didn't really care about horseracing, *A Full Cup*, turns the life of grocer and tea entrepreneur Thomas Lipton into a thrilling story you won't be able to put down. . . . *A Full Cup* tells the story in a breathless style that will keep most readers racing through D'Antonio's account of this extraordinary character." —*Connecticut Post*

"This story of a Scotsman who was born poor in Victorian Glasgow and ended up a self-made millionaire, adventurer, and sailing legend would seem the stuff of fiction. But Michael D'Antonio has written a bracing biography of the man who can be called the original Richard Branson . . . A charming and popular businessman founded the global tea empire that still bears his name, but Lipton's unsuccessful attempts to win the America's Cup, the renowned yachting trophy, were what endeared him to the public on both sides of the Atlantic and made him a true celebrity. A genial man who carefully cultivated his public image without letting ego rule him, Lipton was an innovative businessman, philanthropically minded, and well-liked from the slums of New York to the palaces of Europe, all of which D'Antonio captures with aplomb." —*The Daily Beast*

"An enjoyable book about a larger-than-life character that helps explain the nascent days of brand marketing." —Bloomberg.com

"Entertaining and instructive." —DailyFinance.com

"[Lipton's] story is a surprising and memorable one, and his biography offers readers with an enthusiasm for history a glimpse of American and European life in post–Civil War America and England at the turn of the nineteenth century. Very well-written and engaging."
—The Martha's Vineyard Times

PRAISE FOR

Forever Blue

The True Story of Walter O'Malley,
Baseball's Most Controversial Owner,
and the Dodgers of Brooklyn and Los Angeles

"Michael D'Antonio presents an evenhanded assessment of . . . one of the most polarizing figures in baseball history." —The New York Times

"A complex, nuanced picture of this key baseball man's role in the game."
—Boston Globe

"Unprecedented access to the family's archives gave D'Antonio an insider's perspective . . . nuanced." —Los Angeles Times

"[A] comprehensive account." —New York Post

ALSO BY MICHAEL D'ANTONIO

Forever Blue: The True Story of Walter O'Malley, Baseball's Most Controversial Owner, and the Dodgers of Brooklyn and Los Angeles

A Ball, a Dog, and a Monkey: 1957—The Space Race Begins

Hershey: Milton S. Hershey's Extraordinary Life of Wealth, Empire, and Utopian Dreams

The State Boys Rebellion

Tour '72: Nicklaus, Palmer, Player, and Trevino: The Story of One Great Season

Mosquito: The Story of Man's Deadliest Foe (with Andrew Spielman)

Tin Cup Dreams: A Long Shot Makes It on the PGA Tour

Atomic Harvest: Hanford and the Lethal Toll of America's Nuclear Arsenal

Heaven on Earth: Dispatches from America's Spiritual Frontier

Fall from Grace: The Failed Crusade of the Christian Right

A Full Cup

SIR THOMAS LIPTON'S
EXTRAORDINARY LIFE AND HIS QUEST
FOR THE AMERICA'S CUP

Michael D'Antonio

RIVERHEAD BOOKS

New York

RIVERHEAD BOOKS
Published by the Penguin Group
Penguin Group (USA) Inc.
375 Hudson Street, New York, New York 10014, USA
Penguin Group (Canada), 90 Eglinton Avenue East, Suite 700, Toronto, Ontario M4P 2Y3, Canada
(a division of Pearson Penguin Canada Inc.)
Penguin Books Ltd., 80 Strand, London WC2R 0RL, England
Penguin Group Ireland, 25 St. Stephen's Green, Dublin 2, Ireland (a division of Penguin Books Ltd.)
Penguin Group (Australia), 250 Camberwell Road, Camberwell, Victoria 3124, Australia
(a division of Pearson Australia Group Pty. Ltd.)
Penguin Books India Pvt. Ltd., 11 Community Centre, Panchsheel Park, New Delhi—110 017, India
Penguin Group (NZ), 67 Apollo Drive, Rosedale, Auckland 0632, New Zealand
(a division of Pearson New Zealand Ltd.)
Penguin Books (South Africa) (Pty.) Ltd., 24 Sturdee Avenue, Rosebank, Johannesburg 2196,
South Africa

Penguin Books Ltd., Registered Offices: 80 Strand, London WC2R 0RL, England

Copyright © 2010 by Michael D'Antonio
Cover design by Isabella Fasciano
Cover photograph © The Mariners' Museum, Newport News, Virginia
Spine illustration © Mary Evans Picture Library
Frontispiece photograph: Library of Congress, Prints & Photographs Division, LC-DIG-ggbain-16564
Book design by Michelle McMillian

First Riverhead hardcover edition: July 2010
First Riverhead trade paperback edition: July 2011
Riverhead trade paperback ISBN: 978-1-59448-521-3

The Library of Congress has catalogued the Riverhead hardcover edition as follows:

D'Antonio, Michael.
A full cup : Sir Thomas Lipton's extraordinary life and his quest for the America's Cup / Michael D'Antonio
   p.   cm.
   Includes bibliographical references and index.
   ISBN 978-1-59448-760-6
   1. Lipton, Thomas Johnstone, Sir, 1850–1931.   2. Thomas J. Lipton, Inc.—History.   3. America's Cup—History.   4. Businessmen—Scotland—Biography.   5. Grocers—Scotland—Glasgow—Biography   6. Sailors—Scotland—Biography.   7. Tea trade—History.   8. Yacht racing—History.   9. Glasgow (Scotland)—Biography.   I. Title.
   CT828.L5D36   2010   2010000275
   338.092—dc22

PRINTED IN THE UNITED STATES OF AMERICA

10 9 8 7 6 5 4 3 2 1

*For the girl who shares tea with me
every night*

Contents

Dr. Optimist is the finest chap in the "names" directory of any city or country. He and I have been life-long friends and boon companions. Just try a course of his treatment. It will work wonders. And this doctor charges no fees!

—SIR THOMAS LIPTON

ONE

Glasgow

The yachting cap with the black leather bill was a kind of trade-mark, just like the floppy polka-dot bow tie, the white mustache, and the inch-square patch of whiskers under his lip. For thirty years, on occasions when he met the public, he had placed the cap on his balding head, adjusted it with a little tug, and become in an instant the man who called himself The Great Lipton.

Tall and ruddy-faced, Sir Thomas Lipton had proved that a poor, undereducated boy could conquer the world of business and rise to fame as an international sportsman. His friends included the rich, the famous, the powerful, and the royal. His successes and failures—some quite spectacular—had been announced a thousand times in the press on both sides of the Atlantic and made him one of the most recognized figures in the world.

Even children knew Lipton's story, and in the summer of 1930 they came running from every direction when they heard he was going to give out free cookies and chocolate at his warehouse in the Anderston district of Glasgow. These children of the Great Depression, raised under a cloud of deprivation, understood that Sir Thomas would stay until every last child got a treat. He had done it before.

On that Friday, July 4, 1930, the queue on Lancefield Street began forming in the morning and eventually stretched for a cobbled quarter mile, all the way down to the dock at the River Clyde. Sons and daughters of shipbuilders, sailors, factory workers, and maids waited patiently until a fancy private car wheeled down from busy Stobcross Street and stopped at the curb. When Lipton emerged, unfolding his old body to stand tall and square in an immaculate suit, cheers rippled off the soot-stained buildings and echoed into the air. He replied with a smile that deepened the crow's-feet that framed his sparkling blue eyes.

At age eighty-two, Lipton had lost much of what had been familiar and reliable to him. Once one of the most eligible bachelors in the world, he no longer attracted the throngs of women who had loitered in hotel lobbies hoping to catch his eye. Most of the vast business empire that bore his name—the plantations, factories, warehouses, and chain of grocery shops—was now controlled by a board of directors. Nearly all of his longtime associates and friends, including "Whiskey" Tom Dewar, Andrew Carnegie, King Edward VII, and Queen Alexandra, were dead. He had no close family and, as far as anyone knew, no lovers. But he still possessed an unbroken connection to the working-class districts of Glasgow.

With its smoky air and overcrowded tenements, Anderston was a tough neighborhood. Gangs controlled the streets at night, and life for the law-abiding was a matter of hard work and struggle. It was the same as it had been when Lipton started there in business and began to manufacture himself, story by story, and image by image. The cap, bow tie, and mustache were decorative elements of the Lipton myth, which was relentlessly cheerful and positive. But the real man was reflected in the faces—some dirty and wary, others eager and hopeful—that lined up on the pavement. On the eve of his last great adventure he spent hours greeting them and handing out gift boxes like a summertime Santa Claus. In return he collected their gratitude and heard the sound of his past in their voices.

As a Glasgow boy, Tommy Lipton had received what he called a "liberal education in the give-and-take, the rough-and-tumble of life." With its enormous productivity, the city of Lipton's youth all but vibrated with creative energy. Even the grime in the streets seemed fertile, feeding the ambitions, hopes, and dreams of the working class who labored in dangerous and dirty industries that operated right next to tenements and houses. The most noxious were the foundries, like Dixon's ironworks, where open-pit furnaces glowed so brightly through the night that people called the place "The Blazes." Glasgow's mills produced a million tons of pig iron annually. On drizzly days the acrid smoke from their fires covered everything with a black film. On blue-sky days the smoke was carried by the prevailing winds, billowing over the mills, factories, docks, and sprawling shipyards of the area called Clydeside.

Glasgow made almost everything from locomotives to calico, but the great ships built at local yards were the ultimate symbols of the city's status as the industrial center of the far-flung British Empire. Strong, graceful, and powered by the latest in steam technology, Glasgow ships sailed on every ocean in the world and in rivers and lakes from Australia to America. They were so superior that the term "Clyde-built" became synonymous with quality. The ships established the city's identity as a hub of international trade. They brought cotton, timber, leaf tobacco, and other raw materials and departed with iron, steel, textiles, leather, and heavy machinery. They also enabled the easy flow of people in and out of the city. Scots departed from the Clyde for adventures in the British Empire or to resettle in America. Others, especially poor Irish families fleeing famine and turmoil, came to Glasgow looking for jobs in factories, mills, and foundries.

Thomas Lipton's parents had lived in County Fermanagh in rural Northern Ireland, and then in County Down. After years of poverty, and the deaths of two young children, they fled in 1847—later called "Black '47"—as famine killed people all around them. In Glasgow, Thomas Lipton, Sr., found work in a box factory while the family—including his pregnant wife, Frances, a son, John, and daughters named Frances and Margaret—took shelter in a slum district called the Gorbals. There narrow, shadowy lanes called "wynds" cut between four-story tenements made of local sandstone that had been blackened by pollution. The wynds were barely wide enough for a pushcart, and their gutters often overflowed with sewage. A resident walking down one of these dark alleys would occasionally come upon a little courtyard, called a "close," which would be as cramped and confining as the name suggests. A typical close was both a playground for children and a dump for all sorts of waste. The communal pump found in a close often delivered water teeming with pathogens, like cholera bacteria, washed down into the water table by falling rain.

The slums of Glasgow shocked outsiders. After he toured the city in the mid-1840s Friedrich Engels wrote, "I did not believe, until I visited the wynds of Glasgow, that so large an amount of filth, crime, misery, and disease existed in one spot in any civilized country." By the 1860s, when the famous Thomas Annan photographed the slums, they were considered the worst in all of Great Britain. He found jerry-built additions tacked onto the rears of already substandard tenement buildings and below-ground apartments packed with dozens of men and women. Conditions were so extreme that one visitor wrote that in

Glasgow "there was concentrated everything wretched, dissolute, loath-some and pestilential."

In crowded districts like the Gorbals, outbreaks of typhus and chol-era burned with such intensity that the annual death rate for children under five was more than twenty percent. During the Liptons' first year in the city, typhus killed more than four thousand Glaswegians. In the following year a cholera epidemic killed more than thirty-seven hun-dred. Young Thomas was born on May 10, in the midst of the 1848 outbreak. While his four-year-old sister, Frances, would die by the end of the year, Thomas somehow survived.

A child who thrived in this place and time would have to be extraor-dinarily tough, and that's how Tommy Lipton would recall himself as a member of a gang who called themselves the Crown Street Clan. Among Lipton's fondest childhood memories were the turf-war attacks he led against "boys from other quarters of town" and escapades that ended with him being chased by the local "peeler," or beat cop. Most of the time, Tommy was too fast to be apprehended. But he was caught once when he ran through a close, passed a cowshed, and scrambled up a mound, hoping to then slip over the top of a wall. The mound was a pile of what Lipton called "glaur"—Scottish for slimy mud—and he sank to his armpits. The peeler, deciding the boy had been punished enough, walked away laughing.

Heart-pounding flights from the police lent an air of excitement to a boy's life, but the moment that defined Lipton as a young man of the Gorbals involved a fistfight with a neighborhood bully named Wullie Ross, which he would recall, in vivid detail, seventy years later. (The son of a butcher, Wullie was, in Lipton's account, an ox-strong "lout" who demanded protection payments in the form of marbles—they called them "bools"—from smaller boys.)

When Tommy squared off with Wullie, cries of "A fight, a fight!"

drew boys from all around. The two combatants stripped to the waist as rules were set and seconds were selected. While some boys egged Tommy on, insisting he could end Wullie's reign of intimidation, others urged him to withdraw. "Wullie will kill you," they said bluntly.

As the slugging began, Tommy gamely stood his ground while Wullie landed blow after blow. By the sixth round Tommy was so bloodied that his friends stopped the fight. But, as he would remember it, the unbowed loser gained far more in terms of respect and admiration than he lost. "My stock soared high among all the boys of the district," recalled Lipton decades later. The lesson he learned about the value of reputation would last a lifetime.

More lessons came as Tommy wandered the Clydeside, which was a noisy and dangerous carnival of ships, men, horses, wagons, and steam engines. Here he heard sea shanties and cursing and saw men of all races and types. Rough-and-ready sailors worked next to uniformed officers who exuded authority and privilege. Tommy's mind bloomed with questions and in between their duties on ship and their business ashore, officers, engineers, and sailors gave him answers and told him stories of life at sea and distant ports.

Using what he observed about ship design, Tommy built models from scraps of wood. String became rigging, and he cut paper to make sails. He created a miniature sailing course at the great city park called Glasgow Green, where rainwater collected in abandoned clay pits to form shallow ponds. His *Shamrocks*, as they were named, were joined by boats built by other young hands. Soon the self-appointed Commodore Lipton had organized a Crown Street Yacht Club and was conducting regular races.

There was nothing unusual in Tommy Lipton's hobby. Boys across Great Britain were captivated by yacht racing, which was the preeminent international sport. British racers sailing under the flag of the Royal Yacht Squadron dominated the major regattas in Europe. And everyone in the country could tell the story of the great race of 1851, when the schooner *America* appeared from across the Atlantic and captured a trophy called the Hundred Guinea Cup in a race around the Isle of Wight. Queen Victoria, Prince Albert, and their nine-year-old son, Bertie, had watched in amazement, and the event gave the boy who would be King Edward VII a lifelong passion for the sport. At Glasgow Green, whether they reenacted the race for the Hundred Guinea Cup or invented their own regattas, the *Shamrock*s usually prevailed and Tommy Lipton collected a prize of a few bools.

For poor boys who raced for marbles, models represented the only option for getting close to the exotic realm of competitive yachting, which was the exclusive domain of the titled and the rich. They could, however, fantasize about taking to sea on a working ship, as either passenger or sailor, and becoming part of the dramatic march of history. Throughout the nineteenth century, oceangoing ships represented the height of technology and adventure. People the world over followed the development of larger, faster, and more efficient vessels, which opened the world to ever faster and cheaper communication and commerce.

Tommy Lipton followed the development of the great ships and eventually graduated from model vessels to actual sailing. Using what coins he could save, he would occasionally rent a little boat and head into the Clyde to test the wind and the water and himself. He also invested in a roughly drawn map of the world, which he used to study the routes of the ships he knew. Most went to ports in America, which was the biggest buyer for Glasgow goods and the place most people imagined when they dreamed of a bigger life than the one they knew in Scotland.

L ipton's parents did not dream big. In emigrating from Ireland, Thomas Sr. and Frances had improved their lot, but they still saw life in terms of struggle and loss. Their eldest son, John, who had often been sick, died in 1857 at the age of nineteen. A few years later the Civil War in America disrupted trade and threw thousands of Glasgow men out of work. As Thomas Sr. grappled with the insecurity of his income, the solution that he and his wife, Frances, imagined was to join the shopkeeper class by opening a little grocery store. Humble and wary of overreaching, they wouldn't set out to make a success "in the ordinary sense of the word," recalled their son, but only to make a "bare living."

Tucked into a tiny space a few steps below street level, the Lipton grocery shop offered the most basic wares—eggs, butter, ham—to a community no more than a few blocks square. The provisions came from a friend of the family who farmed in Ireland and packed them onto a coastal steamship that arrived at Clydeside every Monday. Tommy, by now a teenager, wheeled a barrow to the dock, waited for the shipment to be unloaded, and then pushed it back up Crown Street. Inside the shop, he helped with cleaning and offered precocious suggestions, including the idea that eggs be served to customers by his mother, because her small hands made them seem bigger.

The bustle of business captivated Tommy Lipton in ways that school never did. In highly literate Scotland, even working-class families tried to give boys a proper education, but by the time their youngest was fifteen, the Liptons concluded the three pence per week they spent for him to attend the St. Andrews Parish School wasn't buying much. "I cannot say I was either a favorite or a diligent pupil at St. Andrews," he later confessed.

As the family's only male child, Tommy's potential as a wage earner was vital to his family. Soon after he left school he found work as an errand boy at a print shop and brought his pay home to his mother and father. Eager to increase his wages, Tommy moved to a job cutting patterns for Tillie and Henderson, a shirt-making company so successful that Karl Marx would eventually point to it as an example of industrial ruthlessness and gigantism. At the shirt factory, Tommy lost the independence and freedom he enjoyed as an errand boy. He felt confined and frustrated, and wound up fighting with another boy in the pattern department. This time Tommy Lipton, fully six feet tall and strong, won.

Ambition drove the restless Tommy to request a raise, which was denied in writing by a manager named David Sinclair. "You are getting as much as you are worth," he wrote, "and you are in a devil of a hurry to ask for a raise." Sinclair wasn't the only cranky older Scotsman who bothered young Lipton. At a night school he attended for a while he chafed under the rule of a "fish-blooded tyrant of whom Dickens would have made a character." Nicknamed "Auld Specky" because he wore peculiar blue-tinted glasses, teacher Thomas Neil used whippings to keep order.

With the likes of David Sinclair and Auld Specky making his days and nights unpleasant, ships on the Clyde seemed ever more entrancing to Tommy. When he learned that the Burns Line was looking for a cabin boy to sail between the Broomielaw (Glasgow's riverside docks) and Belfast, he rushed to the company's office. The job paid double what he made at the shirt factory and included meals on board. His main duty would be the care and feeding of cabin-class passengers—mostly tourists and businessmen—who boarded in the late afternoon, hoping to relax on the voyage and awake refreshed at their destination.

After the claustrophobia of work in a factory, the open sea intoxicated Tommy. He loved the thrumming of the ship's engines and the choreography of arrivals and departures. At sea he studied every sailor and officer at work, from the bridge to the engine room. And when he was alone on deck he reveled in the stars, the play of the wind on the water, and the blinking messages from distant flashing lighthouses. "I felt that the world was opening up to me," he would recall, "that it was good to be alive and better still to be a cabin boy on a gallant Clyde-built steamship."

The stories that crewmen told to pass the time revolved around voyages to more distant ports. Many spoke of crossing the Atlantic to New York or Philadelphia and then traveling to exotic places like Chicago and seeing prairies and cotton fields. But a young man didn't have to work as a cabin boy to hear stories about the United States. Glasgow was afflicted with a kind of "Ameri-mania," as one writer put it. A popular song about the lure of "the land of the free" evoked the dream many shared about a place where "the poorest may gather the fruits of his toil."

Glaswegians found reinforcement for their dreams in the letters sent by friends and relatives who had gone before them and succeeded. Better educated than most other immigrants, Scots tended to rise once they landed in the States. They were more likely to become supervisors in factories or skilled laborers in the trades. Scots dominated the typesetting business in New York and the dry-goods business in the Midwest. And it was a son of Scottish immigrants—James Marshall—who first discovered gold at Sutter's Mill in California.

Mates and sailors on the Burns liners "had made trips to America and they never tired of telling of its vastness, its wealth, the boundless opportunities, which the great new world across the Western Ocean was offering with open hands to all and sundry," recalled Lipton. "Fortunes were to be picked up for the asking. Millionaires grew at the rate of one a day! I listened eagerly and made up my mind sooner or later to try my luck in America."

A seventeen-year-old cabin boy working on the Irish Sea had reason to hope for the opportunity to transfer to a ship bound for America and work his way across the ocean. Tommy wouldn't get this chance. After a night crossing from Belfast, the Burns Line's chief steward inspected the cabins and found that an oil lamp had been allowed to smoke and stain a white enamel ceiling. With plenty of poor boys eager for a job, it was easy enough to dismiss the one who most likely responsible. Tommy was allowed to work one more week, collect his pay, and go.

In his brief time with the Burns Line, eating free food and working such long hours he barely had time to spend what he earned, Tommy had managed to save a substantial sum. When his last week's wages were added to the pot and he left the Burns Line paymaster, he went straight to nearby Union Street and the offices of the Anchor Line to ask the price of a steerage ticket to New York.

Tommy Lipton's timing was perfect. The American Civil War had ended with the South's surrender one year earlier and Union blockades had been lifted. Ships that had served both the Confederate and Union navies were being converted to commercial use. Public interest in transatlantic travel, long suppressed by the war, had exploded. With both supply and demand at work, prices for the passage fell for a brief period and many more people felt emboldened toward adventure. (Wanderlust soared on both sides of the ocean. At the time Lipton decided to leave Glasgow, Mark Twain persuaded a San Francisco newspaper to pay his fare for an excursion to Europe aboard the converted Union warship *Quaker City*. The resulting *Innocents Abroad* would become a comic classic and signal the beginning of a more open American attitude toward the wider world.)

For a Scottish boy entering a steamship office, the moment brought a rare opportunity. A steamer taking cargo that day was about to cast off for New York. Passage in steerage would cost five British pounds.

With no requirement for a passport or visa, and American laws setting immigrant quotas still years in the future, this was all he needed to begin his pursuit of a new life in the New World. Fearing they would try to stop him, he considered simply leaving without a word to his parents. His apprehension was reasonable. Scottish mothers and fathers knew that although nearly all said they would return, very few boys who departed for America ever came back. A young man could avoid a lot of tears, threats, and demands by slipping away.

After wrestling with the question, Tommy realized he didn't have the heart to simply abandon his parents and his sickly sister, Margaret. Besides, his parents had always supported his ambitions and he had talked often of making the voyage west, to the "Land of Promise." Surely they wouldn't be surprised.

If his mother and father had not made a small success of their little shop, they might have clung to their boy. But in fact they would be able to get along without his help, and his enthusiasm quickly won them over. "The parting was sad," he would write, "but I really think that my mother, at least, had such faith in me that she believed I would soon return a rich man."

TWO

America

Freed from steerage, where three hundred souring, wool-clad bodies made the air sweetly thick, a tall young man with sandy hair moved quickly up the ship's ladder and burst through the hatch onto the open deck. Blinking in the sudden sunlight, Tommy Lipton felt a cold west wind beating on his face. Off the starboard bow a flotilla of stately icebergs, blue-white and gleaming, rose menacingly from the sea. Overhead, black coal smoke puffed from the vessel's single smokestack. Uniformed lookouts scanned the horizon and a V-shaped wake rippled from the hull, adding wavelets to the North Atlantic chop.

In the few minutes he could enjoy before a deck monitor sent him back below, Tommy Lipton inhaled the clean, dry air and checked the careful course the captain followed through the ice field. The ship's single-screw steam engine allowed for steady progress against the headwind and more precise steering, compared with sails. Although Tommy could feel the rhythm of the motor through the steel deck, for the moment, at least, he was spared the relentless bass beat that vibrated the bones of every man, woman, and child jammed into the bowels of the ship.

Sixty-five years later, Thomas Lipton would insist that he first sailed to America aboard the somewhat grand Scottish steamer *Devonia*, a fast ship made famous by Robert Louis Stevenson's account of her passengers "singing and spewing lustily" in a fierce gale. Lipton's memory was the product of a good-natured imagination. He could not have traveled aboard the *Devonia*, because in 1866 she wouldn't be launched for another decade. Instead, he had sailed on a much smaller and slower vessel, the SS *Caledonia*. Nevertheless, he, like Stevenson, witnessed plenty of spewing and singing in the steerage compartment.

Steerage aboard the *Caledonia*, which wasn't much bigger than that stalwart of the Irish Sea, the *Penguin*, would make any voyager ambitious to change his station in life. While just forty people occupied the first-class deck, and a mere ninety were berthed in second, the Anchor Line crammed more than three hundred souls into *Caledonia*'s stifling lowest deck, where noise, darkness, lice, and rats made the two-week crossing a grueling test.

Except for their occasional open-air strolls on the top deck, Lipton and his companions spent their days in shadowy rooms where they amused themselves with games, reading, storytelling, and the occasional brawl. (Tommy, who had acquired a violin and a bit of skill with it, played while others sang.) Meals were a matter of porridge or stew ladled into small buckets. In rough weather, when hatches were closed, steerage became a circle of hell where seasickness and bad ventilation bred wildfire outbreaks of various illnesses. Conditions were so demanding, especially for infants and the elderly, that many vessels reached their destination with more than one dead body aboard. Of course, microbes weren't the only risk faced by a hopeful immigrant. A few months before Lipton set sail, a man was murdered aboard the New York–bound steamer *Scotland*. His mutilated body, discovered in a cranny of the hull near the engine room, was buried at sea.

Lipton's cheery account of his first passage finds him making friends and using his limited skills to write letters for the truly illiterate immigrants who spent the transit feeling homesick. Ships like the *Caledonia* carried Scottish factory workers, farmers and tradesmen, and Irish laborers who had transited through Dublin or Belfast. Some, including master weavers headed for textile mills in New England, had been recruited for guaranteed jobs. They would accept low wages and long days, in order to be freer than they had been under Great Britain's Master and Servant Act, which allowed workers to be jailed for quitting their jobs. Other migrants, especially the farmers, would arrive in America with no plan other than to find work in a big city or head for the vast open country of the West. America's newly passed Homestead Act promised 160 acres of federal land to those who staked a claim and improved the property. This was a stunningly attractive prospect to immigrants from countries where they had no hope of ever becoming landowners.

Dreams of free land and other opportunities motivated immigrants to risk the conditions aboard ship and the dangers of the sea. In thirty years, more than a hundred ships had been lost in the Atlantic trade. Among them was the Anchor Line's first transatlantic steamer, the *Tempest*, which disappeared without a trace in February 1857. One hundred and fifty passengers and crew died.

On this voyage, the *Caledonia* struggled against prevailing winds that added days to the journey. As the ship neared North America, a gale began to blow, further slowing her. On May 1, *Caledonia* finally reached Portland, Maine, where a few passengers disembarked. She then proceeded south along the coast. The ship entered New York Harbor on May 5, 1866, just days before Thomas's birthday. In his memoir he would claim to have turned sixteen toward the end of his first week in America. He was actually eighteen, but this detail would be so well obscured that the year of his birth—1848—would be misstated even at the time of his death.

Although he was older than he later claimed, Lipton was still a bug-eyed youth as the *Caledonia* eased up to dock at Castle Garden, a sandstone fortress that rose out of the water at the very tip of Manhattan Island. Built between 1808 and 1811 to defend the city, the fort was originally called West Battery and was supposed to complement East Battery on Governors Island. After the army abandoned the fort in 1821, it was leased for public performances. The great Swedish soprano Jenny Lind made her American debut at Castle Garden before beginning a nationwide tour promoted by the impresario P. T. Barnum. More than five thousand people flocked to that performance, and in the course of Lind's U.S. tour Barnum cleared $500,000 in profit.

Operas and symphonies continued to draw big crowds to Castle Garden until 1855, when federal officials decided a big secure fort on an artificial island would be the perfect place to receive immigrants. The need for a more formal system to handle newcomers had been apparent for years as rapid improvements in ships and political turmoil in Europe had steadily increased the number of people coming to America. The completely unregulated trade dumped ill-prepared men, women, and families into a city where too many were exploited by criminals, or where their ambitions and needs simply added to the chaos and violence in the poorest corners of the city.

When it opened, the Castle Island immigration station offered voyagers a doctor, a bath, and help making arrangements for further travel. (No longer would dockside crooks sell wide-eyed innocents fake tickets for trains that didn't exist.) All this was accomplished in a big, circular, two-level building that was open at the center, with rows of wooden benches. In 1866, the year Tommy sailed, 750 ships docked at Castle Garden and more than 230,000 people disembarked.

Day after day, hundreds and hundreds of weary voyagers would arrive and gather where concertgoers once gazed down at performers. They would wait for government clerks who stood with a ship's officer to call and then confirm the name of each arrival. Once properly identified and registered, immigrants could change money at an exchange bureau and inquire about rail and ship connections to other parts of the country. When they were ready, newcomers then walked across a causeway to Manhattan, where the first building they saw was a U.S. Army recruiting station. On the street, employment agents and touts for boardinghouses called out for customers.

Castle Garden teemed with crowds of people from around the world as an excited young Tommy Lipton rushed off the ship. The rich tourists were decked out in formal Victorian fashion—crinolines and hoops for women, stovepipe hats and morning coats for men—and hired porters to carry their baggage. The poor immigrants, who spoke many languages and generally dressed in worn clothes, carried all they owned in the world in their hands and on their backs.

Tommy lugged only his violin and a satchel stuffed with clothes. As he slipped through the crowd to the causeway that led to shore, he schemed to make the few dollars in his pocket last as long as possible. In the street he heard a boardinghouse operator named Mike McCauligan who was loudly selling the comfort and value of his establishment. McCauligan spoke in a warm brogue that reminded Tommy of home.

"What will you charge me if I bring you a dozen lodgers tonight?" asked Lipton.

"Not a cent me bold lad," came the answer. "I'll board you free for a week."

Returning to the big crowd of new arrivals, Tommy collected more than a dozen from the *Caledonia*, many of whom had trusted him with their hearts as he wrote their letters, and now readily joined him. They

all followed McCauligan on a walk straight up Washington Street, with
the most densely populated blocks of Manhattan on their right and the
Hudson River on their left. So many ships were berthed along the shore
that their naked masts made the riverbank look like a forest in winter.
On the docks, men wrestled with all kinds of cargo—lumber, cattle,
produce, hides, sugar, flour—which they transferred to horse-drawn
wagons that joined the streetcars, stages, and carriages on crowded
streets. On the sidewalks merchants piled goods under canvas awnings,
and the brick walls of various shops were covered with gaudy signs offering shirts, hats, produce, and printing.

At number 27A Washington Street, the troupe from the *Caledonia*
entered the red-brick building where McCauligan rented beds for pennies per night. The customers were packed eight to a room, and the
comforts began and ended with the fact that the place stayed dry when
it rained. Conversation at McCauligan's was limited by the fact that the
residents spoke so many different languages it was hard for a fellow to
make himself understood. Too often this failure to communicate led to
shouts or a fight.

Outside McCauligan's, Lipton found a busy street lined with cheap
hotels, cheaper flophouses, and saloons catering to sailors and other
transients. Poles hung with dozens of telegraph wires marched down
the avenues and cross streets, casting shadows and cross-hatching the
sky. The air smelled of rotting garbage, horse manure, and the acrid
smoke from the tall chimneys of a big soap factory that occupied several
buildings a block away. More than twenty thousand people in this part
of the city lived in subterranean apartments, and public health experts
called it "New York, the Unclean." The blocks had nicknames like Rag
Pickers Row and Dog Alley.

The rich visited the area around Washington Street with police escorts, and public health officials feared for their lives when they made inspections. Just before Tommy's arrival, a *New York Times* report described the streets as a "disgraceful, dangerous, disease-breeding nuisance" where clogged gutters collected "garbage, vegetables, refuse, offal, straw-beds, children, lazy men and shiftless women." Waste from the city's forty thousand horses joined with "green stuff from the kitchen, ashes, mud and children, all indiscriminate in the congenial gutter."

The neighborhood was a quarter mile west of the Five Points district, where gangs called Dead Rabbits and the Bowery Boys fought pitched battles, and where professional pickpockets worked the sidewalks. Irish-born prostitutes—called "lofters" by local police—loitered in cigar shops, gambling rooms, and gin mills packed with immigrants and recently freed slaves. Nowhere could a young man find more ways to get into trouble or lose his money. If he wasn't taken in a rigged game of cards he might fall victim to "panel thieves," who hid behind false walls and emerged to empty a fellow's pockets while he was distracted by a prostitute. Even the most careful men faced the risk of random violence. Three months before Tommy arrived, a bystander was shot and killed on Washington Street when four men scuffled and a gun went off. Only twenty-five years old, the victim was a German immigrant who just happened to pass by as a fight broke out. The alleged triggerman, a recent arrival from Ireland named John MacDonald, was still at large.

In a city swollen with tens of thousands of recently demobilized Union Army veterans and an even greater number of new immigrants, MacDonald would have had no trouble disappearing into the crowd. At the same time, the police and other city officials had so many big problems to confront that the pursuit of a suspect in the shooting death of a lone immigrant would have received little attention. Rents in the city had doubled in a year, and more than half the population of 800,000 lived in substandard buildings. Merely keeping order in this environment was a gargantuan task.

Tommy Lipton's main goal was to secure a job, and he could hope to find a place in one of the companies operated by his countrymen. The most prominent was a Scots-Irish entrepreneur named Alexander T. Stewart, who employed two thousand people in one of the biggest department stores in the world. Nicknamed the Iron Palace (the façade was cast iron painted white), Stewart's emporium at Tenth Street and Broadway offered thousands of items in a six-floor building topped by a glass dome. It was also headquarters for a network of similar Stewart stores that stretched to Great Britain, France, and Germany.

Stewart's success had been based on the idea that shopping should be a pleasure. Instead of showing piles of goods in his big front windows, he left them uncluttered so people on the street could see the colorful stocks of artfully arranged items displayed all across the gleaming floor. Stewart stressed personal service. Though customers could wander for hours without ever being asked to purchase a thing, hundreds of attentive clerks were always at hand. Stewart was among the first to mark prices on his goods, and he refused to haggle, a practice that brought a new measure of civility to the trade. Yet his biggest innovation was the installation of stools for ladies to rest on while shopping at his counters, thus making his store a social gathering place as important to women as saloons were to men. Shopping to the sound of organ music, Mary Todd Lincoln, who traveled to New York often, had spent $27,000 at Stewart's during the Civil War, acquiring clothes and furnishings for the White House.

When Lipton arrived in New York, Stewart's personal fortune was estimated at between $40 million and $50 million, and the blue-eyed

Merchant Prince was one of the richest men in America. Every immigrant with a brogue hoped to find a job in his company. However, Stewart's workers were loyal and turnover was low. Meanwhile, unemployment was high, and so the majority of applicants never found employment with the great merchandise man. Instead, they tramped door to door, day after day, hoping to find some way to turn their hours into money.

Big, strong, and eager, Tommy Lipton joined the wandering hopefuls but could not rise above the competition and secure a position. The vast number of applicants was only one part of the problem. Another had to do with the overall economy, which would need time to recover from the war. This was especially true for New York City, traditionally a center for the middlemen trading in the produce of southern plantations, which were now producing seventy percent less cotton, tobacco, hemp, and other crops than they had before the war. With the federal government no longer purchasing supplies for a million-man army, New York businesses, especially those that hired unskilled labor, were even more distressed.

As his savings ran down, Lipton began to let go of his fantasies about finding success in Gotham and turned to agents who recruited for employers in other parts of the country. With his name added to the rolls, all he could do was check in periodically and then look for ways to pass the time without getting into too much trouble. Lipton would have found plenty to amuse himself in Lower Manhattan where the streets offered a parade of life. Shoppers bustled in and out of busy stores, among them the various branches of the Great American Tea Company, on Vesey Street, Spring Street, Eighth Avenue, and Broadway. The rich flocked to Delmonico's restaurant on William Street, and tourists trooped to P. T. Barnum's American Museum near City Hall. In May of 1866 the offerings included "a learned seal," a midget named Tom Thumb, and "a mammoth fat infant" weighing almost two hundred pounds.

If he couldn't afford the museum, Tommy could pay a penny to ride a crowded horse-drawn streetcar to the new Central Park, or simply wander the city and take in the spectacle of commerce, contest, poverty, and wealth. Along Broadway, buildings were plastered with advertisements for shows, and music poured out of open stage doors. In the Bowery he'd find "b'hoys" engaged in bare-knuckle boxing and "g'hirls" in bright clothes screaming in support of their favorites. Weekends would bring the wealthy membership of the New York Yacht Club to the harbor for racing and display. Some provided string quartets on the decks of their boats. Others served lavish banquets. Six weeks after Tommy Lipton set foot in New York, Admiral David Farragut, who had damned the torpedoes in Mobile Bay, was the guest of honor for the club's annual regatta.

Events like the regatta, which was witnessed by thousands onshore, were part of the never-ending spectacle available for free to anyone willing to jostle with the crowd. For just a few coins an urban adventurer could feast on the female form by catching a stage show at Niblo's Garden or find a companion for the night at a beer garden where the waitergirls worked overtime in rooms upstairs.

When his energy flagged, a young man loose in New York City could buy a newspaper to catch up on events in his new country. In May of 1866, federal troops skirmished with Indians in the West and the white citizens of Memphis attacked an African-American neighborhood, burning and looting homes, raping women, and murdering dozens of men. Later in the summer the papers were filled with news of a cheerier sort, about a great new effort to span the North Atlantic with a "submarine" telegraph cable. The project was mounted by a colorful American capitalist named Cyrus W. Field, who actually went to sea to supervise the work himself.

News reporters followed the cable project as avidly as they would a great battle. Everyone knew that if successful, the transatlantic wire would mark a turning point in history. Instead of the ten days required for the fastest ships to carry papers and people across the ocean, communication would be almost instantaneous. Commerce, politics, science—all of human affairs—would be affected. But the odds against the endeavor were great. Only one of four previous attempts at laying a line had succeeded, and in that case, in the summer of 1857, the cable failed in a matter of weeks. The breakdown came after a spasm of celebration that included parties, cannon fire, and a song called "The Ocean Cable Gallop." The disappointment led some skeptics to say that the claims of transatlantic communication had been a giant hoax.

This time crews worked with a cable that was twice as big—one mile of the strand weighed two tons—and wrapped in many layers of an early type of waterproof latex made from the sap of Asian gutta-percha trees. They could also rely on the biggest steamship in the world, the SS *Great Eastern*, which was capable of carrying all of the materials required.

The job began with the seemingly miraculous recovery of a previously broken cable that lay ten thousand feet below the surface at a point 560 miles from the Irish shore. The old line was found to be in working order and the new one was spliced to it. In late July the cable reached a point of land in Newfoundland called Heart's Content. Suddenly, as the papers declared, the New World was connected to the Old World and the gulf between them had been conquered.

"We are in telegraphic communication with Ireland!" Cyrus W. Field reported. In New York, investors held lavish parties, ordinary people toasted the cable in saloons, and a printer issued a commemorative poster that featured Poseidon, god of the sea, as well as images of London and New York City, and declared the transatlantic wire the "Eighth Wonder of the World."

By the time the Eighth Wonder sparked to life, Tommy Lipton had left New York or was about to depart. An employment agent had finally found him work as a farm laborer in Virginia, where emancipation and the ravages of war had caused a shortage of willing hands for the tobacco harvest. One-third fewer acres had been planted than in the years before the start of the Civil War, but the crop was healthy and many planters who were angry about the new order of things refused to pay former slaves, preferring instead to recruit white labor from distant cities. A farmer named Samuel Clay paid to bring Lipton and his strong back to his farm in Dinwiddie County.

Named for a colonial-era lieutenant governor, who happened to be born into a family of merchants in Glasgow, Dinwiddie County had been the site of some of the final battles of the Civil War. During the Appomattox campaign, the Union Army crossed the county in order to cut off the one railroad still open to supply Robert E. Lee's Army of Northern Virginia. The much larger Union force, which was led by Ulysses S. Grant and an officer corps that included General George Armstrong Custer, overwhelmed the rebels and ten days later the war ended.

Lipton traveled to Virginia on one of four paddlewheel steamers that worked the coastal route from New York to Richmond. (If lucky he sailed on the new ship called the *Vixen*, which was advertised as "A1.") He passed first through Norfolk and then arrived at City Point on the James River, where General Grant had built the massive camp needed to stage the siege of Petersburg and the concluding battles of the Civil War. Grant had left behind acres of cleared land and hundreds of Union dead who were buried in fresh graves on a hill overlooking the river. From

City Point, Lipton either walked or traveled by stage right through war-scarred countryside including the battleground at Five Forks, where three thousand casualties were recorded in a single day.

In his memoir Lipton would offer no details about recent events or the postwar landscape. Petersburg, where rebuilding had not begun in earnest, lay in ruins and the fields that stretched to the west of the city were still torn in places where battle lines were formed and cannonballs landed. Neither did he mention that for generations the Dinwiddies of his native Glasgow had imported Virginia tobacco—likely grown on Sam Clay's farm—directly to the Clydeside. In fact, the docks at City Point, many of the warehouses in Petersburg, and the small cargo vessels that plied the Appomattox River were all owned by Scottish families with familiar names—Duncan, Gordon, Boyd, and others.

What Lipton recalled instead was the bone-weary exhaustion he felt after a long day in Sam Clay's fields and the "almost instantaneous sleep" that fell upon him as he lay down in a former slave cabin and closed his eyes each night. "Take my word for it," he wrote, "there was no restless tossing on the beds of that Virginia cabin. Its occupants slept like logs until it was time to tumble out for another day's 'hard darg' as we say in Scotland."

In many ways Lipton's days in Virginia matched the experience of the slaves he was recruited to replace. Farms in the area ranged from five hundred to a thousand acres and all the work of planting, tending, and harvesting was done by hand under a hot sun. Although Lipton and his fellow workers were free to come and go and were paid for their time, their labors hardly differed from those of the slaves they replaced. Tommy accepted extra work assignments and saved most of what he earned until an accident forced him out of the fields. He was injured when a hatchet slipped in his hand and struck his right foot.

Sam Clay took the pained and bleeding laborer into his house. His wife, Sallie, tended to his immediate needs while a doctor was summoned. It was probably Clay's neighbor, a physician named Scott who could trace his lineage to the doctor who brought the smallpox vaccine to America at the request of then President Jefferson. The wound was so severe it seemed Lipton might require amputation. However, Dr. Scott delayed using his scalpel and bone saw, and over the course of several weeks Sallie Clay nursed Tommy to a remarkable recovery.

His foot saved, Lipton returned to work, and to the former slave quarters, but his time in the Clay household had changed his perspective. "I would like to try my hand at something else," he told Clay, and the planter agreed that "tobacco fields didn't offer any great chance of advancement." In the late autumn Lipton returned to New York, which had only become more alluring in his imagination. But again he found no work and as "dollars melted down to a few dimes and nickels" he went back to the employment agent. This time he would have to go farther south, to a rice plantation in South Carolina, and once again take up the work formerly done by slaves.

During the trip to Coosaw Island the young Scot was all but overwhelmed by the vastness of this new country. On the map, South Carolina was just a little more than half the distance between New York and the tip of Florida. And yet the sailing took five full days. "What sort of distance lay between the Carolina town and, say, San Francisco?" he wondered. "I recollect my mind reeling at the probable answer."

Just as mind-boggling as the great distances one might travel in America was the variety of cultures, languages, and races found within its borders. At Coosaw Island, South Carolina, Tommy Lipton was deposited in the middle of a community of former slaves who spoke a dialect called Gullah, which blended English, Creole, and various West African languages. Racial tradition would land him in a small cabin with a Spanish laborer and his Irish wife. The woman took a liking to the strapping young man, who reminded her of home, and a casual reader of Lipton's memoir would expect the triangle to lead to trouble. Lipton did find trouble, but not in the way one might predict.

It turned out that Lipton's Spanish host had served at Fort Sumter during the war and there had become attracted to another woman. While in uniform, the illiterate soldier had had another man write his letters to her, but with the end of the war the correspondence was interrupted. When Lipton arrived, his new Spanish friend was eager to resume the correspondence. Lipton agreed to help him, and the two men took ink, paper, and pen into the woods to write in secret. When the letter was finished, Lipton folded it and tucked it into his coat pocket. That night, while he slept, the woman of the house searched until she discovered the note and confirmed her suspicions.

The following day, Lipton and his love-struck friend went, as usual, to the fields. During a break Lipton checked his pocket and discovered the letter was missing. All day long, as the wayward husband and his young scribe planted rice, the anxiety grew. Their evening meal was eaten in silence. When the dishes were cleared, the wife finally turned and confronted her husband. In a fit of temper he grabbed a knife, turned to Lipton, damned him for betraying his secret, and slashed his face. Tommy jumped back and then ran to save his life.

Outside the small cabin, Lipton ran as hard as he could with his angry housemate giving chase. Blood poured down his face as he sprinted toward a foreman's house, got inside, and explained what was happening. The foreman grabbed a pistol and pointed it at Lipton's pursuer, halting him before he reached the doorway. The standoff ended with the Spaniard's retreat, and Lipton received care for his wound from the overseer's wife. When their tempers cooled, the fighting couple resolved their differences, and they both came to the overseer's house to apologize and insist their friend return to stay with them.

Once again, Lipton's misfortune had brought him into close contact with his betters. This time, however, he made more of the opportunity. Writing had gotten him into trouble but it would also get him out of it. His boss moved him from the fields to the office, where his penmanship and bookkeeping skills proved a little bit better than what the firm had seen from other clerks. The easy work and higher pay kept him there for nearly a year. When a large schooner anchored near the plantation, Lipton and another boy persuaded the captain to let them board in the darkness before the ship's dawn departure.

By the time Lipton left Coosaw Island it was 1868 and he was almost twenty years old. He landed first in Charleston and then found passage back to New York, a city he had come to love—but where, once again, he failed to find work. The irony of his failure to find work in the city of opportunity was not lost on Lipton. As he recalled:

> I never tire of New York. . . . All the same I must admit that
> on this occasion I experienced a very thin time of it. I had
> not much money in my pocket, and New York, like most
> other places, does not offer a boisterously warm welcome
> to the man or boy with a decided scarcity of dollars in his
> possession.

When winter arrived, the cold weather propelled Tommy back to the South. He traveled by ship to New Orleans, where he rode the St. Charles Avenue streetcar line to its last stop, in a suburb called Carrollton. Like the rest of Louisiana, Carrollton was struggling to recover from the collapse of the slave-based economy and the political shock of Reconstruction. Cotton production was still half what it had been before the war. Then, in the summer, Congress ratified the Fourteenth Amendment to the Constitution, affirming the full citizenship of former slaves. Mobs of angry whites responded with violence. Weeks before Lipton arrived in town a gang had broken into the Carrollton jail and killed two black prisoners. On the same night whites attacked the black community in nearby Gretna, killing three and driving the entire population into nearby swamps. The next day, army troops assisted the police in turning away four hundred whites who had arrived by boat intent on attacking New Orleans.

As he fell into this cauldron, Tommy Lipton found a secure job with the streetcar company. The trams had once been powered by steam lo- comotives, but in the postwar years the owners had returned to an old technology—mulepower. Tommy took occasional turns behind the rumps of the mules when the regular drivers were sick, but most of his workdays were spent in an office, where he kept the books and handled correspondence. He lived in the home of his supervisor and found after-hours adventure in the shops and saloons of the French Quarter in New Orleans, where he sometimes played the violin. At the famous Poydras Market he would get a huge slice of pecan pie for a nickel and hear soapbox speeches for free.

By the end of a year, Lipton had deftly avoided a confrontation with fellow streetcar workers who suddenly called a strike and weathered high water when the Mississippi River breached several dikes. He even braved the flames when a friend's shop caught fire with his violin inside. He saved the instrument but was arrested and held by police for a brief time on a charge of looting. This much adventure, and savings of $18, moved him to head back to the North for one last try for success in New York City. One newspaper account of his life credited him with a few months of labor at a farm in Dunellen, New Jersey, before he reached Manhattan. Lipton doesn't mention the precise date in his book. But it's certain that he reached the city by mid-1869, and this time he would find not just a job but the path that would lead him to a level of wealth and fame that he could never have imagined for himself.

I f Tommy Lipton wasn't completely hardy and resilient when he left Glasgow, then mule driving, plantation labor, and life in former slave quarters must have given him all the extra toughening he required. After three years in America he was willing to forgo the comparative comforts of Mike McCauligan's Washington Street dormitory for the less expensive shelter of the steerage-on-land accommodations at a place called Casey's Bedhouse.

A typical bedhouse offered customers little more comfort than a book might get on a shelf. In some, patrons were shown to large rooms filled with long double and triple-decked platforms where a pile of straw a few feet wide represented the very best accommodations. In others, actual beds were offered, but they might be occupied by two or three people at the same time. Conditions in these places were filthy at best, dangerous at worst, and always rough enough to motivate all but the most degenerate to rise early and take to the street.

The mood that an eager young Lipton discovered as he roamed the city was much improved. The year had brought a brisk recovery to the national economy, symbolized by the completion of the Transcontinental Railroad. The last spike was driven at Promontory Summit, Utah, on May 10, 1869. In New York, Lipton learned that the founders of the Great American Tea Company had changed the name of their firm, in honor of the event, to the Great Atlantic and Pacific Tea Company. (With designs on a national market, they were also opening new shops and starting a mail-order business.) Tommy also found the first elevated railroad was operating in lower Manhattan, and the second-largest train

station in the world, Cornelius Vanderbilt's Grand Central Depot, was
rising on East Forty-second Street. In a bow to the Francophile trend
raging through high society, the depot sported a mansard-style roof,
just like the one that workmen were completing on A. T. Stewart's huge
new home on Fifth Avenue at the corner of Thirty-second Street. Faced
with gleaming marble, the Stewart mansion all but glowed next to the
brownstones that soldiered down the avenue as far as the eye could see.
It was the largest private residence in New York and the first of the great
mansions on Fifth Avenue. Its main hall, seventy-five feet in length, was
filled with one of the finest art collections in the Americas.

No one represented the ideal of immigrant success more grandly
than A. T. Stewart. Although an inheritance had helped him get his
start—he used it to buy a big stock of Irish textiles to sell in America—
his achievements were mainly the product of his own pluck, and this
won him wide admiration. However, he was hardly a soft touch for
those who hoped he might help them follow his example. A small man,
with reddish-blond hair and plain features, he employed a physically
imposing former judge to keep people away from his office door. Those
who made it inside received an impatient hearing and a gruff response.
Each new employee was assigned a number, which became his identity.
He submitted to a system of fines that reduced his pay each time he
made change incorrectly, reported late, or committed any of a dozen
other sins. He understood that he would be timed as he completed various tasks and that he would be dismissed for any slacking.

Stewart's temperament in business yielded unmatched success where
others failed. As it was being built, his competitors called his big store
Stewart's Folly (this was long before Seward's purchase of Alaska), but
he made it such a success that many of them were forced out of business and wound up in his employ. His strict rules made for excellent
customer service, and his obsessive competitive drive made him alert

to changes in fashion and technology that kept his business up-to-date. When dress styles changed in France, Stewart was the first to make the new lines available in New York. When steam-powered elevators were invented, he installed six of them.

With no children and little taste for social life—one biographer wrote that he didn't have a single "bosom friend"—Stewart's main outside interests, other than his wife, were good citizenship, philanthropy, and art. His collection of sculpture and painting featured major works by the European artists John Martin and Adolf Wagner, and many masterpieces by painters of the Hudson River School, including Frederic Edwin Church's *Niagara*. Stewart's purchase of Jean-Louis-Ernst Meissonier's painting *Friedland*, which depicts Napoleon in victory, set the record for the highest price paid for a single work of art at the time.

As a citizen, Stewart was very public about being a cheerful taxpayer and, unlike other businessmen, never appealed assessments. (By the estimate of *The New York Times*, he paid the government more each year than anyone else in the country.) He served the city and state in certain ceremonial roles—representing New York City at Lincoln's funeral, for example—and he committed frequent and very public acts of charity. During a terrible cold wave in the winter of 1854–1855 he opened a free kitchen in the basement of his store and gave away thousands of meals. In the late 1860s he joined Theodore Roosevelt, Sr. (father of the twenty-sixth president), J. P. Morgan, and William Dodge to found the American Museum of Natural History. Stewart also gave to hospitals and schools, but rarely without receiving publicity in return. Like everything else Stewart did, giving built his good name and contributed to his fortune.

In 1869, A. T. Stewart's business was so good he purchased the buildings that shared a block on Broadway with his store and began construction work to expand his retail floors. The rush of customers demanded more clerks and on the luckiest day he ever spent in America, Tommy Lipton rolled out of his rented space at the bedhouse, made his way to Tenth and Broadway, and was hired to be a clerk in the food department. Suddenly he was a bit player in the biggest retail show in America, and perhaps the world.

The rigors of A. T. Stewart's were no strain for Tommy Lipton, who had survived a tobacco farm, a rice plantation, and Louisiana in the grips of racial warfare. Well mannered and well spoken, he excelled at serving customers and keeping displays neat and appealing. He saw immediately that the way Stewart presented goods, as well as the attentiveness of the clerks, made customers more willing to buy. The quality of the goods wasn't much different from what he saw in Scotland, but "it seemed to me they were 'shown' to fuller advantage." A bit of polish and a smattering of pleasant conversation created what he called an "atmosphere" that wasn't found in a Glasgow shop. He also heard, somewhere in New York, a little doggerel that stuck with him for the rest of his life.

> *The man who on his trade relies*
> *Must either bust or advertise.*

The development of the continuous rotary press, which could print both sides of a roll of paper and produce thousands of copies per hour, was a boon to penny newspapers, which flourished in New York after the Civil War. (The technology didn't work out quite so well for its inventor, William Bullock, who died from gangrene after getting caught in one of his machines.) Along with the new dailies and weeklies came ever more elaborate print advertisements. Big retailers became major purchasers of advertising, and promotion became an important part of their business.

Everything about the retail business appealed to Lipton, and he studied the store's operation closely. Managers recognized his interest and abilities and gave him one promotion after another. As he moved around, he had a chance to see how cash and inventory were handled and how employees were managed. The upper floors at Tenth and Broadway housed sewing shops and offices that dealt with a vast network of suppliers, some of them company-owned and some independent wholesalers. For a bright young man, Stewart's was a twelve-hours-per-day university of modern retailing. When work was finished, he could walk the nearby blocks to see further evidence of the rise of modern retailing on Broadway and Sixth Avenue, as big new emporiums—Lord & Taylor, Stern's, R. H. Macy & Co.—rose to challenge the Stewart behemoth.

Among the many big new retailers, Macy stood out. A failed land speculator and gold prospector, he was friends with P. T. Barnum and used lots of aggressive advertising and fancy displays—including holiday-theme tableaux and an in-store Santa Claus—to promote sales. The red star, which became the store's trademark, was copied from a tattoo Macy received when he was a young man working on a whaling ship. He was also the first to routinely knock a penny or two off the price of an item, charging, for example, $1.98 instead of $2. The practice served two purposes. It gave shoppers the sense that they got a bargain while forcing clerks to register purchases with the cashier—in order to get change—and thereby limiting theft. His clerks, who dressed in blue-gray uniforms, were known to work such long, hard hours, especially during holiday seasons, that some slept in the store. In 1870, Macy's did more than $1 million in business.

While the great merchants became millionaires, Tommy Lipton watched, and saved his money. He got by on pennies a day, and, thanks to several promotions and raises, slowly accumulated roughly $500 (equivalent to about $8,000 in 2010). All around him, immigrants who found such success were marrying, settling in apartments, and establishing families. Buoyed by their great numbers, the Irish were quickly taking over New York City politics and achieving real power through elected and appointed office. Bright, energetic, and personable, Lipton, who was just one generation removed from County Fermanagh, could have floated up with the tide. But unlike the others, his homesickness was more powerful than his attachment to the New World. He had not found love or romance in the States, and letters from home weren't enough to soothe his aching heart. He began to wonder what he might accomplish in Glasgow with his cash and all he had learned. He decided to go home and become a kind of merchant showman, and would start practicing the role as soon as he landed.

To prepare, Lipton bought his mother the kind of gifts—a rocking chair and a barrel of flour—that would make a big impression on people in the Gorbals. As he crossed the ocean he refined his plan for getting noticed right away. The ship eased into a berth on the Broomielaw at midday but he would loiter until he knew that factory workers would be walking home from their jobs. He then descended the gangplank, summoned a horse-drawn cab, and placed the goods on the roof. As horse and driver carried the young man, the chair, and the barrel slowly down Crown Street to his parents' address, a crowd followed on the sidewalk. Old friends shouted to him, and he called back through the window.

The sudden, triumphant return of Tommy Lipton brought a crowd to his parents' home that night and the following day. While his mother rocked, visitors peppered him with questions about life in America, and he recounted his adventures for them. Besides the gifts for his mother he hadn't brought much of material value except cash. But he had acquired for himself two little affectations that might aid him in his coming assault on the local grocery business. First, he had grown a bushy mustache, which made him look more of a man and less of a boy. Second, he was experimenting with the use of his mother's maiden name, Johnstone, as his own middle name. The rough-and-tumble Tommy of the Crown Street Clan was becoming Thomas J. Lipton, a man of the world, a man with both a purpose and a plan.

THREE

Homecoming

A few steps below the sidewalk, the Lipton family's "wee butter-and-ham shop," as Thomas called it, was barely big enough for a display case, a counter, and a clerk. If more than two customers came at once they had trouble keeping out of each other's way. Despite this limitation, business was good enough to support the family and spare Thomas Sr. from working at a dangerous shipyard or foundry. He and Frances succeeded by holding to a routine. A wholesale shipment came from Ireland each week. Thomas fetched it from the Broomielaw and returned to stock the shop. As the days passed they sold pretty much all of it, down to the last egg, and then the cycle started over again.

Given their expectations, the Crown Street shop was everything Tommy's parents had hoped it would be. But compared with A. T. Stewart's retail palace on bustling Broadway, the little underground store felt like a tomb; the final resting place for a young man's dreams. Like every emigrant who returned to Glasgow, Tommy had risked being judged a failed adventurer. This is one reason why hardly any of the young Scots—or Irishmen, Welshmen, or Englishmen—who went to America ever came back. They saw reverse immigration as a matter of personal shame. The exceptions were those who brought home both a fortune and eyes open to the change under way in their native land.

The Glasgow that greeted Tommy Lipton in 1870 was fast becoming the most productive and modern city in Europe as it led the world in the transition from the Industrial Revolution to a gilded age of international trade, finance, and consumerism. The clearest sign of this change could be seen in poor districts like the Gorbals, where a new Civic Improvement Trust was tearing down slum buildings and putting up solid apartment houses with gas lighting and indoor plumbing. In the coming decade more than fifteen thousand housing units would be demolished and replaced by nearly twice as many new, modern apartments. Most were contained in four-story buildings designed to suggest stability and cohesion. These homes would help shelter newcomers, who added more than 105,000 to the census between 1861 and 1881.

Just as tidy new housing blocks replaced the crumbling tenements and divided houses, old commercial structures were being supplanted by new warehouses, factories, office buildings, and shops. The first cast-iron building in Britain (a warehouse with an ornate façade) had been erected in Glasgow, and Alexander Thomson's towering retail arcade, called the Egyptian Halls and Fancy Bazaar, with huge street-level windows, multiple skylights, and a carved ironwork façade, was bringing new energy and life to central Glasgow. A great public greenhouse called Kibble Palace—shimmering glass set in curving ironwork—was soon to open in Glasgow's Botanic Gardens. The University of Glasgow had moved from its original site in the city center (thirteen acres deeded by Mary, Queen of Scots) to a new campus along the River Kelvin. And new mansions were rising in the fashionable West End to house the growing ranks of middle managers and successful entrepreneurs.

To keep commerce sailing, another nonprofit do-good organization—the Clyde Navigation Trust—had built a new quay called Kingston Dock and was dredging the river so it could accommodate larger ships. New factories were opening and old ones were being expanded to serve growing export markets. Some of these industrial plants were built by newly ascendant American firms like the Singer Sewing Machine Company.

Although the American companies would be greeted with some suspicion, their arrival put people to work and did not threaten local industrialists. Indeed, Glasgow businessmen were leading a far broader expansion of British businesses around the world. Between 1870 and the dawn of the twentieth century, thousands of companies would be created for this purpose. Many invested in colonies and former colonies, but no part of the globe was excluded as firms went to Japan, Malaysia, Brazil, Russia, and many other nations to create subsidiaries controlled in every aspect from Scotland or England. Founded in the mid-1870s, the Burmah Oil Company of Rangoon, for example, was run from an office in Glasgow. Australia's most productive source of gold, the Mount Morgan Mine, was operated from London.

As British capitalists followed the spread of the empire to Asia, the Americas, the Pacific, and Africa, they sent back the profits they harvested. Their successes reinforced the idea that British entrepreneurs strode the world with a special kind of brilliance. As their repatriated profits mingled with the vast wealth drained as tribute from India and other corners of the empire, Britain came to dominate world finance. This money stimulated further development of leading technology industries at home in cities like Glasgow. Yes, the Americans were emerging from their Civil War with industrial vigor, but in 1870 the United Kingdom produced more steel by a factor of *twenty*, and twice as much as the rest of Europe put together. More impressive, Great Britain produced far more manufactured goods for export than any other nation. In fact, the factories of England, Scotland, and Wales produced sixty percent of all the capital goods—machinery, ships, locomotives, steel, etc.—traded in the export market worldwide. Glasgow, with the best-educated workforce in the world, was at the center of this trade.

In the Gorbals, where anyone who wanted a job could find one, Tommy Lipton chose to work behind the counter at his parents' little shop, and did his best to turn it into a Lilliputian version of a New York emporium. He wooed customers with respectful attention, dressed up the street-level window, and adjusted the buying to make sure supplies were available to meet demand. Soon the bank account holding the profits from his parents' shop was approaching a hundred pounds sterling, a sum that was roughly twice the average annual salary of a man in the neighborhood. It was also equal to the amount he had brought home from America and stashed safely away. Having learned in America that "money makes money . . . rapidly if it's used properly," Tommy told his parents they should expand their business. "We are doing as well in the Crown Street shop as we can ever hope to do," he told them. "If I open another shop, I can double the profits."

Stunned by their boy's audacity, Lipton's parents answered with equal caution. "What, risk all the hard-won savings of years in a wild-cat scheme of starting another shop, with all the worry and anxiety that would entail?" they asked. They then answered the question themselves. "Not on any consideration."

Having endured slavelike labor, a vicious hatchet wound, a knife attack, and the wilds of Manhattan, Tommy Lipton was hardly discouraged by a little resistance from his mother and father. He still had his savings in the bank, an eye for opportunity, and that American-style hunger for success that Walt Whitman called an "almost maniacal appetite." He would wait for his chance. It came in the form of a storm-battered ship that arrived in the Clyde five days late. The ship's hold contained tons of American goods, which the buyer had rejected on account of the late delivery. The next day an advertisement in a local paper announced that the cargo would be sold at auction on the Broomielaw dock.

Withdrawing all his savings from the bank, Tommy Lipton went to the riverside and joined in the bidding. He won a sizable shipment of cured hams and bacon and then spent the rest of the day hauling the lot around the streets of Glasgow. By evening he had sold every last scrap of the pork to neighborhood shopkeepers and turned 100 quid into 118. The work was hard, but he was struck by how quickly he had realized an eighteen-percent profit.

> Repeatedly I kept telling myself, that if I could make eighteen pounds by selling a few hams, I could make hundreds of pounds by selling a thousand of them. The operation was the same. The quantities didn't matter. All that did matter was the possession of a vision, determination, quickness to see an opening and to seize a chance.

The arguments Thomas made in his own head inevitably came out of his mouth as he worked in the shop with his parents. He understood that "success and fortune seldom come stalking up one's home street uninvited. . . . No, you had to go out and meet them more than half way." Unfortunately, from Thomas's perspective, his parents were not much interested in success and fortune. "We are only humble folks," his father would say. "We should be thankful that we have done so well. If we followed your plan, people would say we were riding for a fall; that the peas were shooting above the sticks. Come back to earth my boy, and stop building castles in the air."

These were the words of a man who had survived famine in Ireland, immigration to Glasgow, work in dangerous factories, and the deaths of four children. The Crown Street grocery store had freed him from the kind of hard labor that shortened men's lives, and it had become the kind of asset that his son could inherit and rely on to support the next generation. From this perspective, which was streaked with tragedy, Thomas Sr. saw God's grace in this modest progress, and great peril in asking Him for more.

Just as God-fearing as her husband, Frances Lipton wouldn't contradict him in their talks with their son, but she had come through life with a more optimistic view. When she was alone with Tommy, either in the shop or at home, she indulged and even encouraged him as he talked about opening his own grocery store in an empty shop on busy Stobcross Street on the other side of the river, nearer the city center. She even allowed herself a little reverie as he outlined his greater ambition to open stores in every neighborhood in Glasgow and then all over western Scotland. Better to have a son with some energy and direction, she thought to herself, than one who was satisfied with things as they were.

As Tommy spun his dream, others were already developing retail chains that could take advantage of bulk buying and distribution. George Huntington Hartford and George Gilman were building a national chain in America under the banner of the Great Atlantic and Pacific Tea Company, and in France, Félix Potin's efficient new markets were selling goods packaged at his own factory. Great Britain had yet to see a chain grocery company, but John James and Mary Ann Sainsbury had started in business on Drury Lane in London and would eventually open more stores. In Glasgow, Tommy tried to jolt his father into the chain-store business with a grand gesture. He walked north over the bridge to Stockwell Street and found, just past an alley called Goosedubbs, the saddlery operated by Leckie & Company. The nineteenth-century equivalent of a truck dealer, Leckie sold custom vans (and the horses to pull them) to Glasgow businesses. Thomas bought a whole kit—van, horse, shiny leather harness—and had the vehicle painted with the name "Lipton" on its sides. When it was ready, one of Leckie's men climbed aboard, pointed the horse's nose toward Crown Street, and clucked.

Thomas Sr. happened to be standing in the doorway of his shop when the van arrived at the Lipton shop. His son watched from inside as Senior spotted his name—Lipton—written in big letters and quickly climbed the few steps to the street.

"What on earth does this mean?" he demanded.

The driver hopped down, made a little salute, and announced the delivery of "your new horse and van, ordered by your son, sir. And I must say," he added, "it's a fine smart turn-out and does your son credit."

"Well I don't want anything to do with it," shouted Lipton the elder. "And you can take it back to where it came from."

The driver did as he was told, climbing back into the seat of the van, clip-clopping away. When he and his father were finished talking about what had just occurred, Tommy followed the van back to the saddlery. Embarrassed but undeterred, he persuaded John Leckie to take back the rig and its hay-burning motor, while promising that he would soon want the same kind of outfit for himself. "I am opening up on my own account in Stobcross Street shortly," he said.

The horse-and-wagon stunt had raised Thomas Sr.'s temper, but it also showed the depth of his son's ambition. Frances could see this, and finally began to challenge her husband on the matter of a new store. As Thomas would one day recall, she said she was happy to see her boy was "pushful, self-reliant and ambitious." These qualities had taken him across the ocean, where he had explored a vast and strange country and succeeded well enough to return with a tidy sum. In his months at home Tommy had used his charm, along with ideas borrowed from

America, to build up the business on Crown Street. He was more than ready to try something on his own, and likely to succeed.

With Frances adding her voice, the argument was finally won. The father gave his son his blessing to open the new business in the Anderston district, on the opposite side of the Clyde. The new store would occupy a busy spot—entirely aboveground—on the north side of Stobcross Street near the intersection of Lancefield, which led directly to the quay where wholesale shipments of fresh food were off-loaded from short-haul ships. It was a good-size space with a wide door flanked by display windows.

The area around Stobcross Street in Anderston bustled with the usual Glasgow mix of commerce and industry. It was best known for the big Clyde Rivet Works, a factory that employed two hundred men. Thanks to them, the spirits shops and tobacconists on Stobcross did brisk sales. However, the location did not guarantee instant success for any business. The space at number 101 was the site of a failed grocery store and had been empty for five years. In that time the landlord had done nothing to keep it up. The sorry conditions allowed Thomas to negotiate an extremely low rent. He then threw himself, and half his savings, into the job of renovating, equipping, and stocking the shop.

The stock got most of Lipton's attention. He believed that if he could find superior products and buy in large quantities, he could undercut the competition and build a high-volume business. Cash, and a promise to buy big, got him the best price. He added to this advantage by arranging for the shipping, and by showing up at the docks and nearby wholesale markets to collect and haul the goods himself. With this effort, an egg or a pound of butter or a rasher of bacon reached his sales counter at a price significantly lower than what his competitors paid. And here he had even more advantages. Young and strong, he would do the work of manager, clerk, cashier, salesman, and delivery boy all himself. Not needing to hire any help allowed him to reserve the part of his savings held in the bank to pay for future promotions and advertising.

The new grocery opened on May 10, 1871. (Eager to pad his claim to the title of Boy Wonder, Lipton would report that it was his twenty-first birthday. In fact, he turned twenty-three that day.) Entering below a sign that announced "Lipton's Market" in letters more than a foot high, the first customers found a brightly lit store with fresh, unmarred paint, gleaming display cases, and a proprietor dressed in spotless white overalls and a matching apron.

Tall and handsome, Thomas now parted his light brown hair in the middle, as was the fashion, and he sported a bushy mustache that made him look older than his years. He was already known, by many, as the young man who had made a showy return from America with both a small fortune and a wealth of wonderful tales. On opening day, shoppers knotted around his window from dawn to dusk. Those who came inside were charmed by the talkative Lipton—who bent slightly at the waist to greet them—and impressed by the quality of the goods and the low prices. By closing time the new shop had rung up sales far greater than the Lipton family's Crown Street store had seen on its best day.

Sales were strong at the Stobcross shop because Lipton offered his customers something new at just the right moment. After decades of stagnation, caused mainly by a surplus of labor, wages across Great Britain were rising at a rate faster than the cost of living. At the same time the real price of consumer goods was actually declining. Although it wouldn't be recognized at the time, Great Britain had begun a fifty-year period of remarkable improvement in virtually every aspect of daily life for the vast majority of people. In Glasgow a new water supply system, which tapped pristine Loch Katrine forty miles to the north, had begun to end the scourge of waterborne diseases. Improved housing, thanks to

the Civic Improvement Trust, further aided public health and contributed to a steady rise in both life expectancy and vigor—measured by
height and weight—of the average Scot.

Settled in places like Anderston, better-paid workers and their
families aspired to a middle-class life and the pleasures it could bring.
For decades the working class had subsisted on potatoes, grains, small
amounts of meat, alcohol, tea, and coffee. Many a breakfast or lunch was
simply tea and bread, and those who couldn't afford tea drank a substi-
tute hot beverage made of powdered grains and beans that was dubbed
"radical coffee" because it was favored by the striking workers called the
Glasgow Radicals, who had battled British soldiers in 1820. More than
fifty years later, the modest rise in the workingman's standard of living
allowed the pursuit of a better diet that included higher-quality tea,
meat, eggs, cheese, milk, and cream. At Tommy Lipton's market they
found these goods, and more, at the lowest price. They also discovered,
for the first time, that shopping could be a pleasure.

Until Lipton, the job of finding unspoiled and unadulterated food
at an affordable price in places like Anderston and the Gorbals was a
tiresome chore. The principle of "Let the buyer beware" governed most
retail encounters, and the typical neighborhood grocery store often ran
out of supplies before the demand was satisfied. When goods were available, prices and quality might vary widely from day to day, or even hour
to hour.

At Lipton's new store customers found reliable quality, low prices,
and ample supplies. They also found a shopkeeper who truly enjoyed
his work. Always dressed in a spotless white apron, he was attentive and
welcoming. When no one was in his shop, he'd stand on the sidewalk,
or clean the front window, and chat up whoever happened by.

He was always ready with an observation, a joke, or a story—perhaps
about something he'd seen in America—and a subtle sales pitch. A

chilly fog has swept up the Clyde and into Glasgow? Perfect weather for a soup with a bit of ham to fortify the body. Your husband's got a new job at the Blazes? A few slices of cheese, set between two slices of the Stevenson bakery's inexpensive new "Machine Bread" (made on a production line), would be a nice lunch for him.

The routine charmed Lipton's customers, who were almost exclusively older women charged with the daunting task of caring for home and family in an era when the job required great amounts of physical labor and ingenuity. Wives and mothers had to know how to feed a family without the benefits of refrigeration or a stove that supplied reliable heat. Coal fires, polluted air, and husbands who brought home industrial filth on their clothes, made cleaning the home a daily and strenuous chore. Raising children in this place was even more difficult. Despite the improved economy and sanitation, life in Glasgow still confronted children with real peril—epidemics, pollution, streetcars, gangs—and gave their mothers tortured dreams.

For these women, who knew too little relief from work and worry, a visit to Lipton's on Stobcross was an opportunity rather than a chore. Since his prices were good, and supplies reliable, what harm was there in walking an extra block or two so their shopping might come with a little chat with the tall and worldly young proprietor? Charm was just one element Lipton added to the retail experience. Light was equally important.

At 55 degrees latitude, Glasgow is one of the northernmost industrial cities in the world. With autumn, and then winter, the days grow so short that on the solstice the sun shines for less than seven hours. In response, Thomas turned up the many gaslights he had installed in the store. The warm glow spilled out the plate-glass windows and onto the sidewalk, inviting anyone who passed to come inside.

This simple act, which turned the Stobcross store into a neighborhood beacon, was remarkable at a time when most British shopkeepers burned just enough fuel to provide dim light and hoped the shadows would obscure the dirt and dust. To be fair, some favored low light because they considered it cozy. The great writer, artist, and critic John Ruskin was one of these traditionalists, and when he opened a tea shop in the mid-1870s he refused, as one observer noted, to compete "in either gas or rhetoric" with more modern competitors. Of course, in the "absence of these allurements" Ruskin's shop was run out of business by others who burned the lights as if the fuel were delivered free of charge.

What Ruskin didn't understand as he clung to a dimly lit past, was that a new generation of merchants had recognized that commerce could be a form of entertainment and bright lights turned a shop into something like the stage of a public theater. In this model, the clerk and the cashier and the customers played roles that became more comfortable when the setting was clean and the goods were fresh and well ordered. Lipton added to the show at his store with his patter, and this worked well enough to draw a loyal clientele.

For the first weeks Lipton did all the work himself, meeting the overnight boats from Ireland at six o'clock in the morning, wheeling his provisions across the bridge and uphill to the shop, and then unloading the lot and serving customers all day long. Determined to outdo the competition, he decided to forgo set hours and simply remained open for as long as there was business to be done. He made deliveries when requested—closing the shop while he ran to some address and climbed the stairs to an apartment—and he made a fetish out of sprucing up the shop. All these responsibilities could keep him busy, sometimes well past midnight, when he would fall asleep in a small back room.

Tommy would later recall that in those first months "I lived for my little business." His mother, though proud of his success, worried about the pace he maintained. "You're doin' fine Tom," she told him, "but dinna kill yersel' workin' o'er hard."

Self-preservation led Tommy to hire his first employee, a boy who could run around the city with messages and deliveries and clean up around the shop. He came from a family as poor as the Liptons had been in 1848 and his clothes were patched and threadbare. Gradually becoming a bit of a dandy himself, Thomas quickly concluded that something must be done about the young man's appearance. He wrote: "A ragged boy in my beautiful shop was so completely out of place that one day I put my hand in the till and took out a bright golden sovereign. 'There Jim,' I said. 'Go and buy yourself a decent suit and put it on during your dinner hour.'"

More than one clothier operated on Stobcross Street, and Lipton took for granted that the boy would be able to get outfitted and return for work in short order. (Since the one-pound coin was the equivalent of $250 in 2010, he may have also expected a bit of change back.) Jim fulfilled the first part of his mission—buying the suit—but got hung up on the rest. After three days passed with no boy in sight, Thomas went to Jim's apartment house and found his mother. Is something the matter? he asked. Is the boy ill? The mother answered that Jim was fit, and "he looked so respectable in the new suit you were kind enough to give him that he now has a better job!"

Jim was followed by another clerk who had a similar problem handling cash. This time Lipton handed over a half-sovereign and sent his helper to spend a few shillings on stamps for an advertising circular announcing "superb value at the lowest possible prices." (Lipton hadn't forgotten the ditty he read in New York about the man who "must either bust or advertise.") This time the boy actually returned from his assignment, but without the change. "The price of stamps has riz," he lied.

The clerk, who failed in his duty, was dismissed but the circular, trumpeting the quality goods at Lipton's store, was employed with great success. Lipton followed with a second, more detailed handbill that listed actual prices, and invited customers to compare them with the charges at other shops. (This one was distributed to a few hundred carefully selected addresses.) Next came a little ad in an evening newspaper, offering special Irish bacon at a price so low it "defied competition."

From this beginning, Lipton would pursue a strategy of nearly constant promotion and advertisement. A few trends were working in his favor. First, the government had relaxed taxes on advertising and newspapers. Second, new technologies were driving down the cost of printing. And third, the working-class public—Lipton's market—had become fascinated by a relatively new form of communication. New cheap cartoon-filled magazines—descendants of the original and more pricey *Punch*—were becoming popular across Britain, and the artists who did the drawing developed loyal followings. In Glasgow one of the most popular was Willie Lockhart, whom Lipton hired to ink up some posters to display in his shop windows.

Lockhart's caricatures were simple and direct. One showed a man being pulled down the street by a pig on a leash. The caption read: "Lipton's Leading Article." Another early cartoon showed a skinny, bedraggled man wearing a "Lipton's" sandwich board and a wealthy woman telling her husband, "No wonder Lipton is a bachelor if that's him!" A third drawing featured a man carrying a pig in a sack slung over his shoulder. The pig was crying and the man explained to a woman that the poor pink fellow was "an orphan. The rest of the family have gone to Lipton's."

In an era before publishers could reproduce actual photographs, this kind of commercial illustration represented the height of popular art for the working class. A new cartoon was posted each Monday. Lockhart was something of a provocateur and occasionally used his Lipton commission to take a poke at the government of Prime Minister William Gladstone. He also used notable local figures as models for his caricatures. A cartoon showing a fat policeman struggling over a wall that a thief had scaled with ease brought every member of the force to 101 Stobcross. (They wanted to see if they recognized themselves.) The exact identity of Lockhart's cop was never established, but Lipton would claim that many of the city's finest became regular customers.

Scenes of Gladstone hoisting a ham, or a policeman falling on a crate of eggs, were popular with Lipton's customers. Popular, too, were the occasional sculptures made out of butter that Lockhart added to the window decoration. (A racy one showed a stout policeman trying to seduce a dairymaid.) But even when he confined himself to the retailer's sales pitch, the weekly cartoons were greeted with some excitement, and hundreds of people visited the window. When he wasn't too busy inside, the genial Lipton would join the crowd on the sidewalk, charm a few of the viewers into his shop, point out a special item, and win another customer.

Two final bits of retail showmanship completed Lipton's promotional campaign. Determined to make his address stand out on a street where plain-fronted shops stood shoulder to shoulder, he labored over the design for a proper sign to hang from a pole that would jut out from the building and communicate at a glance. After discarding numerous ideas, Lipton decided that nothing would work better than a large wooden sign cut in the shape of a huge Irish ham and painted with such precision that it looked real. The swinging ham was installed on a hot summer day. The intense sunlight and temperature softened the paint and made it run just enough to create the illusion of a freshly cooked ham just removed from the heat and glistening with its own juices.

Crowds flocked to see the greasy ham. The improved sales inspired Lipton to add the final ingredient—a bit of performance—to his publicity scheme. To cast his show he went to the sprawling livestock market on the east side of Glasgow, where farmers sold anything that could moo, bleat, whinny, or grunt. Thomas rescued two large pigs from the slaughterhouse, which operated next door, and brought them back to Anderston. Borrowing the use of a private yard located away from his shop, he scrubbed the pigs until their pink skin glowed, put pink and blue ribbons around their necks, and tied matching tassels to their corkscrew tails. When the beasts were ready, Lipton paid a local man to attempt to herd them through the neighborhood to the store while carrying a sign that read "Lipton's Orphans."

The orphans attracted attention and led a small parade to the store. The next day Thomas sent his man and his pigs to a different starting point and had them follow a new route. He repeated this routine often enough to become the talk of the city. To maintain the public's interest, he tried to vary the display. Sometimes, instead of handing his man a placard, he painted messages on the sides of the pigs. "I'm Going to Lipton's," read the words on one side of a pig. On the other side he wrote, "The best shop in town for Irish bacon!"

Lipton added more variety to the show by occasionally hiring an Irish immigrant to play the pigs' minder and costuming him in an outfit— cutaway coat, knee-breeches, derby hat—that suggested a bumpkin from the old sod. (For generations, Irish farm families had kept prize pigs to fatten and sell for cash to see them through the winter. This practice had become such a powerful symbol that "Paddy and His Pig" were staples of comedy and caricature.) Armed with a shillelagh, Lipton's Irishman was supposed to drive the pigs, but they often resisted his direction. Their pigheadedness was part of Lipton's design and added to the enter- tainment of the crowds. The most outstanding display came on the day Lipton dared to start his troupe's journey on the far side of Glasgow Cross, a busy square at the heart of the city marked by a medieval tower and a statue of King William on a rampant horse. Five streets converge at the cross, and in the summer of 1872 traffic included new horse-drawn trams that ran on tracks. Lipton's pigs decided that the space between the tramline rails was a good place to rest, and settled down. Traffic came to a halt, a big crowd gathered, and Lipton had all the attention he could want.

With promotion and advertising, Lipton's business was so strong that six months after opening, he expanded his store into space available next door. At last unable to do all the work himself, Lipton began looking for a helper who would be competent, honest, and reliable. One day, as he walked across the great span of the Victoria Bridge—one of the widest in Great Britain—he spotted a strong young fellow pushing a barrow heavy with machinery and ironworking supplies. To Lipton's eye the barrow was loaded with at least a thousand pounds of weight, and though the young man gamely put his shoulder to the job, he barely made any progress up the slope of the pavement. Lipton fell in beside him and pushed. When the barrow reached the crest of the span he also joined the struggle to keep it under control as it coasted down into the Gorbals.

"What wages do you get?" Lipton asked the young man when they stopped on the other side.

"Seven shillings a week."

Lipton looked him over, thought for a moment, and said, "Come and work for me and I'll give you fourteen shillings a week."

"Right you are," came the answer.

William Love, who was six years younger than his new boss, would become Lipton's first truly loyal and competent employee. Bright and full of energy, he threw himself into his work and absorbed everything Thomas could teach him. As additional workers were hired, William took on more responsibility and Lipton was able to leave him in charge of the shop. Freed from the retail routine, he began to entertain ever more grand ambitions. "I was beginning to realize," he would later write, "that the first aim in business is to secure more business, and also, that the more business you can do, the less profit you can work on. Simplified down to the elemental truths, I realized that it would be far better to make a small profit on a turnover of say a thousand pounds than a slightly larger profit on a turnover of half that amount."

In any previous era, the notion of a Glasgow shopkeeper developing a high-volume business to reap a fortune on a thin margin of profit would have been far-fetched. No single store could attract enough walk-in customers to make such a scheme work, and managing more than two or three shops in an age before the telegraph and telephone would exhaust even the most energetic owner. Then there was the whole matter of supplying stores with quality goods. Obtaining, storing, and shipping large quantities of products, many of them perishable, required reliable transportation, warehousing, and capital.

Fortunately for Lipton, steam power, the dredging of the Clyde, and the ongoing expansion of Glasgow's port facilities promised to make it easier and less costly to import food from Ireland and beyond. The telegraph system, which now reached every corner of the city and most of the developed world, allowed for easy communications.

With these key technologies in place, Lipton only needed to build capital. He began by chasing the business of a single customer—the University of Glasgow.

With its recent move from the city center to Gilmore Hill in the West End, the growing university was establishing new relationships with suppliers of all sorts. Thomas won a contract to supply staples to the university kitchen and made the deliveries himself, early every morning. He then made sure that customers heard about this arrangement and others he made with important local businesses and families. "I did not hide my light under a bushel," he reported, "and I made as much capital as possible out of the fact that Liptons were supplying the famous firm of So-and-so with their household provisions."

As he made "more business" the major focus of his little enterprise, Lipton soon ran up against the limits of the wholesale traders at the Broomielaw and in Glasgow's markets. Determined to guarantee a supply and, perhaps, reduce costs, he began making more frequent trips to meet farmers and market men in both northern and western Ireland. With his pockets full of cash, Lipton traveled from village to village, buying all the meat, eggs, and dairy goods he wanted on the spot. In almost every exchange, buyer and seller made a good match, with Lipton getting the price he needed and suppliers unloading a greater volume of goods than they expected. Sometimes, however, the exchange was less than perfectly balanced.

On one of his earliest buying trips Lipton set out for the farm market town of Lisnaskea, near his Irish ancestral hamlet of Shannock Green Mills. His mother had maintained contact with farmers in County Fermanagh, which Thomas could exploit. He could also rely on the bit of history and fame associated with his name. In the previous century, a small gang of brothers called the Lipton Ones had led an armed farmers' uprising against British authorities. Later they fought a battle of a different sort, using their muscle to unite a young man in love with a young woman whose father forbade them to marry. Their legend grew when they were arrested and tried on kidnapping charges, which were dropped when the fair maiden testified that she had been rescued, not abducted, by the Lipton Ones.

The Ireland that Tommy Lipton set out to explore in 1872 was no longer suffering blight and famine. However, the population had continued to decline—it was about five million in 1872—and prices on farm commodities were significantly lower than in Scotland. This trade had been made easier with the opening of rail lines linking the farm country to the ports of Belfast and Dublin. Faster steamships, which carried both passengers and cargo, further encouraged these exports by reducing rates to the point that, even with the cost of shipping, Irish goods were still cheaper.

On his voyage from Glasgow to Belfast, Lipton met an English businessman bound for the same region he would visit in Fermanagh. When he told this new companion he intended to buy a big supply of butter and eggs, the man replied, "I'll put you wise to a wrinkle for taking a rise out of all your rival butter buyers. I know Lisnaskea. You can collar the market if you do as I tell you."

When Lipton arrived in the town he found a hotel and rested for the night. The next morning he got to the market before the farmers and rented a stall equipped with scales. He then hired a young man to hike along the main road out of the town with a stack of paper slips, with prices written on them in Lipton's hand. The slips guaranteed a good price, paid fully in cash, for all the butter and eggs a farmer could deliver just as long as he came straight to Lipton's stall and bypassed other buyers.

Within half an hour of his scout's departure, the first of the farmers appeared in the town square and headed straight for the man from Glasgow. Soon a line of barrows and pony carts had formed, with each man holding one of Lipton's notes. Weighing and counting as fast as he could, Lipton spent two hours buying every lot and piling the goods in and around his rented space. The plan was working, only too well. With a few of his slips yet reclaimed, and their bearers staring him in the face, Lipton ran out of cash. Sensing his predicament, other buyers who had been unable to get the goods they required began to laugh and jeer. Lipton looked at the waiting farmers, repeated his promise to buy, and asked them to wait for a few minutes.

Dashing across the square, Lipton entered a pawnshop and pulled out his silver pocket watch and its matching vest chain. The watch brought thirty shillings. This, combined with the cash he had brought to pay for his hotel, was just enough for him to honor his promises and corner the entire day's market in butter and eggs. After he gathered his haul and arranged to have it shipped, he sent a telegram home to request that money be sent by wire right away. He received overnight the funds he needed to pay the hotel, get his watch out of hock, and travel home.

Lipton would later cite his experience in Lisnaskea to support his belief that cash was the grease that made business run smooth. He would never again run short in the middle of a deal, and never again see the inside of a hockshop. The lesson about cash served Lipton for the next sixty years or so, and offers some clues about the man's business style. He understood the power of money to make more money. He enjoyed devising schemes, and when it was time to act, he moved decisively, even audaciously.

Less obvious, but just as important, is the clue that Lipton's Irish market adventure offers about his lifestyle less than a year after he entered business for himself. The fact that he carried a silver watch so valuable that it could be hocked to pay three farmers for their day's produce suggests that this young man, who began his life in desperate poverty, was already doing well in business and developing a taste for the finer things.

FOUR

P. T. Lipton

The young grocer Thomas Lipton disappeared for good, and was replaced by Thomas J. (for Johnstone) Lipton, in the year after the shop on Stobcross Street opened. At the time, ordinary Scots rarely used middle names or initials. These extra identifiers, however, were widely employed by Americans, and Thomas had likely gotten the idea in the States. The affectation would make him seem a bit upper-class and sophisticated. It would also distinguish him from his father.

Businesspeople learned the new name when Thomas registered his store with city officials and in various commercial directories. The greater public became aware of it when Thomas J. Lipton made his first big splash in the local press. The Glasgow papers reported that the young provisioner had imported one thousand frozen geese from Canada, which arrived by steamship "in fine condition, ready for the manipulation of the cook." Lipton was expecting thousands of frozen turkeys from the same source the following week, noted the newspaper, and, like the geese, they would be sold at cut-rate prices.

Lipton's birds were news because trade of this sort was just beginning. Thanks to speedier trains and ships and improved methods for keeping meat properly chilled, North American slaughterhouses were beginning to ship not only birds but also sides of beef and pork to Great Britain. This business would be halting at first, but by 1875 (four years before competition arrived from Australia) it involved thousands of tons per year. In Britain the most successful buyers were those who could take delivery immediately—no refrigerated warehouses were available—and distribute the meat before it spoiled.

For Lipton, who avidly pursued the attention of the press and public, the frozen-bird business was another move in what would become a lifelong, multilayered campaign to promote himself—or, to be more precise, an ideal version of himself—as the face of a new, modern, and respectable industry. No longer would shoppers be forced to buy in dark, dingy little shops offering a few basic items of questionable quality. Instead, Lipton would bring them variety and lower prices in a pleasant setting. And he would add enough cornball entertainment—parades, comic posters, and slide shows projected by "magic lanterns"—that P. T. Barnum would surely approve.

None of the showmanship would have worked if Lipton hadn't delivered the goods. So while he encouraged his clerks to laugh and banter with the customers, he also insisted on selling only the freshest, most appealing produce. The emphasis on freshness was comforting to shoppers who had deep concerns, based on real experience, about spoiled, contaminated, or adulterated food. Newspapers often reported on outbreaks of illness linked to milk products, vegetables, or meats, and the government reported that a quarter of the food samples tested were contaminated. As the widely publicized work of Louis Pasteur and Joseph Lister established in the public mind the link between poor sanitation and disease, the ambiance at Lipton's Market, where the air smelled fresh and someone always seemed to be sweeping or cleaning, equaled profit.

With success came enough income that Lipton was able to support his parents when they closed their shop on Crown Street. (Thomas Sr. and Frances were well into their sixties and, given the average life expectancy—forty-one—quite elderly.) Success also allowed Thomas J. to move out of his parents' home and into a series of high-status addresses in the fashionable West End, where construction of the new campus of Glasgow University had sparked much new development.

Lipton's first flat was situated close to Kelvingrove Park, a hilly preserve bisected by the gently curving River Kelvin and anchored by a towering ornate fountain honoring Robert Stewart, the man most responsible for the Loch Katrine water supply system. The new fountain was completed in 1872, at about the same time that the Kibble Palace was opened in the West End's Botanic Gardens. The beautiful park and wondrous glassed-in garden, where plants from the tropics thrived and flowers bloomed all year, spurred the rapid settlement of the neighborhood. Prominent industrialists, bankers, merchants, and professionals moved into houses designed by elite architects, including Alexander "Greek" Thomson. Soon the district attracted a crowd of artists and intellectuals who gathered in restaurants, cafés, and tea shops.

Once he settled in the wealthy and bohemian West End, Lipton invited William Love to live with him. The young man, whom Lipton had met on the Victoria Bridge, had turned out to be a highly competent and diligent employee. He was so reliable that he had risen quickly to be Lipton's second in command, taking charge of the business when the boss was away. The two would stay together in 1877 when Lipton bought and moved into a small manse in the suburb of Cambuslang, a beautiful green village eight miles south of the city and served by a convenient rail line. The house, which he named Johnstone Villa, would also be home to Lipton's parents, who would finally leave their Crown Street apartment.

Lipton would never share a home with anyone except William Love and his parents. And though he made a show of flirting and encouraged rumors about romantic attachments to various women, he would never be seen courting one. He doted on his mother. "She taught me to hold my head high and have ideals in life," he explained. And he had many women friends. But in the fullness of a life that would span more than eighty years, he was closer to his male companions and revealed no true intimacy, or attempt at intimacy, with the opposite sex.

As Lipton grew into a public figure, his romantic life would become the subject of questions from reporters and speculation in the penny press. He would skirt the issue, confessing his admiration for various beauties, but in the end declare he just never found the right one to marry. This was a common pose for gay and bisexual men of his time, and the signs would suggest he found love with his housemate, William Love, and, perhaps, with men he knew later in life. But he would never speak plainly about these relationships.

If he did hide the truth about his romantic life, Lipton had plenty of reasons. As the trial of his contemporary Oscar Wilde would demonstrate, any public man with other-than-heterosexual relationships faced scandal, prosecution, and even imprisonment if found out. (British law prescribed sentences as long as ten years.) Some men took the risk of signaling their sexual orientation by wearing a green carnation—a symbol used by Wilde—in certain social situations. Others, like the cross-dressing stage performers Ernest Boulton and Frederick William Park, signaled their status more openly by appearing in costume in public. But this kind of courage was rare, and if Lipton had relationships with men, indiscretion would inevitably mean the loss of his reputation, his business, and possibly his freedom.

Although he guarded his personal life, Lipton understood that a modern British entrepreneur needed to present a polished self to the public. Eager for self-improvement, he decided he needed better language skills and decided he might acquire not one but *two* new tongues. He bought some books in hopes of teaching himself to speak French and hired a native-speaking tutor—a Professor Schultz—to teach him German. Lipton paid in advance, and the German agreed to come to the Stobcross shop, where they would work in the back room.

On the appointed evening the boss at Lipton's Market, who had found little to like in his school days, prepared himself to become a student again. The teacher never arrived. Night after night, Lipton waited. When he finally concluded that he had been swindled, Lipton set out to find the man. He tracked him to an apartment on St. Vincent's Street near the city center, rang the bell, and confronted him as he opened the door. As Lipton recalled it in his book, he said, "I've been waiting for you to teach me German and now I'm going to teach you." The words led to blows and after about five minutes Lipton departed satisfied, if not fluent.

The next day a sergeant from the Western Division of the Glasgow Police Department visited the market while Thomas was out. Frances Lipton, now working there, was alarmed to hear her boy had assaulted a man at his apartment on St. Vincent's Street and was the subject of a search. A friendly sort who would rather not arrest the local grocer, the sergeant observed that if Thomas wasn't apprehended in a few days the matter might fade along with the professor's bruises. At his mother's urging, Thomas decided it was a good time for a vacation in Dundee, a city on the Firth of Tay, a hundred miles to the east.

In Dundee, Lipton found a hotel and took in the sights. His tour included a stroll along a wide and busy street called Murraygate, in the city's most fashionable shopping district, where new horse-drawn streetcars ran on steel rails. There he noticed an empty store on the south side of the street, between a clothier called Smith Brothers and the Collier &

Sons shoe shop. He found the agent for the owner of the five-story brownstone, inspected the empty store, and concluded the space would make "a magnificent Lipton market."

Until this moment in Dundee, Thomas had not set a firm plan to establish stores beyond Glasgow. Now he started to move in earnest to build a retail empire that would span not only Scotland but the entire United Kingdom. He negotiated a lease on the spot. A telegram from his mother signaled he could return home without fear of arrest, and on the train ride he had a chance to reflect on the future. He thought, "It was only a question of brains and organization, of making profits and conserving them to make other profits in precisely the same way and by the same methods." When he got back to Glasgow, Thomas heard that after the police had learned of other students who had been cheated, Professor Schultz had departed the city. A local judge declared that Lipton had performed a vital public service with his fists.

Safe from the threat of arrest, Lipton gave up the quest for self-improvement and focused his energies on his markets, where business continued to grow. To take advantage of economies of scale, he opened a second Glasgow shop on High Street, not far from the busy and ancient Glasgow Cross commercial district. (Following a rule he would stick to for life, he paid cash for all the fixtures and stock, and demanded cash for every item sold, too.) At High Street, where he found a wealthier clientele, the Lipton Market occupied a much bigger space than the one at Stobcross. It was manned by six clerks, instead of two, and this number grew quickly as business thrived. He often found new employees among the boys and young men he saw on the street, offering, typically, to double the wages paid by their current employers and winning their instant devotion.

Energized by his success, Lipton poured the profits from the new store into yet another, which he opened on Paisley Road in Govan, on Glasgow's western border. As late as 1864, Govan was so small and undeveloped it had no organized police force. By the time Lipton opened there, it was a home to three major shipbuilders, boilermakers, and other factories. Thatched cottages and country homes were being torn down to make way for stone tenements. In the next fifteen years the population would quadruple to more than sixty thousand. Each one of these newcomers—many were Irish or Gaelic-speaking Scots from the Highlands—would be a potential customer for Lipton, who could and would speak as either an Irishman or a Scot, depending on who was in the shop.

Lipton wasn't present at the Govan shop very often, however, as he was too busy employing "brains and organization" in order to advance his business. With William Love typically handling the management of each new shop as it came to life, he quickly opened new ones on busy Jamaica Street in Glasgow and in Anderston on Main Street. With the acquisition of this space, which was much bigger and in a busier spot, he closed his original market on nearby Stobcross.

With four large retail outlets, Lipton did so much business that he had trouble finding reliable sources for finished pork products. To overcome this problem he opened a slaughterhouse and curing facility on Robertson Lane near the city center. Set in a series of industrial buildings, the factory would allow him to cut costs further and control the quality of his products. During full operation, the plant could process twenty-four thousand hams and more than sixty tons of bacon per month. In time, the volume of goods the factory produced became more than his own shops could handle. Happy to profit from his excess capacity, Lipton became a middleman himself, selling wholesale to restaurants and hotel dining rooms as well as mills, factories, and other institutions that operated kitchens to feed their workers. He also began to export cheese and butter to the Caribbean, where British firms enjoyed special access to markets controlled by the Crown.

As he advanced his business, Lipton used every opportunity to put his name before the public. Gleaming horse-drawn Lipton vans crisscrossed the city with his name painted on their sides in giant letters. He sent free hams to the rich, powerful, and popular and then posted their thank-you notes. One recipient, a general, wrote that he had shared his succulent gift with a countess who happened to be the mother of Napoleon III's widow, Eugénie, the last empress of France. Lipton publicized the general's letter, which spoke of how much the ham had delighted the countess. Thus began the grocer's long association with royalty, which he would make sure to publicize whenever possible.

Although he could sometimes seem overbearing, Lipton was pioneering a new form of merchandising in an effective way. Besides borrowing a bit of fame from the elite, he cultivated the press by purchasing lots of ads and staging events that would put him at the center of public attention. It didn't matter if he came across as a bit eccentric. The British public had a well-established fondness for oddballs, many of whom they embraced with pride. In Lipton's time these included the wildly untalented actor Robert "Romeo" Coates, who traveled England in a carriage made to look like a cockleshell, and a raving but popular street poet of Dundee, William McGonagall. Hometown editors liked to publish articles about these characters and were more than willing to add to their reputations. In Lipton's case, the "character" was neither starry-eyed nor delusional, but his colorful persona made for good copy. When he reported selling thousands of hams, tons of bacon, and more than 175,000 eggs every week, the press happily declared him "the largest retailer in the world."

But it was not enough for Lipton to be seen as a big operator with fancy connections. The retail food business served a broad market—everyone eats—and he wanted every segment of it. In wealthier communities he advertised his relationships with prominent customers and made sure to appear as a wealthy and successful businessman. In poor and working-class districts he stressed his impoverished beginnings as a boy of the Gorbals and his undying loyalty to Irish immigrants and the Scottish-born poor. The Irish and the Scots might fight with each other, but in Lipton they shared a hero with a story as potent as the stories of Horatio Alger's characters. Lipton made this point in a handbill distributed all over town when Glasgow shipyard workers were locked out during a dispute over wages. In the pamphlet the addresses of his stores appeared beneath a poem titled "The Master and the Man: Lipton to the Rescue." It began:

> *Says Mr. Shipbuilder to Johnny McPhee*
> *Come here you scoundrel and listen to me.*
> *For twenty long years I've kept you I'm sure*
> *On one pound a week, how dare you want more?*

Before the poem is ended, the everyman McPhee stands up to his boss, saying he'll thrive on low-cost hams and other "dainties" thanks to Lipton, "the hero of High Street, the friend of the poor," who was loyal to the "lockouts" and had assured them they "shall still have their fill."

Poetry of this type was a staple of the Victorian media. Newspapers published regular contributions from self-made bards, and merchants often distributed paeans to themselves. It didn't matter if the writer was anonymous or the sentiment self-serving. If the lines were clever and people liked the message, these scraps of verse did their job. "The Master and the Man" was a bald attempt to connect Lipton's markets to the passions of the working class, and he almost certainly wrote it himself. But it also reflected his genuine affection for the men and women of Glasgow, whose struggles he knew firsthand.

In the city where industrial workers were among the first in the world to organize and demand better pay and conditions, class distinctions were keenly felt. True to Scottish values, honest work was revered by all, and even the rich tended to pledge their respect for labor. Lipton often said he valued a poor customer's shilling as highly as a rich one's pound, and this was probably true. Considered in this light, the ode he wrote to himself was, at best, an honest declaration, and at worst, harmless.

Not so harmless was the other promotional scheme Thomas pursued with great vigor in 1877. It began when he and his housemate William Love hit upon the idea of printing some advertising handbills that resembled the one-pound notes issued by the National Bank of Scotland. In size, color, design, and even texture Lipton's resembled the real thing to an uncanny degree. However, lines of script below the crest explained that they were issued by the "Great Irish Ham Butter and Egg Markets" of Thomas Lipton. The note promised that the bearer would receive a pound's worth of goods for a mere fifteen shillings upon presenting the note at a Lipton grocery. The signatures on the bill, placed where officers of the National Bank signed theirs, belonged to Thomas Lipton, proprietor, and William Love, cashier.

Had the nation issued a single recognizable currency, the Lipton note would likely have done its job as a sort of coupon and attention-getter with no other complications. However, Scots were used to handling a variety of currencies issued by different institutions. As thousands of Lipton notes went into circulation, people inevitably began to mistake them for the real thing. Lipton notes discarded on the street by people who recognized they were handbills were scooped up by people who couldn't believe their good fortune to find a one-pound note in the gutter. Some shop clerks, including those at Lipton's own High Street market, casually accepted them at face value as payment for orders.

Soon after the notes were handed out, Lipton got a sense of the confusion they were causing as he shared a compartment with three strangers on a Monday-morning train from Cambuslang into the city. During the short trip his traveling mates chatted about the previous day's service at their church and agreed that the preacher had made a stirring appeal for a special charity. One of the three, who was a church elder, complained that the donations from the congregation were disappointing, given the cause.

"That's funny, Elder," answered one of the others. "For I just said to Jeems here as ye went 'round wi' the plate that I never seen sae mony pound in oor collection since the church was built."

"Imphm, that's true. There were seven pound notes in the plate. Richt enough, but six o' them were Lipton's!"

Other incidents involving these fake bills were more serious. In a distant suburb called Old Kilpatrick, a man named Archibald McCallum found a Lipton note on the street and used it to buy himself a couple of drinks at a pub. Once the whiskey and ale did their work he used the change he had received to buy a round for the house. The owner of the pub didn't discover the note was a fake until he had poured its supposed value in alcohol. The police were summoned. McCallum was arrested. A guilty plea got him thirty days in jail.

The McCallum case was followed by the prosecutions of Samuel Gemmel, who was sentenced to twenty days for trying to use a Lipton note, and James Carson, who was locked up for two months. William Maxwell, whom the newspaper *The Scotsman* described as "a respectably dressed man," won the sympathy of the magistrate as he blamed Lipton. But in the end, the judge observed that he couldn't imagine a way the shopkeeper "could be got at," and Maxwell went to jail for a month. The courts did show mercy, however, on a woman who attempted to buy meat pies with Lipton scrip. The magistrate could not determine whether Helen Stewart actually knew the money she used was fake, so she went free on a verdict of "not proven."

In only one instance did the trouble caused by the notes involve Lipton directly. This happened when a bank in Glasgow's East End sued him in Small Debt Court over a Lipton handbill that had been accepted as a payment. Expert testimony from the cashier of the local branch of National Bank suggested that one of the fake notes could be confused for a real one by a reasonable, if less-than-alert, consumer. Others, including a rival merchant, testified that they had received Lipton notes in the course of business, which seemed to bolster the argument that the well-fashioned fakes were too easy to pass.

Although Lipton did not appear in court to defend himself, the ever-loyal William Love did testify on the shopkeeper's behalf. Love explained the idea behind the promotion and described how the papers had been distributed as handbills on the sidewalk. Unlike the bank cashier, Love was certain that no one in all of Scotland, where the literacy rate was higher than almost any place on earth, would reasonably offer or accept a Lipton note in trade. (Given that the handbills bore the message "Try Lipton's fresh eggs" and the firm's addresses on High Street and Paisley Road, Love had a point.) The magistrate grudgingly sided with Mr. Love, chiding Lipton for a caper that was "reprehensible in the extreme" but finding too little cause to let the case go further.

After the claim made by the bank, Lipton stopped distributing the handbills and collected those he could, and the furor subsided. He escaped responsibility for the losses suffered by bankers and businessmen, and for the long days spent in jail by men who might have been innocent of any malign intent. Rather, he reveled in the success of a stunt that made headlines in papers throughout Great Britain. In the years to come, Lipton the raconteur squeezed more value from the notes as he entertained the people he met with stories about them. In one he callously teases a beggar by giving him a fake one-pound note. The gleeful man disappears so quickly Lipton can't give him the "copper or two" he intends to offer once the joke plays out. In another he hears a tale of woe from a down-on-his-luck comedian working at the Scotia Music Hall in Glasgow. The comic says his pals at a bar named Shelly's took up a collection on his behalf that included thirty-five one-pound notes, all issued by the grocery store. After hearing of the man's disappointment, Lipton gives him a few real bills to make him feel better.

The old comedian's experience notwithstanding, no one profited more from the Lipton notes than the man whose name was plastered all over them. The trouble they caused, and the subsequent press attention, had people all over the United Kingdom talking about the Glasgow grocer. Even as some newspapers scolded Lipton, he found the general public was thoroughly amused. Already inclined to think of himself and his business in bold and dramatic terms, the promotion confirmed what Lipton had learned in America. All things being roughly equal, a person would rather spend money in a place where a little amusement might be part of the bargain.

Almost immediately after the Lipton notes were withdrawn, Glasgow's best-known shopkeeper installed funhouse mirrors beside the doors at all his stores and started a new advertising campaign. Over the concave mirror, which made a person's image look tall and thin, he placed a sign that read "Going to Lipton's." Over the other mirror, which was convex and made a viewer look short and squat, he posted the message "Coming from Lipton's."

Once he liked an idea, Lipton had a tendency to exploit it fully, and in this case he built a complete advertising campaign around the mirror images. Cartoons in store windows and notices in the paper used the figures of gaunt and then plump customers. On some busy shopping days he hired a dozen "cadaverous males" and a dozen of the fattest ones he could find. The thin ones paraded down one side of the street, carrying placards that read "Going to Lipton's." The portly fellows paraded in the opposite direction with placards announcing they were "Coming from Lipton's." In a variation on this display Lipton abandoned humor and went for simple sex appeal as he hired a number of the "buxomest" women he could find, dressed them in identical outfits, and had them parade to his store carrying baskets and signs reading "I'm Going to Lipton's."

By 1878 the people of Dundee, on the opposite coast of Scotland, could parade themselves to a new Lipton Market in the space on Murraygate that Lipton had discovered during his fugitive days. The first of his shops outside the Glasgow region, the Murraygate grocery, designed by William Love, was organized around a horseshoe-shaped counter that ran down both sides of the shop and along the back wall. Hams were suspended from the ceiling, and counters were piled with butter, eggs, cheese, and other items. Bright tiles covered the floor and the sides of the display cases. On high shelves cans and jars were stacked in pyramids.

In the future, all Lipton Markets would be outfitted according to Love's design for the one in Dundee. Most were identical to the Dundee shop, but a few, in wealthy districts, would get marble in addition to tile, and extra brass fittings. (These fancier stores also got clocks that displayed a series of pictures as the hands moved and "magic lanterns" that operated like slide projectors, displaying photos of famous places.) In daylight these shops bustled with activity. At night, thanks to the many gas lamps covered with opal globes, the stores glowed, as writer Alec Waugh reported, "like a fairy cave."

Each new cave was opened only after weeks of advertisements and then the arrival of The Great Lipton himself, decked out in white overalls and a white apron. The tall, handsome, and gregarious young man stayed long enough to demonstrate his charm and hand out a free ham to the first customer. He then left the supervision of the shop to William Love, who would stay until a competent manager was trained. Staffed by eighteen men and boys, the Dundee store, for example, was an instant success as it brought to the city the same combination of service, quality, and low prices that had won the loyalty of the hardworking city of Glasgow.

In many ways Dundee was like a small Glasgow. It was a center for shipbuilding. (Vessels that could survive whaling in the Arctic were a specialty of the shipyards.) And, like Glasgow, it was growing fast, thanks to Irish immigrants, who had helped raise the city's population fivefold between 1800 and 1870. Textile production was a major industry in Dundee, but instead of weaving cotton cloth, the local factories hummed with the production of jute, a versatile fabric generally used to make heavy products like burlap and carpet backing. Some of the wealth produced by this business found its way into infrastructure and civic improvements. A month before Lipton arrived, a new bridge over the Firth of Tay had been opened to rail traffic. At the time it was the longest bridge in the world.

The people of Dundee bought, literally, tons of meat and cheese and more than a million eggs from Lipton during his first year in business there. Pressing the advantage he had with the efficiency of scale, Lipton soon covered the town of Greenock with posters that declared "Lipton Is Coming!" He repeated the scheme in the town of Paisley and at both sites did enormous business when his stores opened. Cartoons, pig parades, and butter sculptures brought in the curious, and low prices moved them to become loyal customers. The colorful Lipton and his markets became so well-known that they were the subject of songs and jokes heard in theaters from Glasgow, where a popular comic sang "Lipton's Butter and Ham," to Aberdeen, where "Can Anyone Tell Me Where Lipton's Is?" became a music-hall favorite.

In Paisley and other communities, Lipton's biggest sales came during Christmas and Easter, which had only recently been recognized as legal holidays by the British government. For generations, Presbyterian Scots had marked Christmas in sober style, but thanks to the great efforts of merchants and Charles Dickens, the celebrations were becoming more elaborate and warmhearted. While *A Christmas Carol* gets much of the credit for reviving Christmas in Great Britain, Lipton can be credited with giving Easter a major boost. As the man most likely to profit from these customs, he put lots of time and energy into promoting Easter-egg decorating and ham feasts. During his first Easter season in Dundee he sold a quarter million eggs and twenty-five thousand hams.

The huge volume of business financed the opening of one store after another. By the start of 1880, Lipton had twenty shops in a dozen Scottish cities and was preparing to move into England with a market in Leeds and into Ireland with an outpost in Belfast. Although the newsagent W. H. Smith had more actual outlets scattered around Great Britain—thanks to small stands at railroad stations—no other general retailer even came close to matching the number of stores in Lipton's chain. In America, the Great Atlantic and Pacific Tea Company had about a hundred stores, but it was still just a tea and coffee company and not a general grocer. A few small chains of grocery stores did business on a regional basis, but none approached the size of Lipton's. With the profits collected from so many shops, Lipton found it got easier to finance new ones. He regarded these stores as both business outposts and public amenities for the benefit of all. When a reporter asked him about his politics, he said, "My politics are to open a new shop every week."

Not surprisingly, in many communities the public viewed Lipton's arrival as a sign of civic progress and considered his low prices to be a capitalist's form of grace, bestowed upon them by a smiling, smooth-talking man dressed all in white. Some competitors struggled and failed, but in general they got by because they sold the kinds of lower-quality staple items—herring, cheap cereals, and bread—that Lipton considered beneath him to sell. Positioned squarely between these down-market shopkeepers and the few very exclusive ones who had long catered to the rich, the new stores tapped the growing demand for better food—made more affordable by declining prices—expressed by working- and middle-class customers.

This seemingly insatiable demand became Lipton's biggest problem as he used the profits collected from his far-flung empire to reach out even further into the countryside for sources of supply. Although he insisted on getting top quality for his money, too much of the butter he received from Ireland was inferior. He saw trouble in the way farmers handled and shipped the product, and published articles in the Irish press that suggested improvements they might make, "beginning at the fountainhead—the cows" and extending to the methods used for salting, storing, and packaging.

Similar problems with supplies of eggs, hams, cheese, and other items caused Lipton to make several big moves. He built a depot at Ballina, in Northern Ireland, where he could improve handling and shipping. He then moved his Glasgow processing plants and warehouses from narrow little Robertson Lane to a large block of stone buildings on Lancefield Street, not far from the site of his first store. The buildings were close to the quay at the foot of the street, where freighters arrived with goods. They were also big enough so that he could expand his processing operations to produce more ham, bacon, and other delicacies. Hundreds of people worked at this complex, earning higher-than-average wages for twelve-hour shifts. Overtime—performed after the usual long day's work—was routine as the volume of sales grew faster than new workers could be hired and trained.

A decade after returning to Glasgow from America with a sack of flour, a rocking chair, and a few hundred dollars, Thomas J. Lipton was a rich man. At age thirty-two (he claimed to be just thirty) he was known to people all over the United Kingdom. And word that he might open a market could set an entire village abuzz with excitement.

The trends that had allowed Lipton to achieve so much, so quickly—falling wholesale prices and a growing middle class—were still strong. And remarkably, no one else seemed to be matching Lipton's strategy. The Sainsburys of Drury Lane, for example, were still confined to London. With the field to himself, Lipton was poised to conquer all of Britain. All he needed was to expand his wholesale sources. He had sent buyers "with open checkbooks" to Russia, Sweden, and Denmark, and found the Danes especially well prepared to ship high-quality goods.

FIVE

The Big Cheese

Thomas J. Lipton finally got to sail for America on the Anchor Line's luxury steamer *Devonia* in July 1880. Fourteen years after his first trip to the New World—a grueling two-week passage in steerage—he traveled to New York as a first-class passenger who was so prominent that after the lines were cast off and the ship took its initial heading for the Irish Sea, the purser made a little speech in which he announced to all the passengers that the merchant prince of Glasgow was among them.

Although it was not one of the newer Clyde-built "Atlantic greyhounds" that had begun to set new speed records, *Devonia* was a fast ship, and in calm summer seas the crossing would take just a little over eight days. During the voyage Lipton ate sumptuous meals in the saloon, which was bathed in the glow of a massive stained-glass skylight. The courses were delivered on china plates decorated with the Duke of Devonshire's crest, which showed two stags garlanded in roses. Between meals he could listen to music—the first-class parlor was equipped with both a piano and a pipe organ—while lounging in an upholstered chair. He was able to read in a well-stocked library, and fresh air was always available on the main deck, where passengers could stroll or play quoits, which was like horseshoes except that players tossed rings made of rope instead of iron shoes.

The Devonia arrived in busy New York Harbor on a clear, sunny day when scores of merchant ships rode at anchor waiting to dock. Among them was the schooner *N. H. Burrow,* with half its foremast missing and the stump charred by lightning. Near the Brooklyn shore a steam-driven dredging machine mounted on a barge poured black sludge into the holds of flat-bottomed mud-scows. In the open water, dozens of pleasure boats loaded with kegs of beer and cases of champagne moved lazily in a light breeze as the Hudson River Yacht Club conducted its annual regatta.

At Castle Island, Lipton met immigrant crowds far larger than he had seen in 1866. The half-year total of newcomers entering New York—almost 178,000—was triple the number recorded in the first six months of 1877 and represented the heaviest flow in twenty-five years. Many still arrived from the British Isles, but the numbers from Germany, Italy, and Scandinavia were rising quickly. A few days earlier, six hundred Mormon converts from Sweden and Norway, shepherded by twenty returning American missionaries, had passed through on their way to Salt Lake City.

After clearing official checkpoints and leaving Castle Garden, Lipton entered a city that was substantially cleaner and less dangerous than the one he knew in 1866. Police reforms had brought a semblance of order to even the roughest neighborhoods, and great sanitary and public-health projects led by Dr. Elisha Harris had yielded vast improvements in conditions on the street. This was accomplished despite a rapid growth in the population, which had risen to 1.2 million, making New York the sixth-largest city in the world.

Everywhere Lipton went in New York he could see and hear growth and development. The city's newspapers had begun to publish photographs in their daily editions and phonograph music drifted out of theaters and saloons. Typewriters, a new invention, clacked in offices, and Bell's telephones rang in hundreds of locations served by the world's first working exchange. (Glasgow had just two telephones, which connected Lord Kelvin to an assistant at the new university site and were only used experimentally.) Although electricity was not yet lighting New York streets at night, transmission wires were being strung and Thomas Edison was designing the nation's first power station, which he would soon build on Pearl Street.

Invention had produced great new fortunes in America, and this wealth was concentrated in Manhattan, which was quickly becoming the national center for finance and investment. By 1880 the richest men in the country, led by Andrew Carnegie, had begun to move to the borough from every corner of the nation. When he traveled uptown, Lipton passed their new mansions and others under construction as the phenomenon the *Times* called "mansard mania" drove the newcomers to surpass one another in the construction of their palaces. A more cosmopolitan place than the one he had left in 1870, the city now had a museum of natural history, and its museum of art had just been installed in a new building in Central Park. On the day Lipton arrived, more than one thousand people visited to see the special exhibit of glass, silver, and gold from ancient Cyprus and modern paintings by both Americans and Europeans. When they are seen side by side, noted one critic, "you feel that American art is not so bad after all."

Beneath this high culture, New York still offered something for every taste. A brand-new shipment of assorted primates from Africa was on display at the Central Park Menagerie. And up on the corner of 116th Street and Sixth Avenue crowds packed a newly built wooden arena to watch a traveling troupe of Spanish bullfighters battle steers purchased from nearby stockyards. The show opened three days after Lipton arrived and thousands of New Yorkers took trains to the arena. In the end, only one of the bulls had a taste for the fight and he sent the brightly costumed matadors running. As one observer noted, the show was, if not fearsome, "quite funny." Predictably, the whole thing would end badly, when, months later, the police were compelled to shoot two escaped steers—one absorbed a hundred bullets—and the arena went into foreclosure.

Thomas had, in fact, come to America to chase steers, and other prey, himself. By early August he was on his way to Cincinnati—then the eighth-largest city in America—where he would look for wholesale suppliers. The train from New York passed farms bigger than any Lipton had seen in Great Britain and small cities bristling with new factories and commercial districts. In Cincinnati he found a bustling center for agricultural products and manufacturing served by fifteen railroads. Fancy steamboats with orchestras, calliopes, and glittering chandeliers plied the Ohio River. And at Hunt's Hotel (recommended by *King's Pocket-Book of Cincinnati*) Lipton found himself on raucous Vine Street, where hucksters sold patent medicines, and men of all ranks, including the famous boxer John L. Sullivan, came to indulge their every appetite.

Having come to Cincinnati seeking reliable sources of meat, cheese, and butter, Lipton surveyed the options and discovered that local slaughterhouses, especially pork processors, were actually in decline. Pork being his most urgent need, he then pressed on to Chicago, which had almost completely recovered from the Great Fire of 1871. Growing faster even than New York—the population would rise from 100,000 in 1860 to 1 million in 1900—Chicago was bursting with development paid for with the profits from railroads, steel, and the ever-growing meatpacking industry. Thanks to Gustavus Swift's invention of a reliable refrigerated railroad car, the business of collecting and killing animals and shipping the edible parts to distant buyers had become concentrated in the hands of five giants, including Swift and P. D. Armour—"We Feed the World" was his motto—who were moving quickly to dominate the global trade in meat.

A ferociously competitive businessman, Armour had used new methods for canning and shipping meat to make his first profits, and gained more by making such products as glue and bonemeal out of the hair, hooves, skin, and bone other packers discarded. However, Armour's success was not just a matter of pluck and thrift. He also used his position as a major shipper to gain unfair secret discounts from railroads and to block shipments of his competitors. And he reaped still more profit when he leased his refrigerator cars to carry fruit from California without paying government fees. Lipton would one day compare the boisterous Armour, who wore huge muttonchop whiskers, to Theodore Roosevelt. They may have resembled each other personally, but in fact Armour was the type of businessman bully Roosevelt despised.

The full truth about Armour and the others who created the big meatpackers' trust wouldn't be revealed for decades. In the meantime, tourists in Chicago—Lipton included—accepted the idea that these giants were creating a new era of food improved by technology. The industrial meat complex was Chicago's greatest tourist attraction. Rich and poor alike eagerly paid for a few minutes in one of the observation towers near the stockyards and to walk through the huge sheds where the most gruesome work was performed. At the typical slaughterhouse, animals entered mooing, bleating, and oinking. Just past the doors they were met by men who were paid piece-rate and for this reason killed with furious speed. With steam power driving much of the machinery, carcasses were then disassembled with astounding efficiency. The meat was salted, cured, and packed for shipping to markets around the world. By-products were sent to rendering plants, tanneries, soap works, and glue factories. Waste went into the Chicago River, which became so polluted people called it Bubbly Creek.

Shocking as it would have been in another setting, the polluted river rarely got a mention when people described what they experienced in Chicago's meat district. More typical were the recollections of the great actress Sarah Bernhardt, who would visit a few months after Lipton. In her memoir she recalled "the almost human cries of the pigs being slaughtered" and the "sanguinary mist" in the area where they were skinned. Bernhardt also wrote that hours after her tour, as she struggled to get the sight, sound, and smell of the place out of her mind she wound up fainting onstage.

No cloud of blood or cries of agony would disturb Thomas J. Lipton as he visited the South Side. Having toured many smaller slaughterhouses and packing plants (including his own), Lipton was a connoisseur of butchery and he was captivated by what he saw. Day after day he wandered the sprawling complex, and he asked so many questions that he was certain the "employees must have thought I was the most keenly interested stranger they had ever seen on the premises. I was." Eventually Lipton introduced himself to higher-level officials at the packing houses, among them one of the partners in a midsize firm called Kingan and Company. The man happened to be from Belfast, Northern Ireland, and knew about Lipton's business. He would become a trusted advisor as Lipton bought Chicago pork and then, years later, when he decided to open his own packing plants in the United States.

As an old man, Lipton would claim he joined the Chicago meat trade during his first businessman's tour of the United States. In fact, five years would pass before his Cork Packing House opened there, but the old man might be forgiven the mistake since this time in his life was a blur of activity. From 1880 to 1900, Lipton would literally dash around the world in pursuit of new markets and entirely new lines of business. During this time he seemed also to have developed a knack for appearing, Zelig-like, at important places or events and with prominent people. Hardly accidental, these associations were the product of his determination to build an appealing public persona and of his talent for attracting publicity.

In 1880 when he treated himself to a few days of tourism in Washington, D.C., he inevitably wound up with the American president's hand in his own. This encounter, and another involving a troupe of con artists, would be added to the trove of anecdotes that helped to create the public Lipton.

According to his own account, on the morning when he arrived at his hotel in Washington, Lipton learned that President Rutherford B. Hayes often received the public during special visiting hours. Hearing that this was one of those special days, and that Hayes might see anyone who appeared, Lipton hired a carriage and driver and rode quickly to the White House. He walked to the front door unmolested and rang the bell. A servant appeared, and when Lipton asked if Hayes was home, the man answered, "He is sir! Will you please follow me?"

A surprised Lipton was led directly to a spacious first-floor chamber where a man he assumed was a secretary greeted him. The fellow looked to be in his late fifties. He was stout and wore a bushy mustache that covered his mouth and flowed into a long, graying beard. Seizing Lipton's hand, he shook it warmly and asked his name and where he was from.

As Lipton gabbed about coming to America from Scotland, his interlocutor said he had cousins in the city of Perth, which was southwest of Dundee. He wondered if Lipton might know them. Having never visited Perth, Lipton cut him off before he could tell him their names. After a few minutes more, Lipton felt so charmed that he suggested they eat lunch together "after I have had the honor of meeting the President."

"But I am President Hayes," came the answer from the man with the long beard.

The story ends with Lipton's profuse apologies to the president and an explanation for the confusion. It turned out that the White House was not really open for a public reception that morning. Rather, the president had an appointment with someone neither he nor his doorman had ever met. One assumption had led to another, resulting in a great story.

Lipton's other adventure in Washington yielded a tale that was even more convoluted and, since it ends with him playing the clever hero, of uncertain veracity. As he told it, the story begins with a bright young man on the street clapping him on the back and mistaking him for a long-lost friend from Indianapolis. The two decide to tour the Capitol Building together, where they meet the young fellow's older friend, whom he calls the Colonel. According to the Colonel, two famous Lakota chiefs—Red Cloud and Spotted Tail—were in town to attend the unveiling of a statue. One thing led to another, until Lipton, who was excited to see real Indians, found himself alone on the Virginia side of the Potomac, where he discovered no statue and no Indians but rather a crowd of crooked gamblers. Lipton tricked them into returning to the city, where his bankroll supposedly awaited, and then turned them in to the police.

After visiting Washington, Lipton went north for a few more business meetings—cheese was the main subject—and the ship that would carry him home. The British economy was suffering from a brief downturn, caused in part by cheap imports from the New World. Although domestic farmers suffered from the pressure these supplies put on prices, almost everyone else benefited from the competition. As a retailer who sold the ultimate necessity, food, Lipton gained more. As of 1880, British consumption of eggs, butter, and cheese was nearly double what it had been two decades earlier. This trend, and similar growth in meat consumption, would continue for another decade as trade transformed the national diet. As food prices declined by thirty percent, better nutrition raised life expectancy. All of this was very good for Thomas J. Lipton, who sold what people wanted, at the best prices, and saw his customer base grow larger every day.

Although other grocers were creating small, regional chains, none grew at the pace Lipton would maintain as he blanketed Scotland with stores and moved into Ireland, Wales, and England. His first English outpost was established in Leeds in early 1881. This opening, like all the others, was preceded by a blizzard of publicity, including numerous newspaper ads and posters declaring "Lipton Is Coming!" as if he were a stage attraction or an evangelist. (D. L. Moody, the great American preacher, happened to be crusading through Britain at the time, generating so much attention that in every city the crowds were bigger than even the largest halls might accommodate.)

The old tricks of advertising worked well enough, but Lipton worried that both he and his customers would grow bored without a new type of promotion. Not long after the Leeds opening he hit upon the idea of buying the two largest wheels of cheese he could order—the world's largest, he hoped—to display in Scotland and England. Given that local newspaper editors could never resist reporting on anything that claimed to be the biggest or best in the world, the press was sure to come running. Nevertheless, Lipton alerted them as soon as the order he placed with an American cheese maker named Wight was confirmed by cable.

Famous for factory cheese that tasted handmade, Dr. L. L. Wight of Whitesboro, New York, was an officer of the American Dairy Association and a frequent champion in cheese competitions. Dr. Wight prevailed because he had pioneered the use of primitive air conditioning and carefully controlled steam heat. Cold water piped from deep wells chilled his storerooms to prevent the cream in his milk from separating in storage. Specially controlled heaters allowed him to then cook his cheese evenly. As he gradually increased the scale of his equipment, Wight had been able to produce ever larger wheels of cheese without sacrificing quality.

Ceremonial big cheeses (hence the common expression "big cheese") had been popular in the United States since 1802, when dairymen in Massachusetts presented Thomas Jefferson a 1,200-pounder named Mammoth, which they made with the help of a cider press and steel bands. (Wary of gifts, Jefferson insisted on paying for it, at sixteen cents per pound.) Andrew Jackson's inaugural cheese weighed 1,400 pounds, and in order to get rid of it he allowed visitors to carry as much as they liked home. His successor, Martin Van Buren, received a 700-pound wheel from Orange County, New York. Careless guests dropped so many crumbs in the East Room, where the cheese was served, that carpets and upholstered chairs were ruined.

While Americans were familiar with them, Britain had seen relatively few big cheeses. Wight had previously supplied Lipton with 500-pounders, but this time he promised to exceed his previous efforts by a factor of almost seven. As the newspapers reported, two hundred milkmaids gathered four thousand gallons of milk from eight hundred cows to produce the so-called monster cheeses. When finished, the two disks were each eleven feet across and twenty-four inches thick. Wight's workers had to wrestle them onto wagons and then onto a barge, which carried them down the Erie Canal to the Hudson and the port of New York. There the monsters were hoisted onto the SS *Surania* and dispatched for the Broomielaw.

All the publicity about Lipton's special order caught the public's fancy. Customers at his Glasgow stores were alerted to the transatlantic progress of the big wheels, and when they arrived at the quay on December 12, hundreds of curious Scots stood waiting to see them hoisted from the ship's hold. One was transferred immediately to a railcar for shipment to the London Royal Aquarium, a giant hall where, because of design flaws, no fish (other than a dead whale) were ever displayed, but huge crowds came to attend concerts, stage plays, and animal acts.

The Glasgow cheese, which like its twin weighed almost 3,500 pounds, was winched down onto a wagon that was hitched to a smoke-belching steam traction engine. The engine looked like a small locomotive equipped with wide wheels that allowed it to navigate slowly and clumsily down Clyde Street and then up to Lipton's High Street shop. With British law restricting their speed to the pace of a man at a brisk walk, traction engines were used only when draft horses and oxen were not up to the task. For this reason, they generally attracted attention when they did appear on city streets. Giant cheeses were even less familiar, so people came out of buildings along the route to gawk and point as the white-aproned grocer and his prize passed.

By the time the engine and cheese reached the shop, Lipton had begun to call the thing Jumbo—in honor of the famous twelve-foot-tall elephant at the London Zoo—and a crowd of perhaps a thousand filled the street. To Lipton's apparent dismay (but perhaps his secret delight), after they hoisted the thing down to the sidewalk, workmen were unable to wrestle the cheese through the door. When the shop window proved too narrow as well, Lipton jauntily announced it would be loaded back onto the wagon and pulled slowly to the bigger Lipton's on Jamaica Street.

Much of Glasgow would have had a chance to watch the traction engine crawl through the city streets. At Jamaica Street, Jumbo was finally installed in the window. There it would spend the rest of the day undisturbed. That evening at Cambuslang, as Thomas regaled his mother with the story of Jumbo's journey, she reminded him that "it would be a better advertisement still, Tom, if the cheese is good cheese."

Having nicked a sample already, Tom could assure his mother that Dr. Wight's creation was, indeed, quite tasty.

The delicious giant would be displayed until Christmas Eve, when Thomas himself would carve it up for his customers. (After a few days in London its companion was sent to Lipton's store in Edinburgh to be sold the same way.) But since he was never one to pursue anything halfway, Lipton kept thinking about his cheeses and the opportunity they represented. He thought about the British tradition of adding silver coins to Christmas puddings and the widely held belief that the person who found one in his serving would enjoy good fortune in the year to come. Why not do the same with the cheese? thought Lipton. And instead of silver coins, why not gold?

With great care, and a long tool used to take samples from tubs of butter, Jumbo and his brother were soon transformed into Golden Cheeses, each loaded with sovereigns and half-sovereigns. Fresh notices in the newspapers and window posters announced that once the cutting commenced, buyers would be allowed to purchase pieces ranging from half a pound to four pounds. In his advertising Lipton noted that he had arranged for a dozen police officers to keep order on the big day. Of course this warning was issued for dramatic effect rather than out of genuine concern about public order.

As it turned out, Lipton's theatrics were also a good precaution. On Christmas Eve, Jamaica Street was jammed with people eager to buy a bit of Jumbo in the hope of striking gold. While the police struggled with the mob, the merchant showman in his white suit actually seized a knife and jumped onto the big disk to announce that the carving would commence. For the rest of the day he would listen for orders, carve off the proper amounts, and pass them to clerks who would do the wrapping and transfer payment to the cashiers.

The crowd grew so large that it spilled onto High Street and stretched for more than a block, a scene Lipton would later describe as one of "perfectly good-natured pandemonium." Inside, many customers began digging for coins as soon as they got the cheese in their hands, tearing at the wrapping paper while they stood at the counter. Most sighed with disappointment when they found they had purchased nothing more than a chunk—now a crumbled mess—of moderately good American cheese. However, Lipton had been true to his word. Gold awaited a lucky few, and their cries of discovery arose often enough to keep the mob motivated. Many who found no coins at their first purchase returned to the line for more. Others, who found coins in their first go-round, became convinced that it was their lucky day and so got back in line for another chance. Even the police officers caught the spirit and joined the queue. One who found a sovereign lost his helmet while celebrating with a dance.

Golden Jumbo was so good for business that Lipton decided that for the next Christmas each one of his stores would display a giant cheese loaded with coins, and conduct the same preholiday carving ritual. Obtaining this many big cheeses would require that Lipton find additional suppliers and, in some cases, pay for special manufacturing equipment. These investments were repaid in free advertising as the huge wheels attracted attention around the world. In 1886, Richardson, Beebe and Company of East Aurora, New York, became the subject of national pride when it filled Lipton's order for fifteen cheeses that were more than four feet thick and twenty feet in circumference and weighed roughly two tons apiece. The successful transport of these monsters to Britain was hailed as an accomplishment equal to the U.S. Navy's remarkable transfer of a 180-ton stone obelisk from Egypt to New York and its installation in Central Park.

Lipton spared no effort when it came to exploiting this promotion. In each community the Big Cheese received a parade from the train station to the store. If a circus happened to be in town, Lipton or his local manager would rent an elephant, which would then be decorated with Lipton banners and employed to haul the cheese wagon. Lipton also made a stunt out of the ceremonial cutting, accepting proposals from groups who volunteered for the chore and making a fuss over his choice. Students, mayors, and stage stars were all enlisted. (Lipton also hired entertainers for other publicity grabs. One of the most unlikely involved the famous mesmerizer Carl Herrmann, whose Vandyke beard gave him a truly devilish appearance. Lipton brought the press to his Lancefield Street office to see two local physicians take the telephone and become hypnotized by Herrmann, who was on the other end of the line. The first demonstration of hypnotism by phone had nothing to do with ham or eggs but it got Lipton's name in the papers.)

With every Christmas, Lipton honed his talent for attracting attention and turning apparent setbacks into advantages. In Sunderland, on the North Sea, police decided that the hidden coins made the cheese stunt an illegal lottery and tried to stop it. Lipton got around this problem with signs declaring that the hunt for coins was merely a game and all that were found should be returned to the shop's manager. (Naturally no one followed this instruction.) In nearby Newcastle, where authorities tried to discourage people from trying their luck for fear they might choke on a sovereign, Lipton paid to advertise the danger under a banner headline that read: "Police Warning." The alarm brought even more people to the store on Christmas Eve.

During other seasons Lipton tried to keep his name before the public and attach it to whatever excitement might be at hand. When shipbuilders in Liverpool launched a new ocean liner, he commissioned a replica, carved out of butter, for display in his central city store. In Dublin he celebrated spring by hiring a newly married couple to sit in his shop window and serve customers tea. When he heard that a famous aeronaut named George Higgins was preparing to ascend over Glasgow in a basket tugged by a hot-air balloon, Lipton proposed to have the ever-faithful William Love float along and drop thousands of leaflets— he called them "sky telegrams"—on the city and country.

Higgins's main purpose was to demonstrate a new hobby— parachuting—but he accepted Lipton's payment and welcomed Mr. Love aboard. With a crowd gathered to watch, the balloon was released from a park south of the Clyde. With a third man serving as pilot, the big gas bag was quickly blown too far south for the crowd to see Higgins and his parachute fall, so the jump was postponed. William Love did manage to throw the leaflets into the wind before the basket descended on a farmer's field. Later some were returned to local Lipton shops and the bearers collected small prizes. Lipton would repeat the stunt in Liverpool, Leicester, and Birmingham. (Two years later poor Higgins would die from injuries suffered when his aircraft hit telegraph wires in Leeds and he fell to the ground.)

The English cities that Higgins showered with Lipton's rain of advertising were among scores that saw Lipton's arrival in the mid-1880s as he opened stores at a rate of roughly one per week. During this time he employed a full-time architect and a full-time attorney specializing in real estate, and he kept them moving around the country so fast they complained about never sleeping in their own beds. The boss, who pursued no hobbies and seemed to have no friends outside of business, maintained an even more hectic pace himself. (Often impatient, he would sometimes bolt out of a hired carriage that was slowed by traffic, leaving a pile of coins on the seat.) He took personal responsibility for making sure every new shop was set in the best available space and decorated in such a way "that it stood out like a jewel from amongst its drab neighbors."

With all his frenetic activity and with his empire growing so rapidly, the rank and file in his organization came to see Lipton more as a symbol and an inspiration than an active part of their daily lives. No businessman appeared in the newspaper more often, and a typical clerk or store manager saw the boss's picture far more often than he would see his actual face. Lipton, who took naturally to the role of the distant shining star, tried to counteract the sense of separation his workers might feel by instituting an annual company meeting—he liked the Italian term *conversazione*—that would give him a chance to shed his glow upon hundreds of employees, ranging in rank from secretaries to executives.

The Conversazione of January 1887 set the tone for many that followed. Lipton rented a hall in Glasgow and sent formal invitations in pink envelopes. He gave a humorous talk, welcomed a duet who sang a few songs, and then presided over a dance. The big boss mingled happily with the crowd and after the last waltz made sure each of his guests enjoyed the banquet. When he gave his closing remarks he made a joke about Jumbo cheeses and then promised his workers that they could advance in the company by doing their job and serving every customer with unswerving civility and attention. Wealth, class, race, and appearance meant nothing. To him, and his army of employees, every face across the country belonged to a king or queen.

With the actual queen, and Britain's most particular consumers, residing in London, Lipton delayed opening a store there until he was certain he could succeed. The biggest and most powerful city in the world was already served by top quality retailers including the venerable Fortnum & Mason, the Royal Warrant holder that supplied the monarch's table. A newcomer would have to find the right niche and perform flawlessly to win business. A year before establishing his store in the city, Lipton tried to work his promotional magic by offering Queen

Victoria his most monstrous cheese ever—an eleven-thousand-pound behemoth—for her upcoming Golden Jubilee. The queen declined, as he must have expected she would, but the offer did get him some publicity, especially after he shared his own letter and the reply from Buckingham Palace with the Fleet Street press. This was followed by a letter from relief officials in Birmingham, who hoped the cheese might go to families of local striking workers.

The cheese, as Lipton replied, would not be ready for months. Instead he sent the Birmingham strikers hundreds of pounds of meat and thousands of eggs. A prominent baker joined the effort, sending a huge quantity of bread so the strikers could have a complete Easter breakfast. At about the same time, Lipton made a similar effort for striking coal miners in Lanarkshire. The charity was heartfelt. As he later wrote, he considered miners "the worse paid and most ill-treated men of Europe." Their meager pay, for such dangerous work, was a "disgrace to a civilized country."

Due, perhaps, to his early life among the factory and foundry workers of the Gorbals, Lipton's affection for hardworking laborers and their families never flagged. As an employer, he paid better than most, while demanding an almost devotional level of loyalty. As a political benefactor, he favored candidates of the Liberal and Labour parties. Later, in a similar show of support for the oppressed, he would make secret donations to the cause of Irish nationalism.

Lipton's political leanings were not part of the public record that he carried into Greater London as he opened his first market there on a busy shopping street called Westbourne Grove, not far from Portobello Road. The shop was opposite a sprawling, high-end department store operated by William Whiteley, who soon found in Lipton a competitor who offered the same quality foods at lower prices. Success led to a second store, in Islington, near an ancient and well-known inn called the Angel. There he showed his political leanings by inviting an Irish nationalist member of Parliament to preside at the opening ceremony. The decision to honor a harsh critic of British policy didn't harm his cash flow. Instead, price, quality, and service filled the store with customers.

Like most of the new Lipton stores, the Islington branch was overseen in its early weeks by William Love, and an incident from this period became fodder for a story Lipton would tell for the rest of his life. The tale begins with Lipton's number two cabling a building contractor with instructions to meet him for an after-hours conference. "Meet me at the Angel at eight tonight, Love," read the wire. Of course the contractor's wife received the telegram, kept it from him, and even visited the inn where she struggled against the desire to assault a "huzzy" she assumed to be her husband's secret "love." Only an intervention by the true Love who sent the cable would calm the contractor's angry wife and put work on the Islington store back on schedule.

The Islington shop was followed by a series of London start-ups from Westminster to Lambeth Walk to Greenwich. By the late 1880s, as the Lipton chain grew to 150 stores, William was cemented as the founder's most valuable man, and the two worked in remarkable harmony. With his hair parted in the middle and a bushy mustache of his own, William resembled Thomas in appearance as well as in the way he dressed, moved, and spoke. The two continued to live together with Lipton's parents, in Cambuslang, although Thomas spent many of his days traveling in the pursuit of new business. He also saw to the development of a great distribution network, which included a new warehouse and factory complex in Liverpool.

The ambitious grocer didn't always get what he wanted. On a mission to Novgorod, for example, he failed to win a contract to help feed the

Russian military. Lipton also seemed to struggle to find success in the Chicago meatpacking business, where his plant began to operate in 1885 but produced just a trickle of goods. The following year a big strike in the stockyards sent him traveling west in search of a site where he might find labor peace and lower costs.

Lipton wound up in South Omaha, Nebraska, a railroad and agriculture center that was quickly growing into its new nickname, Porkopolis. The town was closer to key western hog farms, and therefore the cost of shipping animals to their deaths was lower than it would be in Chicago. And it was already doing business with the United Kingdom through the Anglo-American Packing Company. Ever charming, Lipton quickly made friends among the locals, among them the local beef-packing king, W. A. Paxton, who also owned a downtown hotel and was a leading force behind the development of the community. With Paxton making the arrangements, Lipton was offered a newly built slaughterhouse for five years free of rent by the Union Stockyards, which he accepted. The deal was set on Independence Day, 1886. The Lipton plant, named Johnstone Packing, was running by January 1, 1887.

Employment at Lipton's Omaha plant rose quickly to more than four hundred men, and output topped a thousand barrels per day. But something about the operation didn't quite work. According to some reports American hogs, fed on huge amounts of grain, didn't yield the lean meat preferred in the United Kingdom. Whatever the reason, Lipton soon made a deal with the giant Armour company to take over his business in Omaha. By this arrangement he was able to uphold his commitment to keep the plant running but let others, who knew the American market well, make it profitable.

The setback in Nebraska wouldn't slow Lipton down for long. He returned to Chicago, where, despite competition from other places, the owners of the big packing companies enjoyed almost constant growth in both the volume of business and their profits. The Chicago cartel controlled prices, apportioned sales, and colluded with railroad companies to force ranchers and their middlemen to sell in the Illinois yards. As one cattleman explained it to a congressional committee:

> Years ago, we had plenty of buyers. If a man could not get his figure he went on to New York or Albany with his shipment. But the railroads stopped this by crushing out these shippers, and the wrecks of many of them are to be seen about the yards today as the result of the old monopoly. The railroads all had their pets and they ruined Western shippers. The dressed beef trade has killed the live-cattle dealers of today.

With cattlemen and hog farmers denied the option of shipping animals east of Chicago, the big packinghouses increased the volume of their business while cutting the price paid for livestock by nearly fifty percent. (In 1881, fewer than 1.5 million cattle were slaughtered on the South Side. In 1888, the number exceeded 2.6 million, but in the course of the year the packers actually paid $1 million less for steers than they had seven years earlier.) The processors passed along some of their gargantuan savings by reducing what they charged retailers for canned products, but prices for prime meat were kept artificially high. In this way the packers got the best of everything: an expanding market for low-end products, and high prices for better goods. Add the efficiencies of new steam- and electric-powered tools, and meat monopolists enjoyed a very comfortable existence with profits that might make a loan shark blush.

No one could operate in the Chicago meat business without ample wealth and guile. Lipton had both. After learning that the Myer Packing House was for sale, he hired a veteran of the Chicago industry to accompany him to negotiate the sale. Pretending to have a cold, the advisor blew his nose every time the seller quoted a figure or contract term Lipton should reject. By the time the talks were done and his companion was cured, Lipton had acquired a fully equipped killing shed covering four and a half acres of land. Like the bigger members of the meat cartel he also bought a fleet of refrigerated cars—each one painted with the single word "Lipton" on its sides—to carry meat and other foodstuffs across the nation. Soon he was disassembling more than two thousand hogs per day.

Some of what Lipton killed and carved in Chicago wound up in the stomachs of the folks back home, but most of Lipton's meat was eaten in America. Consumers were largely unaware of his sizable operation because the product was distributed through other firms. He did get some attention when he won a contract to supply miners working the Klondike gold strike in Alaska. Spurred by press reports of ships filled with gold arriving in San Francisco, more than fifty thousand miners headed north that year and Lipton killed thirty-two thousand hogs to help keep them fed. (The business gave Lipton an excuse to travel to the Alaska territory, and soon he would open a cannery in British Columbia to exploit one of the region's other great resources—salmon.)

But as much as he enjoyed the publicity that came from the Klondike adventure, the headline-hungry Lipton made little effort to publicize his meat business. For one of the world's first image-conscious industrialists this was a strategic choice. By the time he got involved at the Chicago stockyards, the business was under constant scrutiny by government regulators and early trust-busters. John Harvey Kellogg and other vegetarians were already crusading against meat. And conditions were ripe for some enterprising journalist or writer to expose all of the industry's dangerous secrets. (Upton Sinclair would fill this role as author of the blistering novel *The Jungle*, which revealed the packing plants to be circles of hell where animals and men suffered and died and contaminated meat was sold without regard for public health.)

Although he became one of the ten largest operators and a member of the Board of Trade, Lipton's low profile helped him avoid being tainted by the scandals of the Chicago meat industry. He was protected even when rumors circulated about his scheme to inflate prices by cornering the market on packed barrels of pork. At one point in 1900, Lipton actually controlled nearly all of the available supply and the price went from $14 to $20 a barrel in two weeks. This little price-fixing episode gained scant attention, however, and was soon forgotten as Lipton pocketed an extra $660,000 (more than $16 million in 2010) and then let the price return to normal. Given his powerful position in the market, Lipton had actually let his buyers off easy and earned a bit of praise from a Chicago newspaper that said he had proved that "a man who has cornered the pork market need not be hoggish."

Profits made quietly in America financed Lipton's drive to corner the business of feeding the masses in Great Britain. Even though he had more than 150 stores in 1890, millions of poor and working-class Britons were not yet served by a Lipton grocery. Captive to old-fashioned shops, they paid far too much for inferior products that provided inadequate nutrition. Hunger was common among poorer children who still subsisted on thick slabs of bread—called "doorstops"—slathered with jam or perhaps margarine. Their parents would make it through the day on porridge and a dinner of cheap stew.

In the decade to come—the 1890s—Lipton's markets would be established in many poorer communities and provide competition that would drive prices down. The great grocer would also devote himself to charitable work—some quite public—that would make him a hero to the working class. But before he could do all this, he would have to enter and then dominate the business of delivering to the masses, around the world, the one product most closely associated with British culture and taste—tea.

SIX

Tea Tom

For as long as his parents and William Love lived in his Cambuslang house, which he'd named Johnstone Villa, Thomas Lipton had sentimental reasons for keeping his company headquarters and his residence in Glasgow. These were the three people in the world who occupied a place in his heart. With them he could let down the showman-millionaire pose and relax. This was most true with William, who was involved in all the critical aspects of Lipton's business and understood the demands and designs of his ambition. In dealing with contractors, suppliers, and even the press, William actually spoke on his behalf and with full authority.

Love and the elder Liptons lived free of financial worry and want, a state that would have been impossible for Thomas Sr. and Frances to imagine a decade earlier, when they lived on Crown Street. Their easy old age was filled with such luxuries as a fancy carriage and a team of beautiful gray horses—the equivalent of a Rolls-Royce today—which they used with the reluctance of a poor Irish couple worried about calling attention to themselves and thereby tempting the fates. People who always knew them to be thrifty and selfless found them unchanged.

Lipton the younger showed no similar Irish superstition about wealth and fame. At every chance he pushed his name before the public and retreated only when blocked. (Clyde port authorities, for example, refused his offer of cash in exchange for permission to put his name on navigation buoys.) Between his shops, warehouses, and factories Lipton employed more than a thousand people in the city, and this success, combined with his fame, made him a most happy favorite son. When officials announced that Glasgow's Kelvingrove Park would host an International Exhibition, he planned to steal an idea from the Chicago meatpackers and offer tours of a hog plant that would show the whole ghastly business, from squeal to meal, two hundred times a day.

The notion of a slaughterhouse demonstration excited Lipton's loyalists when he announced it at the next Conversazione. All of Glasgow was buzzing about the coming fair, which was planned to demonstrate the industry, art, and genius of Great Britain's second city. In time the exhibition season would be remembered as the moment when a band of local artists—designers and architects including Charles Rennie Mackintosh—gained international renown. But in the short run, businessmen and boosters in the city were most interested in making themselves and Glasgow seem successful, powerful, and technologically superior.

With Japan opening up to the West (and ordering Clyde-built ships), Great Britain was in the grip of one of its periodic manias for all things Eastern. The organizers of the exhibition chose an "Oriental" theme for the architecture, and the temporary buildings for the event were designed with towers, mock minarets, and domes, many of which were topped with flagpoles and banners. (Locals called it "Baghdad by Kelvinside.") More than two thousand exhibits were housed in the halls built on both sides of the Kelvin River. The attractions, which drew six million viewers—among them Queen Victoria—included a replica of medieval Glasgow Castle and a tea house shipped from Ceylon and pieced together on site. Sponsored by the Ceylon Planters' Association, the exhibit was intended to improve the image of that island's young tea industry, and their goal was accomplished when the queen herself accepted a cup.

Near the center of the fairgrounds, visitors gaped at the most fanciful decoration of the fair, an electric-powered "Fairy Fountain." With a hundred water jets and scores of colored lights, the fountain would reign as the world's great marvel of iron art for just a year before it was eclipsed by the Eiffel Tower, erected in Paris as part of the Exposition Universelle of 1889.

The fountain marked an oasis of rest for visitors who struggled to absorb the exhibition's endless offerings of products, artwork, and industrial processes from around the world. Exciting as it was, Lipton's public slaughterhouse idea was set aside (fair officials were squeamish) in favor of a Lipton model dairy, where visitors could watch a butter-manufacturing line in action and sample the end product, which was also provided to restaurants on the fairgrounds. (Lipton was their sole food supplier.) Unlike most other exhibits, which were housed among many others in vast temporary buildings, Lipton's dairy would get its own freestanding home near the footbridge that led to the Fairy Fountain. Just before the fair opened, Lipton installed in this dairy his most monstrous cheese ever—five tons of American curds—and planned for it to be cut with great ceremony.

On opening day, May 8, 1888, crowds lined the streets leading from Glasgow's lavish new city council chambers on George Square to Kelvingrove and cheered as the Prince and Princess of Wales passed in a parade of carriages that entered the park beneath an ornate triumphal arch—the Prince of Wales Gate—built for the occasion. At the exhibition's Grand Hall the lord provost of Glasgow handed the prince a golden key, which he used to open the door. Thousands crowded inside to hear prayers, the national anthem, and the words of the future king. He hailed the city as the "cradle" of the "steam carrying trade with America" and a manufacturing, research, and commercial powerhouse. At the end of his remarks, when he declared the exhibition open, the Glasgow Choral Union sang the "Hallelujah" chorus from Handel's *Messiah* and cheers filled the great space.

Although tourists may have been surprised, Glaswegians knew that Tommy Lipton wouldn't miss an opportunity to make a grand gesture after the prince performed his. Once the celebration ended at the Grand Hall, many in the exiting crowd found their way to Lipton's dairy for a second ceremony. When an adequate audience had gathered, the great grocer, clad all in white, climbed on top of a big yellow cheese—called Jumbo, naturally—spoke for a few minutes, and then whacked away with an ax. Once the first few chunks were distributed, he made way for his assistants, who were dressed in similar clothes and who would give away bits of the cheese until all ten thousand pounds were gone.

At an exhibition filled with marvels, the enormous cheese was not as unusual as the solid-silver perfume-spraying fountain at the Paris exhibit, or as exotic as the fancy tearoom in the India Court. However, there was something about Lipton's Jumbo cheese that appealed to average Scots. Their sentiment was heightened, moreover, by the recent death of the cheese's namesake, Jumbo the Elephant. Purchased by P. T. Barnum in 1882—even though a hundred thousand children begged the queen to intervene—the elephant died a few years later, after being hit by a train in Ontario, Canada. His death was felt around the world, but most especially by the British public. Ever after, the name Jumbo would be evoked with pride and in the service of commerce, even to sell castor oil.

Lipton's Jumbo cheese found a similar place in the Glaswegian heart.

Long after the last bits were cut, locals still sang a ditty that memorialized the event. It began with the lines:

> *Great Jumbo the Monster does folks surprise.*
> *Wi' his fine yellow coat an' prodigious size*
> *Ower a fairy grotto or fancy bazaars*
> *He stans oot as clear as the moon 'mang the stars.*

The laughter inspired by Lipton's stunt was also the sound of a city filled with a sense of possibility and adventure. In 1888, Glasgow was entering a period of wealth and influence such as it would never see again. The exhibition was just one expression of this spirit. The new building for the city council was another. One of the greatest examples of Victorian architecture in the world, the council's home was constructed of marble, granite, and exotic woods, and its ceremonial rooms were among the most extensively decorated spaces in the United Kingdom.

Even more extravagant, considering its use, was the carpet factory that James Templeton built at this time alongside the Glasgow Green. Templeton wanted the exterior of his manufacturing plant to be as complex and beautiful as the carpets he made for Europe's royal families and American presidents. His architect gave him a design influenced by Venetian palaces that included spires, arches, circular windows, and parapets. Built to house dyeing vats, mechanical spinning machines, and huge looms, the Templeton building was a monument to both design and industry.

In the same period Glasgow would see the construction of the People's Palace, a free cultural center, and the Kelvingrove Museum, which would house one of the greatest civic art collections in Europe. This boom in development was matched by a surge of what came to be called "municipal socialism." Private trolleys were replaced by one of the best public transit systems in the world. It would be followed by the development of a municipal electric utility and other services that reflected a Scottish-style philosophy that joined industrial ambition with a "my brother's keeper" kind of commitment to the social good. This sentiment also supported a powerful temperance crusade that found its ultimate expression in a development called "tearoom culture." This movement offered a stimulating alternative to alcohol that came with little cakes and sandwiches and a pleasingly ceremonial routine of service, polite conversation, and graceful manners.

Tea culture would spread through Europe and cross the Atlantic, but its epitome was found in Glasgow, where the famous Catherine "Kate" Cranston elevated the preparation, presentation, and service of tea to a degree worthy of the work done by the city's great artists, whom she commissioned to decorate her rooms. The best of this work was done by Charles Rennie Mackintosh at Cranston's Willow Tea Room on Sauchiehall Street. (The name Sauchiehall derives from old Scottish words meaning "willow" and "meadow.")

With free rein over everything from the building's exterior to the design of the menus, chairs, and staff uniforms, Mackintosh used willows as an organizing theme and made every element graceful and elegant. He created dark-paneled spaces where men could smoke and play billiards or dine without the presence of women. But the big attraction was the "room de-luxe," done in tones of gray, purple, and white, where silks decorated the walls and light poured in through leaded glass. Open to all, the room de-luxe was both a democratic and a luxurious experience. No public space in all of Scotland felt more welcoming, and eventually these rooms would gain international fame and imitators.

Miss Cranston's tearooms, which combined good business with art, sophistication, and the notion of doing good, reflected the values of a city reaching the height of its wealth and influence. Lipton, the poor-boy-turned-international-businessman, fit comfortably in this setting. Although he wasn't a temperance crusader, he hardly ever drank or smoked. He believed in the common good and he reveled in the city's commercial and industrial energy. Ultimately, profit and growth were his two real passions. These interests kept him grounded in Glasgow, yet they would also draw him away after his parents died.

Frances Lipton, who had long struggled against respiratory problems, died of bronchitis in early 1889. Her passing was registered with authorities by William Love, and she was buried in a family plot near her daughter Margaret and son John. The widowed Thomas Sr. quickly declined into dementia and died little more than a year later. At the time of his father's death, the younger Thomas had reached the midpoint of his life—age forty-one. With his parents and siblings all gone, his one deeply personal connection to Glasgow was William. This wasn't enough to hold him. With a new and exciting stream of business calling, he finally abandoned Glasgow for London, leaving Johnstone Villa to William. Before the end of the year, Lipton would expand a regional office on Bath Street near City Road to accommodate hundreds of transferred staff at a new world headquarters. One newspaper in Glasgow mourned that "the Great Lipton is evacuating our city," but the move would prove to be the key to Lipton's success in a new line of business, and help make him one of the most recognized figures in the world.

Sometime around the year 1000, a Chinese poet named Lu Tung wrote of a drink with a flavor more compelling to contemplate than immortality. Five hundred years later, tea came to Continental Europe with Dutch traders. In 1660, the former Portuguese princess Catherine of Braganza made it a most fashionable beverage in London society after she married King Charles II. The informal patron saint of British tea drinkers, the queen won much admiration for the way she endured her husband's many sexual affairs with quiet dignity, but outside the most elite circles her tea habit was considered extravagant, if not degenerate, by ordinary Britons, who were suspicious of anything that came from Catholic Europe. While the Dutch writer Cornelis Bontekoe greeted tea as a kind of Prozac/penicillin that could make all mankind healthy and happy, British politician Henry Savile called tea drinking a "wicked" and "filthy" custom. A century of argument would pass before the drink was widely accepted, even if it remained too costly for most people to drink with any regularity.

Tea was expensive in the 1700s because it had become a kind of controlled substance, heavily taxed by the government. (American revolutionaries had once made a dramatic reference to this problem in Boston Harbor.) But the taxes were only part of the problem. Made from the leaves of an evergreen that grew mainly in China, tea was costly to ship and spoiled easily. These factors, combined with the East India Company's official monopoly of the China trade, meant supply was always limited. While the rich could afford the product delivered through this system, others turned to tea smuggled by gangs who defied the monopoly and the tax collector.

Following timeworn tactics, the smugglers arranged for large shipments that were generally routed through Scandinavia to avoid British customs. Oceangoing ships were met offshore by smaller, faster boats that received the divided cargo and delivered it ashore, where it was spirited inland. Although many regarded them as Robin Hood types, the tea smugglers intimidated entire communities with threats and violence. The notorious Hawkhurst Gang, for example, actually raided a customhouse to recover confiscated tea and then kidnapped two officers who were going to testify against them. The officers were whipped and dragged behind horses. One was then buried alive. The other was hurled down a well and then crushed under stones and logs dropped from above.

The violence and the persistence of the illegal tea trade eventually led the crown to reduce tariffs, which made legal tea more affordable. (It also reduced the incentive for crooks who sold "tea" made with everything from dung to black thorn leaves dyed with lead.) The price dropped further after the East India Company lost its official monopoly in 1833 and competition arose. Finally, in the last quarter of the nineteenth century, tea became a household staple throughout the United Kingdom. Not coincidentally, the rise of this habit as a truly universal addiction and the quintessential symbol of its culture came precisely as the British Empire—the largest the world had ever seen—reached the height of its power.

It was the empire's policy to exploit the land and the labor under its control to produce goods and wealth for the mother country. In the case of tea, where China's hold on the supply was an expensive irritant, the mountain slopes and valleys of northeast India suggested an opportunity for the imperial strategy. As early as 1840, the British agriculture expert C. A. Bruce argued that if Chinese plants could be acquired and cultivated, tea plantations in India and Ceylon would "enrich our own dominions and pull down the haughty pride of China." The trouble was China's strict control of its tea plants and foreign visitors. Outsiders were barred from the growing regions, and authorities promised that anyone who was caught aiding the transfer of seeds, plants, or even expertise related to tea would have his or her head chopped off.

The threat of beheading was a fierce deterrent to tea espionage, but addiction, wealth, and patriotism can drive people to take extraordinary risks. In 1848 a Scottish adventurer, appropriately named Robert Fortune, traveled in disguise to Fujian Province to steal some tea tree seedlings. Fortune, who had been a botanist in Edinburgh, spoke Chinese fluently and with a combination of nerve and stealth managed to acquire some plants and smuggle them out. He crossed the oceans with special glass cases filled with soil that kept the plants growing.

Fortune delivered his sprouts to the Royal Horticultural Society, where they were propagated and became the basis for a new tea industry in British-controlled India. This scheme, which was led by C. A. Bruce, put vast tracts of land in northeast India into the hands of favored loyal subjects at little or no cost and with no compensation for members of the local "wild tribes" who were driven out. The new landowners used Chinese advisors, lured by Fortune, to establish large successful plantations. Their operation required great numbers of workers to handle the delicate crop. Thousands of Indians, often entire families, came from cities to enter into serflike arrangements that offered them little more than subsistence on plantation land.

By the 1870s, tea plants grew on more than a quarter million acres in northeast India and the region shipped more than eighteen million pounds of tea per year. Most of this product traveled by steamer through the French-built Suez Canal, which had opened in 1869 and significantly reduced the journey from the East to Great Britain. An engineering and economic marvel, the canal shortened the time required for tea and many other goods to reach Europe, while hastening the end of the exciting era of the clipper ship. (Designed and constructed first in America, the streamlined clippers were built with knifelike bows and were tapered at the stern. They carried huge amounts of sail—forty thousand square feet was common—and with a properly balanced load and an able crew, clippers could reach speeds as high as eighteen knots. Their speed records made headlines around the world but the small wind-powered clippers could not compete with reliable steamers that could carry several times more cargo.)

The millions of pounds of tea shipped at lower cost from India through the Suez Canal drove down wholesale prices worldwide. Most of the benefit from this bonanza, however, was held by middlemen and dealers who controlled the British tea business from offices near an auction house on central London's Mincing Lane, which was near the bank of the Thames.

Once the financial center for Great Britain's opium trade in Asia, Mincing Lane had a lock on the importation and distribution of tea throughout the empire. Wholesalers in places like Manchester, Birmingham, Liverpool, and Glasgow turned to the lane to purchase tea that had already been blended, either abroad or locally, by professionals who adjusted the mixture of dried leaves from different sources to create a reliable taste from batch to batch. This product was then distributed to groceries, department stores, and specialty shops such as tea houses.

Like many foods and other drinks, tea became an object of obsession. Connoisseurs pursued expensive, tender leaves that would be sold in special blends or as "single-leaf" products. Health fanatics insisted that certain exotic blends, including the "meat teas," aided digestion. But the drink that would become a national emblem in the Victorian age was a basic mongrel blend, which made a strong, reddish liquid that could taste woody, fruity, and, thanks to the tannin, slightly tangy. At its best, this common tea was bright-looking and offered flavors described as toasty and brisk. Bad tea, and there was much of it, could look dull and taste musty, bitter, and even fishy. Fortunately for those who sold it, every cup—good and bad—came with a dose of energizing caffeine that was perniciously addictive.

With supplies growing and prices falling, the denizens of Mincing Lane continually searched for new outlets. Lipton's many stores, visited by tens of thousands of people every day, seemed a natural fit, but the firm's eccentric owner was, at best, ambivalent about the retail tea trade. With a little figuring he realized he could sell a basic tea for less than his competitors, and he bought a modest amount for his chain of shops. But the more he considered the business, the more problems he saw.

Ordinarily, chests of loose, blended tea were delivered to retailers, who opened them to make packets for their customers. The chests were neither airtight nor waterproof, and tea imperfectly stored for any length of time was subject to rot and mold. But even when a customer got what appeared to be dry, fresh tea, she had to worry about twigs and other contaminants, and she couldn't be certain she was getting the right amount. It all depended on the seller's practices. Some delivered pure goods fairly measured. Others would mix moldy leaves with good ones and put a thumb on the scale. The worst collected wet dregs from dining rooms and other places, dried them, and sold them as new.

With all the bad and potentially dangerous tea on the market, health warnings became a staple of tea advertising campaigns and of the daily press. These alerts were often colored by xenophobia and even racism. "The Chinese had to be policed," was the subtext, even though British hands had both the motive and ample opportunity to tamper with the product. With addicted Victorian consumers fearful of the foreigners who controlled their fix, at least one early marketer was ready with a solution. "Honest" John Horniman, a Quaker from Jersey, began selling tea in sealed packets in the middle of the nineteenth century. To emphasize the health benefits and science behind his idea, Horniman put his product in chemists' shops, where people trusted they would find pure goods.

The association with Quakers and good health also made packaged tea attractive to temperance crusaders, who began to advocate it as an alternative to alcohol. By the 1880s, Horniman was selling five million packets per year, and at least one competitor, Mazawattee Tea, used the same type of sealed packaging, which it sold with aggressive advertising that included enameled tin signs in almost every railway station in Britain. Mazawattee, which also operated cozy tearooms, was among the first to take one further step, stressing its use of supposedly superior leaves from Ceylon.

While he dabbled in the sale of loose tea, Lipton studied the methods of Horniman, Mazawattee, and others and visited Mincing Lane to charm the agents and wholesalers to gain as much information as he could. He was surprised to hear how little they paid growers for the product they stocked, and astonished by the profits they earned. As he gathered this intelligence, established tea men, wary of his ambitions, tried to warn him away from the business. Blending was an art, they said, and Lipton would go bust before he mastered it. "Why not let well enough alone?" asked a friendly broker. "You don't know one tenth of the difficulties and dangers of the tea trade."

The commercial dangers, it turned out, were fast fading. All the hard work of establishing a steady and growing supply of Indian tea— selecting plants, creating farms and other facilities, hiring workers, and building transportation networks—had been accomplished in the previous twenty years. (And thanks to British rules, wages were solidly fixed at rates sixty percent lower than those paid at plantations elsewhere in the empire.) In this same period the British public, from the poorest of the poor to the royal family, had been thoroughly hooked on the buzz and comfort of a frequent "cuppa." Consumption had risen from roughly 77 million pounds in 1860 to 200 million in 1890.

A mild stimulant, tea cast a spell over drinkers, who found that regular doses made them feel alert, while withdrawal soured their mood. But the appeal was not merely physiological. Making, serving, and drinking tea required you to stop other activity and focus on a very deliberate task for at least ten minutes. The best results came when you followed the recipe carefully, and the repetition had a soothing effect, not unlike prayer. As with all ritualized activities, people set standards for every aspect of tea making and drinking, and many developed fetishistic approaches to the process and the tools.

As every consumer in the United Kingdom learned, the steeping had to be done in a china pot. Water was to be boiled first in a kettle. When this was done, a small amount would be poured into the pot to warm it. After the warming water was discarded, loose tea was then spooned into the pot—one "teaspoon" per cup, plus one extra—followed by actively boiling water in the proper measure. With the cover on the pot, the mixture would be allowed to steep for three to five minutes, depending on the strength desired. The beverage would then be poured through a strainer into waiting cups. Milk, sugar, or lemon were added by some. Although the process could seem complicated, it was simpler than the recipe for making coffee, which helped explain why tea supplanted this earlier caffeine-bearing import.

Whether you made it yourself in the morning or sat in a hotel dining room at four p.m. and let an expert handle the job, the British tea ritual evoked feelings of calm delight. The design, feel, and decoration of cups, saucers, and pots became a source of fascination. Small bowls imported from the East were supplanted by British-made cups with handles and fancy sets that included everything from the pot to the milk pitcher. These were often decorated with floral or Asian themes. Expensive sets were gilded. Companies such as Doulton, Wedgwood, and Spode dominated the high-end market, but dozens of others made certain that tea could be served well in every home. Snobs, of course, believed that most got it wrong, opting for extra-strong brews further spoiled by too much milk and sugar.

By the late 1880s, the average Briton drank thirty-five gallons of tea per year. Thomas Lipton, having noticed the drink's growing popularity, captured some of this business with the help of Mincing Lane dealers, and he happily applied his theatrical flair to this new line. The opening of a new Glasgow warehouse devoted solely to tea gave him a stage for a parade of wagons that carried eighty tons of tea packed in chests from the Broomielaw to Howard Street. The procession was led by a brass band and bagpipers and the horse-drawn wagons were flanked by a costumed army called Lipton's Life Guards, who were dressed in vaguely Indian-looking outfits of white and red silk. The real Life Guards were a famous cavalry unit of the British Army formed in the seventeenth century. The army's original horse-mounted regiment, the Life Guards were considered to be among the fighting elite. (They continue to this day as both a modern armored combat unit and a ceremonial cavalry.) The Lipton Life Guards, whose ranks ranged from fifty to two hundred, became a staple of Lipton pageants, appearing at store openings along-side any other attractions—circus elephants, pigs, marching bands—that might be available. But they were associated mainly with his tea business, which he began to refine with some of the same principles he had earlier applied to ham and eggs.

Low price and consistent quality became Lipton's main goals, and he pursued the first by paying cash up front, and receiving discounts for large shipments arranged through Mincing Lane. He then focused on the problems inherent in the way tea was kept and sold at shops. Years of experience with adulterated and spoiled tea, not to mention run-ins with merchants who cheated them at the scales, had made consumers wary of the whole tea-buying endeavor. Lipton could solve this with a product that was inspected and packaged in a controlled and sanitary setting. To accomplish this he designed small paper packets that he decorated with the motto "Direct from the Tea Garden to the Tea Pot." His print shop on Lancefield Street, which already made labels and packaging for a host of products, was set to work on these "yellow label" containers, while the company hired hundreds of young women for the new tea-processing plant. Once it got into operation, they worked at tables where they measured and packaged the tea that was dumped out of chests sent from India. The rooms where they worked were scented with the bright aroma of the tea and bustled with the traffic of men bringing in chests and printed sheets from the press and removing finished packages.

In Lipton's clean, airy shops, the brightly colored packets were stacked on counters and shelves and priced lower than tea sold anywhere else. (Lipton's price per pound was the U.S. equivalent of thirty cents, while most other retailers were charging about fifty. This was a big difference, considering that most people lived on less than thirty cents per day.) Customers were drawn by the value and guaranteed measure, but because Lipton was dependent on his vendors, they couldn't rely on the taste from one purchase to the next. Ever confident, Lipton decided he could solve this problem without the experts, whose years of experience and delicate senses were supposed to be indispensable.

Setting himself up in the executive dining room at his big Lancefield Street complex, Lipton had his workers brew an assortment of blends sent from London tea masters along with some mixed on the premises from raw teas. He then gathered his managers from various departments and they sat together, sipping, sniffing, and exchanging amused glances and honest opinions. When the grades were tallied, a lower-cost tea made from the Lipton raw stock scored about as well as the most expensive ones from the dealers.

When steeped the proper time—about four minutes—the Lipton tea had a bright orangey color and a slightly tangy or brisk taste. The flavor was crisp, which meant it didn't stay on the tongue very long, but strong enough to handle a little milk, sugar, or lemon. On balance it was substantial enough to serve as an eye-opener in the morning—

like English Breakfast tea—but smooth enough to enjoy in the afternoon, when most people preferred a lighter, cleaner drink.

As with all blends, any special quality in the Lipton tea depended on the plant material used. In general, new growth from the end of a tea tree's branches—including the flowers, leaf tips, and buds—yields better flavor. Leaves labeled orange pekoe come from a section of the branch slightly closer to the main trunk and are substantially better than their coarse, trunk-side neighbors, the souchong. In the sorting process, where batches of leaves are shaken through a series of screens, the best orange pekoe will be trapped in the mesh made to isolate small-to-medium-size leaves.

With all leaves, extra flavor can be produced if they are broken to expose more surface area to the water, but broken leaves also leach additional bitter tannin into the pot. A similar problem arises with small bits called "fanning" and the dust collected after all the sorting is done. When these are used, the taste of a tea becomes more woody. In general, a particular brand's flavor is established by the size of the leaves used, as well as by the proportion of buds, flowers, tips, broken pieces, and fanning included. It is also affected by how well it is handled, dried, and otherwise processed.

In Lipton's tea, drinkers got a high proportion of orange pekoe—OP for short—that had been handled with the kind of care a good wine-maker applies to fine grapes. In the days before machinery took over much of the work, pickers plucked the leaves with the pads of their fingers, avoiding the creases and cuts that their nails might make. (Women and children were considered best for this task.) Rushed from the field, the leaves would be laid on racks and allowed to wither in the heat, becoming sweeter and drier. In less than twenty-four hours they would be ready for "rolling"—that is, gathered together into bunches by workers who then rolled them between their hands. Rolling left the leaves slightly crushed and broken, which released sap and promoted oxidation. When the color of the leaves turned from green to copper they were quickly dried with the aid of hot-air furnaces. Proper drying produced a light, airy mass of plant material that could be packed tightly into wooden chests and still resist mold and rot, even as it was shipped all the way to Great Britain.

Because he bought so much tea, and paid cash in advance, Lipton got the best OP, which was the product of "fine" rather than "coarse" plucking. (This practice was favored in Ceylon, which was a major source of Lipton's raw tea.) Although the precise recipe was kept secret, he may have also added to his mid-quality leaves a few tips and flowers and likely limited the amount of fanning and dust that were mixed in. The result was a drink that was not quite FTGFOP (finest, tippy, golden, flowery orange pekoe) but compared very well to all the others. When he was sure he could offer this mix reliably, Lipton mounted an advertising blitz, plastering cities with signs and buying space to sell it in every major newspaper. When the product debuted, at a price below all other common teas, Lipton's shops had trouble keeping up with the demand. Sales of more than a thousand pounds per week became the norm even in his smaller outlets. This business also drove increased sales of everything else, including Lipton's own brands of jams, canned goods, and biscuits.

Competitors didn't lie down in the face of Lipton's assault on the market. One major importer, United Kingdom Tea Company, fought back with advertising that included patriotic images of the goddess Britannia and a Mandarin with long braided hair serving tea from a steaming pot. Another of the company's ads used a quotation from the famous seventeenth-century diarist Samuel Pepys, who had referred to tea as "a China drink." The point of the marketing campaign was to remind customers of the connections between older firms and the tea tradition.

By contrast, the British-sponsored industries in India and Ceylon eagerly promoted the quality of their product and played on the fact that they came from lands where the Union Jack proudly flew. The Indian Tea Bazaar Company even went so far as to advertise in Glasgow that "Indian Teas can be relied on for their PURITY, Chinese teas cannot." Unlike China, which had been closed to the West and struck many Britons as an uncomfortably foreign place, India and Ceylon were widely viewed as sunnier, more welcoming lands. The people may have been "lazy" and required a lot of "looking after," as the planter George Barker observed, but they accepted Anglo-Saxon leadership. They were in the family, so to speak, and deserved an extra measure of trust.

Reading both the politics and the marketplace, Lipton would throw his lot in with the suppliers from India and Ceylon, choosing to avoid Chinese tea entirely. His tea advertising, which showed happy people with vaguely Indian or Sinhalese features working plantations, conjured a European's idea of a tropical industrial paradise. To link his product with the comfort of home he called his plantations "gardens," and to make sure everyone knew who kept things orderly and controlled, the name "Lipton" was written on every drawing of a factory, wagon, or crate. And to give his tea a little sex appeal, his advertisements often featured a drawing of a beautiful, long-haired Sinhalese woman who appears draped in jewels with her head cocked, her mouth slightly open, and a cup labeled "Lipton's Tea" in her hand.

Gradually, Lipton's promotional efforts would result in the development of one of the earliest global consumer brands. Through quality control, advertising that stressed his name, and wide distribution, he continually pushed consumers to associate tea with the Lipton name.

(Other early brands in Great Britain and America included Cadbury, Heinz, Coca-Cola, and Gillette.) As Lipton's strategy gained traction, owners of specialty shops, where tea and coffee were the main goods offered, warned customers about being poisoned by cheap inferior products found next to piles of sausages and bacon. They mocked Lipton's slogan, noting that no one's tea went directly from the plantation to the pot, and some temporarily undercut his price. In one Irish town a war of posters broke out, with a local shopkeeper covering walls with anti-Lipton ads only to see them mysteriously ripped down. But whether the broadsides were made on the street or in the press, merchants who sold ordinary tea couldn't overcome Lipton's quality product or his advantages of scale. Many of them simply went out of business.

With tea money pouring into Lipton's London office from more than three hundred stores, bankers with global interests took notice and approached him with suggestions about how to spend it. Bad loans had left some of them holding title to bankrupt coffee estates in Ceylon. The culprit there was *Hemileia vastatrix*, a leaf fungus that first appeared on the island in 1869. Also called "coffee rust," the disease marched from plantation to plantation, and by 1890 the island's production of coffee had been cut by more than three-quarters. The fungus did not affect tea, however, and many parts of the mountainous island of twenty-five thousand square miles, which sits twenty miles off the southeast coast of India, offered perfect conditions for this alternative crop. The island saw heavy rain in summer and enjoyed warm, dry winters. In its valleys the soil was deep, acidic, and well drained, which suited a plant that likes to set its taproot deep in the earth.

Ceylon's potential for tea had been established by a Scottish immigrant who traveled to the island at age sixteen to work for the Harrison and Leake coffee company. The firm had assigned to him the job of establishing an experimental tea plantation. James Taylor's nineteen-acre plot at the Loolcondera estate near the city of Kandy produced its first usable tea in 1870. It was processed in a small bungalow where drying was done in clay stoves and helpers rolled the balls of leaves on the veranda table. Taylor's first export to Britain—a shipment of twenty-three pounds—came in 1873. Soon tea plantations were established all over the island.

As the bankers told Lipton, Ceylon was about to eclipse China to become the second-greatest source of tea—behind India—imported to the United Kingdom. Books and government reports of the period confirmed this projection, and a well-read international businessman would have been aware of the opportunities available there. In 1887, an Asia expert named John Ferguson wrote that Indian tea planters already recognized Ceylon's superior climate and soil and lower cost of production and shipping. Ferguson noted that "hard-headed Scots" had built the roads and railroads needed to support their plantations. Ceylon was ready for a tea boom, and old coffee estates were still available for purchase at bargain prices, wrote Ferguson.

Lipton, who was already buying big shipments of tea from Ceylon, surely knew the country produced a good reliable product, and he was always eager to control every link in the supply chain of any item he sold. In May 1890 he announced he was sailing for Australia on vacation. Colleagues and competitors who understood Lipton's obsession with business—the man didn't seem to think about anything else—assumed his announcement was a ruse and speculated he was off to establish a grocery chain down under. They were right about the deception but wrong about the purpose. Lipton had already sent a trusted man to Ceylon to scout plantations and decided, based on reports back, that he would go there, too.

As he sailed for the port of Colombo, Lipton's sense of adventure was heightened by the prospect of visiting the Far East for the first time. Few places were more exotic in the British imagination than Ceylon, which came under the empire's control after two wars against local rulers and the suppression of a native insurgency. Roads built for war became routes for development and shipments of spices, precious stones, coffee, and tea. Steam-powered ships and trains allowed wealthy tourists to visit in greater numbers, and travelers returned with art pieces, antiques, and tales of dramatic hunts in which giant elephants—"tuskers"—were tracked and killed. To them, Ceylon was a blossom-scented paradise where native men wore their hair in long braids, tropical fruit grew wild, and life was a sleepy idyll. The truth was a bit more complicated. Tea workers, for example, faced periods of forced labor for the government if they left the plantations without approval from their bosses. When they did work, they struggled to feed themselves on their scant wages. Clearly the good life of the few in Ceylon depended on the exploitation of the many, but this reality was so much a part of the society, and had been for so long, that it usually escaped notice. It was simply the way things were.

Lipton, who found the island "lovely and delectable," rested briefly at the Grand Oriental Hotel, which overlooked the harbor of Colombo and the Gulf of Mannar. While getting acclimated he enjoyed the company of one of Colombo's most controversial citizens, Arabi Pasha. A child of poverty, Arabi had risen to the post of Egypt's defense minister at a time when his countrymen were seething under the weight of British rule. When several Europeans were killed in a riot in Alexandria, he wound up at the center of a frenzy of accusations from London. The Royal Navy bombarded the city and British troops were sent to secure the Suez Canal. The occupation of Egypt would last for decades, as the military defended British commercial interests and kept the canal, a lifeline for the European economy, open.

The confused and bullying response to the Alexandria riot mounted by officials and the British press would have made a fine satire if it had been a story written by Evelyn Waugh. As a moment in history, it would stand as a prime example of a colonial power's myopia and over-reaction. One early critic of this policy, Lord Randolph Churchill (Winston's father) stood against a rush to punish Arabi Pasha. As Churchill and others brought the facts into the open, Arabi was granted a gentle exile in Ceylon. But only the best-informed Britons understood what had actually happened. The British public generally considered Arabi an enemy.

Lipton admired Arabi in the same way that he admired Irish nationalists. On a subsequent visit to Ceylon he would make him the manager of his estates, with a big salary, despite the fact that Arabi knew no more about tea than anyone else who drank it.

The two men would maintain a relationship for decades, a choice that reflected Lipton's complex personality and politics. An aggressive British capitalist who curried public favor and grew wealthy in part because of his association with the powerful, he couldn't resist certain rebels who, like him, rose from poverty to prominence.

During his first stay in Ceylon, Lipton spent a few days in Colombo, and then traveled east through a forest of rubber trees and cinchona (quinine) plantations to the island's old capital of Kandy. (Famous for the annual Esala and Kumbal Peraheras—processions of elephants and dancers—the city was a religious center and had been home to the island's last independent rulers.) From there Lipton ventured out to inspect property in almost every direction. On the way to estates in Haputale, which was in the south, he passed through Nuwara Eliya, which a planter had developed as a model English town, complete with cottages, mock-Tudor houses, and a brick Victorian-style post office. Nicknamed Little England, it was a popular resort for expatriates who, thanks to the climate, found fresh strawberries served year-round at the posh Planters Club.

South of Little England, where the landscape was carved by rivers and streams, Lipton caught sight of Ceylon's most significant landmark, a dome-shaped mountain locals called Sri Pada, or "sacred foot," and Britons called Adam's Peak. At the summit a small shrine guarded a rock believed to bear the imprint made by Buddha's left foot. Some Muslims believed the mark belonged to Adam of the Bible, who stopped there to weep after being expelled from the Garden of Eden, which they thought had been in Ceylon. Local Christians claimed the footprint was made by the apostle Thomas, and Hindus said it was Shiva's. For all four faiths the mountain was a popular pilgrimage site, and during the dry season—January to May—thousands made the three-to-four-hour hike up along lantern-lighted footpaths, hoping to reach the shrine at sunrise to watch the mountain's shadow recede across the plain.

After passing Sri Pada, Lipton continued south toward a plantation called Dambetenne, which was one of three offered for sale by a company known as the Downhall Group. It occupied land that rose to more than six thousand feet above sea level. From the highest point he could see rolling green hills and, at night, beacons from two lighthouses on the coastline about fifty miles away. Lipton was impressed by the healthy tea shrubs that marched in lines across the hills. He saw promise in two other Downhall properties, Laymostotte and Monerakande. His advance man told him he would be able to buy them "for a song."

"I cabled off a very low offer to the London bankers," recalled Lipton, years later. "When they replied 'Can't you do better?' I knew the plantations were mine. Within a few hours and at the small additional cost of one or two more cables, I became their sole proprietor."

This version of events, involving a shrewd low bid, was employed by Lipton when he wanted to impress people at home with his thrift. It also was confirmed, as time passed, and as industry insiders reported that Lipton paid around 25,000 pounds sterling for five thousand acres tended by more than three thousand workers. But at the moment he made the deal, Lipton engaged in a little image building by telling locals he had paid more than eight times as much. This exaggeration, perhaps intended to seal his reputation as a big man in Ceylon, was duly reported by the press on the island. A correction followed later, with Sinhalese editors scolding Lipton for his manipulations, but by the time the truth was revealed, the new prince of tea was already steaming for home.

Before he departed, Lipton had made a point of visiting the venerated pioneer of the Ceylon tea industry, fellow Scotsman James Taylor. By now an old man who wore a bushy beard, Taylor resembled Lipton's father in appearance as well as in his conservative approach to life and business. Since coming ashore in 1851 he had left the island only once, and that was to go to Darjeeling, India, on a busman's holiday. But though he had steered the development of the local tea plantations, Taylor never became a landowner. Instead he advised and served a succession of British adventurers who came, developed plantations, and formed a caste of self-important men who declared themselves brave heroes who brought civilization, virtue, and prosperity to a primitive land.

As men of wealth and authority who operated under the protection of the empire, estate managers enjoyed an exotic lifestyle and a status almost equal to the headmen who had run English-owned plantations during slave days in the American South. (These farms would serve as the model for British development schemes worldwide.) Most were highly educated military veterans who brought commanding personalities and social skills to their lives as expats. Long days of supervising thousands of workers were followed by veranda parties with their immediate subordinates, and with the Europeans who held similar positions at neighboring properties. Planters would freely trade ideas for improving yields as well as gossip about trends in the international market. Weekends were spent at private clubs, where tennis was followed by gin drinks and sumptuous banquets.

On their isolated properties, planters wielded great power. Typically they were the sole source of employment and housing for thousands, and in some cases the individual planter was so feared he was celebrated as a god during religious festivals. Even when he was regarded as a benevolent figure, an estate manager would be treated with as much deference and respect as the Bishop of Rome. For a man like Lipton, who loved being in command and had for some time been developing a larger-than-life social persona, the role of part-time planter was a nice fit. He couldn't actually run an estate as Taylor did, but that wasn't his goal. As a wealthy investor intent on consolidation and efficiency, Lipton represented the next phase of an industry that had outgrown its founders.

His business there concluded, Thomas Lipton departed the hill country for Colombo, where he sailed into a future that would see his business empire grow until it covered so much of the world that the sun always shone upon it. In a year's time James Taylor would die of dysentery at his home in Loolecondera. He was buried beneath a stone inscribed with praise for his service to Ceylon and its economic development. Although his fame would scarcely approach Lipton's, locals would honor Taylor a century later with a small museum at the site of his experimental tea plot, where some of his original plants continued to produce. Parts of Taylor's original cabin were unearthed and preserved alongside the granite outcropping where he often sat to smoke his pipe and gaze over the plantation. Both became favorite spots for pilgrims, who came to honor a man who died with little wealth but changed a nation in a profound and lasting way.

$\mathcal{A}$stride the $\mathcal{W}$orld

As a man who made money by linking his persona to his products, a good story was Thomas Lipton's stock-in-trade. When it came time for his assault on the American tea market, he developed a fine one. It began on an ocean liner headed for New York. During the long trip, Lipton walked the deck and reflected on the success of his newly integrated tea business and the reliable supply at his disposal thanks to his purchase of the estates in Ceylon and falling prices in wholesale markets. What better place to sell it, he thought, than in the fastest-growing country in the world?

At just over 62 million, the population of the United States was already greater than that of the British Isles, Canada, and Australia combined. Indeed, for three decades America had grown by more than 1.2 million citizens per year. This rate was four times greater than the pace of growth in the United Kingdom. Just as important, the country was getting richer and more cosmopolitan at the same time. These developments were most obvious in New York, where, every day, throngs of immigrants arrived from every corner of the globe, making for an incredibly rich and diverse culture.

In the Lipton-brings-tea-to-America saga, he started scouting the territory at his hotel on his first morning ashore. After taking a seat in the dining room, he requested tea for breakfast and the waiter responded with "an expression of blank amazement," as Lipton recalled.

"Tea sir? Did you say tea, sir?"

A bit of confusion was followed by a cup of coffee delivered with an explanation that the "stuff" Lipton had requested was not served in the hotel. Lipton said he met the same response at other hotels and restaurants. Servers were not quite as outraged as the colonists who once tossed tea into Boston Harbor, but they made it clear that this most British beverage wasn't ever served.

Lipton would report better success when he searched for tea in the city's grocery stores. New York was, after all, home to quite a few branches of the Great Atlantic and Pacific *Tea* Company. But here again he also found trouble. Most of the tea he encountered was made from inferior leaves, and "many of the store keepers regard tea as on the same level with barley, rice and maize and kept their supplies in all kinds of open receptacles." He found tea kept in even worse conditions in Chicago, where, at a State Street shop, it was made to "suffer the horrible indignity of complete exposure to all kinds of weather at the open shop door." Nowhere did Lipton find high-quality orange pekoe from Ceylon. And nowhere did anyone handle the precious commodity with the care—or flair—he felt the product deserved.

With his research done, Lipton concluded there was no real tea trade in the United States. This wasn't true. Americans, many of whom came from tea-obsessed countries such as Ireland and Russia, consumed nearly eighty million pounds of it in 1890. The Great Atlantic and Pacific Tea Company handled much of this business, but small wholesalers could be found in almost any city or town. Many suburbs and villages were served by horse-drawn "tea wagons" operated by salesmen who sold tea, coffee, and other items door to door. And bad as much of what they sold was, some good tea was available if customers were willing to pay the price.

On a per capita basis, Americans used less than one pound per year, far below the rate of consumption of the addicts in Lipton's main market. The difference was not a matter of rejecting hot drinks or stimulants. Americans drank huge amounts of hot coffee, importing half a billion pounds of beans annually. The problem—and here Lipton was absolutely correct—was in the quality and taste of the tea that was generally available in the States.

While Great Britain was winning its long war against Chinese tea, developing a protected industry in India and Ceylon, America had depended on supplies from the losing side. Faced with declining world prices, Chinese producers had tried to make up for the loss in revenue by selling a greater volume. However, the only way to produce more tea from the same plantations was to pick the tougher, woodier leaves that grow closer to the tree trunk. At the time Lipton made his tea tour of America, the Chinese greens and blacks he encountered were quite inferior to the most ordinary brew available in any grocery or tea shop in Britain. As a result, most of what was consumed was weak or bitter, and in some quarters it was regarded as a feminine—or, to be precise, effeminate—drink. This was why tough old party hacks of the era called do-good temperance preachers "namby-pamby, goody-goody gentlemen who sip cold tea."

Even American retailers had to acknowledge that their handling of the product was abysmal. Consider this snippet published in the magazine *American Grocer* in the spring of 1890:

SALESMAN IN THE BOWERY OVERLAND UNDERLAND TEA
COMPANY—I couldn't help it sir. I was a'cleaning the

canister when the whole pail o'vinegar upset into
the chest . . .

PROPRIETOR—Sorry but I'll have to dock you $5.

(TWO MINUTES LATER)—Yes mum, it's the rarest kind
o'brand. Forty cents a pound. Why, er, les' see. Imperial
Pungent Java. Two pounds? Yes mum.

America had suffered with bad tea for so long that many consumers
couldn't tell the difference between a good tea and an awful one, and
millions had given up trying.

If they received a decent product, reasoned Lipton, Americans would
drink far more. Confident as he was that he had the product to do the
trick, the only difficulty he faced was in deciding whether to take on the
entire grocery business, by opening a new Lipton's chain, or to peddle his
brand of tea as a wholesaler. A&P already operated more than a hundred
grocery stores and was opening new ones at a rapid pace. Dozens of
other companies claimed chains covering more than one city, and almost
all of them were growing as well. In the end, Lipton chose to stay out of
the American general grocery trade and start selling his tea through
contracted local agents.

Lipton would say that his initial goal was to "teach" Americans how
to drink tea, and he did this with his "yellow label" orange pekoe, distributed in sealed packages. The low price, bright packaging, and consistent quality made for an instant success. Business was so good that
Lipton immediately opened an office and warehouse in Manhattan at
the corner of Franklin and Hudson streets. This part of the city (now
known as Tribeca) was then New York's grocery district, and if Lipton
walked a few blocks south he could have visited the headquarters of his
chief competitor, A&P. The docks serving oceangoing freighters sat a
few blocks to the west.

From his New York base, Lipton did teach Americans to like tea. To be precise, he persuaded them to like *his* tea, which was smooth but also strong enough to stand up to milk and sugar—as coffee did—and consistent in quality. Lipton's timing was good. The American temperance movement was gaining strength and, like its British counterpart, promoted tea as an alternative to alcoholic beverages. The Woman's Christian Temperance Union served it at events, and "tea dances" were rising as a wholesome alternative to saloon culture. To make tea the product of choice for teetotalers and others, Lipton did all he could to put his name before the public.

Much of this brand-building work was done through paid advertising, which included spots in the newspapers and on billboards, in addition to the free exposure garnered by the six hundred refrigerated railroad cars that crisscrossed the country with the name "Lipton" emblazoned on them in six-foot-high red letters. When the organizers of the World's Columbian Exposition announced plans for the fair to open in October 1892—marking the four-hundredth anniversary of Columbus reaching the Americas—Lipton made a bid to display his tea for the world to taste.

The largest world's fair to date, the Chicago exposition was set on six hundred acres along the shore of Lake Michigan. The vast complex of temporary buildings—called the White City—drew 27 million visitors to marvel at the greatest collection of art, food, technology, manufactured goods, and amusements ever assembled. Among the world's "firsts" that appeared at the fair were the Ferris wheel, the metal zipper, and the Colt machine gun. The fair would announce America's arrival as a world economic power and express the exuberance of a new material culture. The Golden Age was, among other things, a celebration of the new for consumers who learned to expect better, cheaper, and more stuff every time they went to the market.

When ambassador Robert Todd Lincoln invited the British government to join the exposition, it responded by establishing a commission that worked for more than a year to select exhibitors from more than a thousand applicants. The great shipbuilders, machine companies, and railcar manufacturers all sent their wares along with those from distilleries, mines, and bicycle makers. In the food department, the committee collected goods from, among others, the British Bee Keepers Association and the Birmingham Vinegar Brewery. Lipton the tea man would be permitted to display both his regular brand and a special "golden tip" tea made from the most tender leaf buds.

Tea companies in London often offered exclusive products like "golden tip" on auction at Mincing Lane and coveted the bragging rights that came with setting a record high price. In recent competitions the United Kingdom Tea Company and the Gartmore Estate had pushed the record from a little less than $30 per pound to $53. As tea provisioner to the common man, Lipton then shocked the lane when a wholesale pound of his Ceylon-grown golden-tip tea brought well over $100. Since the buyer wasn't named, some suspected it was the old publicity hound himself. "This ridiculous price was merely the result of a vulgar advertising trick," declared C. H. Denyer, in the *Economic Journal* of London.

At the Chicago fair, Lipton enjoyed the status of representing the entire British tea industry, an astounding achievement for someone who, five years earlier, sold very little of the stuff in his stores. In his advertisement, printed in the British program, he claimed to be the "Largest Tea and Coffee dealer in the World." Lipton owned more than sixty shops in London alone, and others in "all towns of Great Britain and Ireland." It is possible that he was the largest dealer in the world, but he couldn't have known this for sure.

Fairgoers discovered Lipton's most expensive tea in a special hall constructed by native builders from the island of Ceylon. The Ceylon Court was a favorite of Chicagoans, who had followed closely the travails of the fifty-three Sinhalese who had arrived in mid-winter to erect it. The visitors came only with their lightweight traditional dress and were shocked by the cold, snow, and wind. They struggled gamely, however, to turn three hundred tons of materials into the beautiful pagoda-style building where Lipton's most precious tea was poured in the midst of displays of art, jewels, and spices.

At the end of the exposition, when the judging was done, Lipton tea won three gold medals. Before he departed, the proud merchant bought a 22,000-pound cheese that had been exhibited throughout the summer by the Canadian government (which had been forced to repair the floor of its pavilion after the mighty cheese crashed through it). The pride of Perth, Ontario, the cheese had been dispatched to America by a crowd of five thousand, and Lipton's purchase assured them that their Elephant Fromage, as it was called, would enjoy continued fame and admiration. The cheese, which was twenty-four feet around, was transported to Britain at great expense. When it arrived in London, Lipton announced that the cheese had spoiled and he left it at a railway depot. Canadian honor was restored when the great wheel was rescued by a caterer who said the beast was still good and edible at its heart. He trimmed it and returned it to Ottawa, where it was consumed at the House of Commons.

The adventures of the great Canadian cheese were chronicled in the British press to the delight of the public and to the benefit of Lipton's business. When established competitors whispered about Lipton selling tea that was not just inexpensive but of cheap quality, he responded with a campaign that stressed his product's superiority and warned consumers of the dangers posed by imitators. Suddenly every container of Lipton tea came printed with his signature and the caution, "Not genuine without this signature."

To emphasize the notion that he personally controlled the quality and
purity of his tea, Lipton also began calling himself a "tea planter" and
generally listed Ceylon among his addresses. Although he hardly worked
the fields with a hoe, Lipton did make the long journey to visit his plantations every year, and his investments spurred rapid growth in the
industry. In his first few years as a planter he built housing for his thousands of workers—described by various writers as "Tamil coolies"—and
a twenty-thousand-square-foot factory. At the entrance he posted a quotation from the failed tea shop owner and successful writer John Ruskin:
"Quality is no accident. It is the result of intelligent effort."

In Ceylon, Lipton's most important technical innovation was a
system of cables and pulleys—he called them "wireways"—that he had
slung across the hillsides. These cables relieved workers of the chore of
hauling heavy baskets of leaves to the factory he built below the groves.
The wireways also increased productivity and, by cutting the time between a leaf's being plucked and the start of its processing, actually
made for more flavorful tea.

As Lipton expanded his landholdings and steadily bought more
leaves from other growers, the Ceylon Planters' Association also worked
to increase demand through its own promotional campaigns in the
United States and Great Britain. They scored a big victory when the London caterer J. Lyons accepted a payment—a bribe, really—in exchange
for a pledge to serve only tea from Ceylon at the prestigious new Imperial Institute, where research and education related to the needs of the
empire would be conducted. The Planters' Association also built a Ceylon Tea Garden and Rest House at the institute, so that staff and visitors
would associate *their* tea, and not the Chinese competition, with the
welfare of the nation. With their combined effort, Lipton and the association helped boost Ceylon's sales from 4 million tons per year in the
mid-1880s to 36 million per year in the 1890s.

The business was good for Lipton and for the island of Ceylon's over-all economy, creating hundreds of thousands of jobs and a flood of new revenue from abroad. The jobs were low-paid, physically demanding, and sometimes dangerous, and the British planters like Lipton relied on government policy to aid their effort. Nevertheless, the planters' capital was essential in a business that required up-front spending to grow a crop, harvest it, and ship it, and enough wealth besides to wait for payment from the buyer. Without this kind of financial strength, which men like Lipton provided, agriculture in poor countries would rarely get past the subsistence stage. With it, plantations flourished, subsidiary businesses grew, and new infrastructure evolved. In Haputale, which was the town closest to Lipton's estates, new businesses arose to provide services and supplies to his workers and factory. Oversize two-wheeled ox-carts (shaped a little like American prairie schooners) clogged winding mountain roads, bringing tea to the rail depot. One hundred miles of new track were built to establish additional service to ports. All of this activity meant a rising standard of living for Haputale, but also, to the dismay of one writer, the appearance of "beer and gin shops, to say nothing of an opium den, all of which are responsible for a grave amount of crime and lawlessness."

Nineteen miles east of Haputale, Lipton's plantations were safe from whatever lawlessness gripped the town. Governed mainly by the rhythm of the sun and the seasons, his workers—men, women, and children—mustered early each morning outside their company houses, worked in the fields and in the factory until the day grew too hot, and then retired. When he was present, Lipton followed much the same routine, although his rest came in a luxurious home he built on a cool hillside high above the plantation.

Though he referred to it as a "bungalow," Lipton's estate house was hardly humble. It had seven bedrooms, two parlors, and a large dining room where exposed beams echoed the Tudor country-house style. The exterior design was tropical colonial, with massive columns marking a broad front veranda and tall windows cut into thick walls of white-washed stucco. Although it was a one-story house, the tall, steeply pitched roof made it look imposing and allowed for high ceilings that permitted air to circulate. Tall trees shaded the house and it was sur-rounded by lush gardens. On one side a green lawn stopped abruptly at the edge of a steep hillside that dropped almost straight down for more than a thousand feet to a valley below.

With hummingbirds flitting among the tropical flowers and a house snake patrolling for mice, Lipton's place became a truly exotic escape for the busy millionaire and, as time passed, a place his friends and associates were desperately eager to visit. Most arrived with a dread fear of leeches, mosquitoes, and poisonous snakes but rarely actually saw any of these nuisances. Instead, they gawked at the men, women, and children who worked the plantation, many of them shirtless, and indulged in every sight, sound, and taste a tourist might find in a land of temples, festivals, and spice. When it came time for more risky adventure, men went into the forest to hunt leopard, elephant, and a local species of the Sambar deer that reached weights of six hundred pounds or more. On one of these outings Lipton would discover an overlook high above his factory where one of the best views in all of Ceylon—mountains, rivers, and the sea beyond—could be enjoyed. The spot, which he revisited many times, came to be called Lipton's Seat.

During harvests the view from Lipton's Seat would include hun-dreds of workers bent over tea plants—*his* tea plants—and dozens of overloaded wagons snaking their way along narrow switchback paths carrying *his* product to Haputale. The sight was enough to inspire in any man a sense of power, if not dominion over the world. It was a feeling common to high-ranking colonialists of any era who came and conquered a foreign land. (Certainly the ancient Romans experienced it when they ruled England.) In the days when Britain controlled a fifth of the world's land mass and a quarter of its people, adventuring Britons typically returned home from abroad with a certain worldliness, if not a swagger, and tastes broadened by the culture they had discovered. This would be demonstrated in a man's words, his dress, his diet, and his possessions.

After Lipton made himself a Ceylon tea planter he began to live in a style that mimicked the displays of wealth, worldliness, and taste that distinguished the educated, upper-class gentlemen who occupied the social circle he hoped to enter. He filled his new home near London with bronzes and wood carvings from Asia and big-game trophies, including an elephant's head, which he hung on the wall in his billiards room. He brought young Sinhalese men to London to staff the house (and his office) and made rice a staple of almost every meal. The home itself was a rambling three-story mansion with an irregular roof and multiple chimneys. Called Osidge, it was set in the northern suburb of Southgate, about ten miles from City Road.

The land surrounding Osidge had first been granted to a local abbot by Henry II in 1176. The king's only stipulation for the grant was that the forest on the property supply wood for the burning of heretics. The house Lipton occupied had been built in 1808 and, while large, held many small, cozy rooms. The Osidge stables sheltered thirty horses, including a few imported from Kentucky. Following a fad of the times (at least among the rich), Lipton built an adult-size playhouse in one of the oldest trees on the property. Visitors climbed a stair built out of branches that wound around the trunk until it reached a platform. Once settled on benches, a party of four could enjoy tea at a table made from rough-hewn wood.

Looking between the branches, they could see brilliant green lawns, pe-
rennial gardens, and big specimen trees covering sixty acres.

The grounds at Osidge were more than adequate for the hundreds
of Lipton office workers who made their way to the estate in ten big
horse-drawn wagons from the Palmer's Green railway station one July
morning in 1894. The women dressed in copies of the dresses worn by
the Princess of Wales—tight bodices, wide skirts—while the men appeared in a variety of styles. Those ready for the games came in the
breeches they wore for bicycling (a current craze) or striped blazers and
flannel pants. Others came in the more formal clothes they wore for
work, including silk hats. With William Love at his side in a Scot's bon-
net and kilt, Lipton received them decked out in the outfit he was making his trademark—light-colored pants, open frock coat, white shirt
with a high-winged collar, and a loose, dark-colored bow tie with white
polka dots. To mark this festive occasion he chose a vest of shimmering
lavender.

Still tall and slim, Lipton's age showed mainly in the white of his hair
and droopy mustache and in the faint crow's-feet spreading from his
eyes. Although he was barely known in London society, and wasn't ever
seen in town with friends, through his travels and the development of
his business Lipton had begun to fashion a playful personality—a big
smile, colorful stories, encouraging quips—for use outside the office,
where he generally presented a commanding personality. The sunnier
Lipton was on full display at the staff party, where he personally took
charge of many of the games, declared the winners of various races, and
made sure that every guest was well fed and watered. (The service included a luncheon, afternoon strawberries and cream, and high tea.)

But even as he charmed and entertained, Lipton worked. Sprinkled
among his employees, and blessed with a private room where they alone
could indulge in drinks more potent than ginger ale and tea, were a

dozen or so newspapermen who received his most focused attention. They heard about Lipton's beginnings in Glasgow, his early publicity stunts—orphan pigs, hot-air balloons, elephants, and giant cheeses— and about his adventures around the world. When asked, "What's the secret of your success?" Lipton replied, "Secret of it? Make no secret of it. Advertise all you can." Lipton repeated these same lines a week later at a second company picnic, held in a public park in Essex for two thousand factory workers.

Previous articles about Lipton in the London press had announced his record sale of golden-tip tea and, more recently, reported a huge monthly customs check—the equivalent of $4.5 million in 2010—for his tea imports. In the days immediately after the Osidge party, the papers were filled with descriptions of the games and the guests and the great house. These notices served as a kind of coming-out for the millionaire tea merchant, letting the rich and powerful who had never set foot in a Lipton's market know there was a new presence among them.

As a mere grocer, Tommy Lipton would have been too common for high society, no matter how many stores he owned. But as an importer, international businessman, and empire builder in Ceylon, Lipton enjoyed higher status. His entry into elite circles wouldn't be automatic, but if he continued to rise financially and made himself more visible, he might attract the kind of friends who could be helpful in many ways. For a son of the Gorbals who never even had a thought of attending the right schools, this goal may have seemed the most outlandish one he ever set. And as he began the pursuit, he seemed to lack the instincts to catch the prize.

Still addicted to work, Lipton spent his days at his office and his nights at home. Aside from the crowd at his annual staff picnic, the guests he welcomed at Osidge were invariably business associates who quickly discovered they had been invited to a working dinner. In 1895 his one notable social appearance was at a dinner party hosted by a fellow Scot, the Marquess of Breadalbane, Gavin Campbell, who as lord steward held power over the management of the queen's household. Though a peer, Campbell did not possess the kind of wealth generally associated with nobility. Nevertheless, in acknowledging the great grocer, he granted Lipton a stamp of social approval. He most certainly played a role in securing a royal warrant for Lipton, which recognized him as an official supplier to the Crown. The honor came with permission to display the royal family's coat of arms. Lipton posted it over the door to his office building, adding the motto "Work Conquers All."

Aside from the marquess and his wife, who were friendly enough toward Lipton to visit him in Ceylon, Lipton didn't have a social circle. He almost never went to dinner or the theater in the city. His one cultural indulgence was a device called an "electrophone," which allowed him to hear performances from theaters in his home via the telephone line. Queen Victoria was the most famous subscriber to this service—£5 per month, free installation—which offered as many as thirty selections per night from sites as far away as Paris.

Although Lipton loved new technologies, it's difficult to imagine he spent much time listening to the electrophone. Instead he was occupied by expanding business—new products and new stores, from Newfoundland to South Africa to New Zealand—and the construction of a sprawling London factory/office complex that occupied a triangular property that was bounded by Bath Street, City Road, and Old Street. At roughly fourteen acres, the property was immense, especially considering it was just a couple miles from the center of the most important city in the world.

The centerpiece of the Lipton complex was an office building faced in red brick and white stone with a slate mansard roof. From the street, a visitor was met by a doorway that was forty feet high and framed by white marble. The name "Lipton" was carved in stone over the door, and above it rose a clock tower. Inside, on the first floor, about three hundred clerks occupied a six-thousand-square-foot hall with a vaulted ceiling. A large oil portrait of the founder gazed down from the wall. The room was lighted with electricity generated on-site and was connected by dedicated telegraph lines to distribution centers in Liverpool, Glasgow, and Dublin. One division of clerks took orders from all over the world and arranged for shipments to reach either Lipton's own shops or other retailers under contract. Another group did nothing but receive and post checks from retail outlets and wholesale customers.

On the next floor up, accountants worked their pencils and typists clacked away at their keyboards to complete correspondence that would be mailed, through an in-house post office, to five thousand different Lipton operatives around the world. Above the clerks, in quieter reaches, senior executives labored in formal rooms lighted by large bay windows facing the street.

On the very top floor at City Road, The Great Lipton's own office was reached via a hallway decorated with Asian art, including frescoes and figures copied from ancient Buddhist and Hindu works and statues of elephants draped with silks and jewels like the ones paraded in celebrations in India and Ceylon. Visitors were welcomed and then guided by one of the young Sinhalese men who served him at work and at home—he employed four in all. They were led by D. D. "Johnnie" Johanis, who would become an institution in his own right, serving until Lipton's death. At City Road, Johnnie and the others dressed in flowing white trousers and tunics topped by colorful vests decorated with gold thread. These costumes would not have been as startling as one might expect. At the time more than a few well-known Britons displayed a taste for outfits with a foreign flair. In warm weather, for example, James Keir Hardie, a member of Parliament, wore a Japanese kimono as he conducted business in London.

The grandeur of Lipton's headquarters—the great hall filled with clerks, the busy hive of typists, the hushed executive suites, and the uniformed Sinhalese attendants—prepared first-timers to be awestruck when they finally got behind the door of the inner sanctum. But instead of entering a great big office, they discovered a comfy, not commanding, little room that was a souvenir-filled jumble, more like your eccentric grandfather's attic than the center of an industrial and commercial colossus.

The heavy ceiling beams and wood paneling in Lipton's office suggested a cozy ship's cabin. The walls were decorated with photos of Ceylon—mostly tea estates—and a framed canceled check for more than £35,000, issued to cover government fees for importing tea. Lipton's roll-top desk and matching chair were made of hand-carved mahogany finished to a golden glow. The big Oriental carpet bore a flowery design, and the large fireplace was ornamented with carvings that echoed the Asian artwork in the hallways outside. This was, distinctly, Lipton's place. It reeked of his passions and peculiarities. And like the man, it was theatrical. It was a stage setting that would make visitors feel as if they were being welcomed to the man's heart.

While his personal office revealed his sentimental side, Lipton's raw ambition hummed in the collection of factories he built behind the City Road office building. In one, five hundred women nimbly packaged a million containers of tea per week. In others, workers made and packed cocoa, candy, meat pies, sausages, and cured hams. The print shop that once hummed on Lancefield Street in Glasgow was moved to this site and turned out a variety of paperboard boxes and labels in more than a dozen languages. These were glued onto barrels and other containers that were also manufactured here. By the end of the decade a fleet of motor trucks would scurry around the city delivering goods. Among the first commercial vehicles ever seen on the streets of London and Glasgow, they were decorated with Lipton's name, as were city trams, railway stations, and shop windows as the nation's biggest retailer became one of its most prominent advertisers.

With promotions that emphasized cheap prices and better quality, Lipton left the high end of the market to others and solidified his attachment to everyone else. In a country where fewer than five percent of the workers made more than three pounds (roughly $18 in 1890) per week, "everyone else" constituted a very large clientele. Thanks in part to Lipton, working-class Britons were consuming ten percent more calories and twenty-five percent more protein than they had in 1887. The price of tea was at an all-time low, and heading further down, and the variety and quality of food in the nation's diet was rising every month.

Thanks to American-style merchandising, Lipton had secured a favored position on the table of the typical British home. At the same time, his American-style biography—poor but plucky boy makes good—earned him a place in millions of hearts. The Lipton legend inoculated him and his firm from class resentments and from the effects of certain social and political movements that were challenging the old order. Throughout the century, a series of reform acts had made more people eligible to vote and introduced more democracy, and labor leaders had begun to gain support especially among Scottish miners and workers in heavy industries like shipbuilding. More recently a few prominent Victorians in the upper classes who felt pangs of guilt and fear, or flashes of conscience, had veered toward socialism and called for a gradual but steady shift of power away from the old elites. Finally, modern trade was reducing the power of the landed gentry. Centuries-old estates were being broken up and sold by squires who couldn't compete with imports, arranged by the likes of Lipton, from America, Australia, and other countries.

In the churning politics of the day, poor and working-class Britons who were radicalized by new union and Labour Party leaders fixed their ire on men who owned and operated traditional heavy industries where work was grueling, dangerous, and underpaid. They were less resentful of the more modern capitalists like Lipton, whose plants offered work that was generally lighter and less perilous. Lipton wages were not significantly above the going rate—although he claimed they were a bit higher—but his shops, plants, warehouses, and offices were good places to work. He campaigned on behalf of laws limiting shop hours—workers deserved time off, he said—and built morale with his annual Conversazioni and picnics.

Altogether, Lipton was the kind of businessman people preferred. His name was synonymous with a common comfort—people on both sides of the Atlantic spoke of having "a cup of Lipton's"—and his reputation was so playfully positive that some people argued that he wasn't a real man but rather the product of some advertising man's imagination. Like "Kilroy," the figment of the World War II years, Lipton's name appeared in so many places and with such frequency that a skeptic might believe he was a fiction. This belief was common enough that several articles were published in the mid-1890s by men who simply had to declare they had met the actual Lipton and he was real. And if his low prices, publicity campaigns, employment practices, and compelling story weren't enough to win over the public, his leap into large-scale philanthropy would cement his reputation around the world.

By 1897, Mark Twain had already begun to let go of his anti-elitist impulses and was treating the rich and powerful with a little less comic scorn. (He was, after all, becoming quite powerful and rich himself.) Many of his regular readers, however, were not prepared for his reporting on Queen Victoria's Diamond Jubilee. Instead of writing as an American, a democrat, and an intellectual, Twain was so affected by the spectacle that he reported the events of the jubilee celebration with the awe and reverence of a loyal subject. "All the nations seemed to be filing by," he wrote in a *New York Journal* piece about one procession. "The Queen Empress was come. She was received with great enthusiasm. . . . She was a symbol, and allegory of England's grandeur and the might of the British name."

Not everyone was thrilled by the jubilee. Irish Nationalists protested, and the kimono-wearing Keir Hardie declared it a big propaganda event that promoted royal excess. But for the huge majority of Britons and admirers of Britain worldwide, the jubilee was a sensation. No event in living memory was as grand as, or captured more wild public enthusiasm than, the weeklong celebration of Victoria's ascension sixty years earlier. All of the empire, indeed most of the world, was riveted by the occasion, which honored not only a sovereign but the most powerful empire since ancient Rome. For Britons, jubilee week allowed a release of excitement that had built for more than a year as various events were planned and every citizen tried to get involved.

Amid all the preparation for the jubilee, it fell to the queen's daughter-in-law, the glamorous Alexandra, Princess of Wales, to raise the idea of including London's poorest. In an open letter to the lord mayor of the city she called for donations to fund a banquet open to everyone unable to afford a celebration meal. She seeded the fund with £100 and called on her friends and others to join in making donations to "provide these unfortunate ones, those beggars and outcasts, with a dinner or some substantial meal during the week of the jubilee commemoration."

Coming after many others, including a hospital drive started by the princess's husband, Alexandra's appeal drew few contributions. With less than a month to go, only fifteen percent of the money required had been donated. When this was reported in the press, Lipton saw both a duty and an opportunity. He wrote a check for the balance needed (the equivalent of more than $3.2 million in 2010) and sent it to the lord mayor with a note. The money would "enable the Princess's kindly and considerate scheme to be successfully carried out," he explained. Then he asked that the gift be registered as "Anonymous." The mayor complied, keeping the secret.

With the impending jubilee promising to be an ostentatious extravaganza, an impulsive gift that would bring so many poor Britons into the celebration warmed many, including a newspaper writer in Birmingham, who hoped it would indeed remain an anonymous, and therefore selfless, act. Elsewhere the press speculated about the donor, raising the names of various men of wealth and fame. Newspapers and wire services competed over the story, advancing one name and then another. A cartoonist published a drawing of a mysterious white knight delivering the gift to Alexandra at the tip of a lance. One writer penned a parody of the folk rhyme "Who Killed Cock Robin?" to float a host of suggestions about the identity of "Anonymous." When a journalist finally asked Lipton if he had given the gift he denied it, adding, "I wish you could tell me where I could borrow 25,000 pounds."

After more than a week, as the energy behind the inquiry began to flag, Lipton at last told the lord mayor he could reveal the true identity of "Anonymous." Since this selfless act had already won public approval, the revelation had to be accomplished with care. Accordingly, friends in the press said that a bank clerk who had seen the check spilled the secret. In light of Lipton's obsessive self-promotion, a skeptic could be excused for assuming that the man *would* have made sure his identity was revealed and developed a plausible cover-up involving a story about an "unnamed bank clerk." But in the glow of the impending jubilee, most observers chose appreciation over cold analysis and focused on Lipton's generosity. His connection to the poor was unassailable. He had been born into the slum life, had grown up amid death and deprivation, and had made himself into a stunning success by feeding the masses. Who else would make such a donation?

Under the gaze of the world press, Lipton added his expertise to his cash, throwing himself into the planning and execution of the great feast, to be offered on June 22. The fund would be enough to feed 400,000 people—almost ten percent of the city—a meal that included cheese, bread, meat pies, plum pudding, and cake washed down with ginger ale, lemonade, and, of course, Lipton's tea. This task, to be accomplished on a single afternoon at nine large halls around the city, would require 1.4 million pounds of food, and more than 100,000 hours of labor to prepare and pack it. The operation would resemble the effort Napoleon had made daily to feed his Grand Army, which also numbered 400,000, except that the jubilee crowd would not be so disciplined, and the food would have to be better than battlefield rations.

On the night of June 21, Victoria's subjects began gathering in parks and along the six miles of road where the formal procession would pass. In streets cleared of traffic, brightly uniformed troops from India, Canada, Egypt, and every other corner of the empire ran through their parade routines. The Bengal Lancers mounted their horses and balanced their pikes while the muffled sound of military drummers rose from various parts of the city. By morning, three million people filled the streets, each of them eager to see the displays of power and pomp and perhaps glimpse the short woman in mourning black who was their queen. Vendors moved among them, selling drinks and food and souvenirs including medals, mugs, cards, and coins decorated with the queen's image.

As the legions took their places for the procession and latecomers jostled for space on the sidelines, horse-drawn vans hired from a company called Pickford's lined up on the streets near loading docks at factories on the outskirts of the city. Workmen began loading thousands of boxed meals onto the vans, which were then dispatched to the halls where London's poorest were already gathering for their jubilee celebration. Inside the halls, hundreds of male and female volunteers set up tables and benches and acted as servants for a day.

Operating as overseer and cheerleader, Lipton spent the day flitting from one hall to the next, making sure all were served, and that his activities were observed by the press. At some of the halls he appeared with Princess Alexandra. But as much as he enjoyed the attention, Lipton was nevertheless struck by the condition of the people he fed. Forewarned that cutlery was in short supply, most showed up with knives and forks in their hands. The sight "was at once ludicrous and pathetic," he would note weeks later, adding that "it was more pathetic, however, to see these half-famished people devouring the only good meal thousands of them had had in years and that some had ever had." Alexandra was so taken aback by "the state of things which was revealed," reported Lipton, that she began to think about making a more deliberate and sustained attack on hunger.

Somewhat fewer mouths—360,000—were fed than anticipated on Jubilee Sunday, but no matter the count, the effort was a spectacular vehicle for publicity as newspapers around the world ran accounts of the poor people's banquet alongside reports about fancy balls and banquets attended by aristocrats. Overnight, Thomas Lipton became known as Jubilee Lipton and members of the Liberal Party began touting him as a candidate for Parliament. For the moment, at least, no commoner in Britain was more popular with more classes of people, from the Gorbals to Buckingham Palace.

It was Lipton's direct and practical charity that captured hearts, and nowhere did this act have a greater impact on the press than in the United States. Americans had read of the planning for the jubilee in their newspapers, where they learned that tens of millions of dollars were being spent to spiff up the city, transport troops, erect monuments, and conduct every kind of celebration from fireworks to balls. The prospect of the jubilee was simultaneously awesome and galling to a people who rejected monarchs, and, with the exception of a few Anglophiles, Americans viewed the whole extravaganza with, at best, ambivalence. Then came Lipton. The press across the United States told the story of the princess who wanted to feed the poor and of the urchin-turned-millionaire who paid the bill. Suddenly a name that decorated railroad cars and packages in shops represented a real person, a man delightfully chivalrous and generous. In an era when a dog in a diamond collar hosted a Manhattan dinner party and Sherry's Restaurant in New York served millionaires on horseback, Lipton's personal charity was cheered by the poor and admired by practically everyone else.

Three weeks after the jubilee, Lipton arrived in America aboard the Cunard steamer *Campania*. A throng of sweating reporters greeted him on one of the hottest days of the summer and followed him to his office in lower Manhattan. There he welcomed them inside for a question-and-answer session that gave him a chance to tell his story of a poor childhood, a rise through the grocery business, and then international trade.

Although doubters in Britain suspected Lipton never intended to be an anonymous donor, they were an ocean away and Lipton was free to explain that during tea with the lord mayor he had decided to make a secret gift to make sure everyone could celebrate the jubilee and rescue the Princess of Wales from embarrassment. While everyone else was focused on entertaining foreign princes and princesses and preparing pageants, "Princess Alexandra alone had this gracious thought about the poor." Of course, by describing Alexandra's kind-hearted impulse he was also calling attention to his own virtuousness. Taking his cue, the reporters diligently wrote about Lipton's sincere desire to make a secret donation and about his admiration for the princess, which made him only more appealing.

In the *New York Times* report on the great philanthropist's arrival, Lipton was not only a man of the people but also a superior physical specimen who was "cool as a jellyfish" in the searing July heat that had emptied "most of the offices in the city . . . as their owners had gone to seek cool retreats." Though he would be fifty on his next birthday, Lipton was, according to the *Times* account, forty-five years old and remarkably robust. Not a single bead of sweat appeared on his ruddy face, the paper noted, and his "accent and manner of speech are distinctly British."

The picture of Lipton painted by the press was of a man who represented the best of both America and Great Britain. He came from the humblest background and his wealth was self-made. A bachelor, he was a friend to princesses and paupers, and he was both physically strong and handsome. Small wonder, then, that after the publicity rush, reporters and curious New Yorkers—many of them eligible young women—began to stake out the lobby of the Waldorf Hotel, where he had taken a room. Now everything about the man, from how he dressed (impeccably) to his marital status (single), was news. He was an enthusiastic admirer of American women, he said, noting the short skirts they wore when they rode bicycles.

The attention didn't cease as Lipton traveled west on business. In

Chicago a writer whom he never met nevertheless reported that Lipton was tired of being "a confirmed old bachelor" and eager to find an American wife. As soon as the story appeared, the lobby of his hotel was filled with women and he was deluged with letters. The outpouring was so surprising that for a moment Lipton seemed to actually resent getting so much attention. On his return to New York, the *Herald* noticed he had a "haunted look in his eye and a nervous dread of women."

Lipton was now an international celebrity. When he returned to London he appeared as an honored guest at the Lord Mayor's Ball and was then formally presented to Prince Edward and the Princess of Wales. Two days later, on Christmas, Lipton received a package at Osidge sent by Alexandra. Inside he found a scarf pin decorated with diamonds. The gift memorialized the beginning of a long and close relationship between Lipton and Britain's most visible couple.

Albert Edward (called Bertie by friends) and Alexandra were charmed by the handsome Lipton, who was self-assured but respectful, worldly but earthy. Rarely did they meet someone who was so comfortable in his own skin and such good company. Not surprisingly, his name appeared on the list of honors issued by Buckingham Palace on January 1, 1898. He was noted last, after an expert on seals in the Bering Sea and a diplomat in Seoul, and was identified as the "millionaire provision merchant." Of course last did not mean least. Although one paper sourly suggested the honor had been purchased, the knighthood was real, and would attach a title to his name that would be invaluable to his social standing and his business interests worldwide.

The news of Lipton's honor brought cheers in the great hall of his office building. When the staff finished singing for the jolly good fellow, he gave them all the day off "to recover." On January 18, he boarded a train for Portsmouth and then climbed aboard a royal yacht to cross

The Solent to the Isle of Wight. The elderly queen was at Osborn House, the palace she had built with her beloved Albert, and was receiving in the Durbar Room, which had been decorated in stunning Indian style by a Punjabi architect. After being called into the room, Lipton knelt on a tasseled pillow, accepted the tap of her sword, and then stood on the queen's command of "Rise, Sir Thomas."

EIGHT

A Real Shamrock

In more than three decades spent building his fortune, Thomas J. Lipton—now Sir Thomas—had generated plenty of playful press notices about elephants and cheeses and parades. The public admired his success, and consumers were grateful for his low-price wares. Thanks in large measure to Lipton, food prices in Britain had reached historic lows and poorer families were adopting the middle-class ritual of nightly family dinners. But until his gift to Alexandra's jubilee fund, Lipton had been ignored by the wealthy, the powerful, and the notable. It was only in spending his fortune on others that he became a man who mattered to them.

As he approached age fifty—though he admitted only to forty-seven—charity had revealed to Lipton a life beyond business. And he saw in Alexandra's continuing desire to do more for the poor a chance to continue both his philanthropy and his relationship with the princess and her husband, who also happened to be the king-to-be. Although it may be gauche to say such a thing, Thomas knew that Alexandra and Bertie could bring him into a social circle so far from the Gorbals that it would hardly seem real. And in this realm he would enjoy even greater celebrity, which would benefit all of his businesses.

Edward's more liberal—some would say modern—attitude toward welcoming new types of people into high society came at a moment when the barriers between the classes were being lowered, if only a little. At street level, this liberalizing trend meant that anyone who could pay a penny for a newspaper could learn some gossip about the rich and powerful, or follow the successes and failures of sporting men. For someone like Lipton, who was rich enough to afford any diversion in the world, a more liberal society offered the opportunity to actually participate in elite sports.

As he got to know avid racers such as Edward, Lipton gave himself permission to consider one other great ambition that would have seemed impossible in his younger days. What would it take, he wondered, to enter the world of international yachting? To be more precise, what would it take to build a racing yacht—a real *Shamrock*—and capture the most prized trophy in all of sport?

The trophy was the America's Cup, which went to the winner of a series of challenge races between boats from the United Kingdom and the United States. The silver cup—actually a two-foot-tall ornate bottomless pitcher—had begun life in 1851 as the prize for an annual regatta around the Isle of Wight. (Then it was known as the Hundred Guinea Cup.) It was snatched in that first race by a radically designed new yacht called *America*, which had been sent to Great Britain by the New York Yacht Club. Hence the emended name for the trophy—the America's Cup.

From the start, when the New York team arrived at the Isle of Wight, the challenge had been laden with patriotic meaning. The Americans were led by John Cox Stevens, the son of a Revolutionary War officer. He was aided by a group that included James Hamilton, who, as Alexander Hamilton's son, could also claim a distinctly personal kind of patriotism. A man of great wealth (his family owned *all* of Hoboken, New Jersey), Stevens spared no expense to create a boat to beat the British. By the time she was sent across the Atlantic, *America* had been the subject of great publicity and was a symbol of the young nation's daring. So much hope and hype sailed with her that the famed newspaper editor Horace Greeley warned that the country would feel "abused" if she were to be defeated.

The patriotic romance that surrounded *America* began with her design. Instead of copying famous European yachts, Long Island shipbuilder George Steers based his plan on the lines of the common pilot boats that worked in New York Harbor, where, by custom, the first vessel to reach an incoming ship won the job of guiding her to a berth. Competition had led pilots to build boats with knifelike bows and rounded sterns. This shape was the very opposite of the style used by British yacht builders, who made their vessels look like blue whales, sleek but rounded in the fore and tapered aft. When she arrived in Britain, *America*'s ultra-sleek appearance had shocked opposing crews, thus giving her the advantage of intimidation. Moreover, in the water, the challenger was so obviously superior that the New York team had trouble finding Britons who would accept a one-on-one race. When a test was finally scheduled in the Isle of Wight race, she beat fourteen British yachts. This achievement was so stunning it immediately spawned the myth that when Queen Victoria inquired about the second-place finisher, she was told, "Your Majesty, there is no second." Although the exchange never occurred, the story accurately reflected feelings on both sides.

The loss of the Hundred Guinea Cup so rattled British yachtsmen that they fell prey to all kinds of suspicions, including the idea that *America* was secretly steam powered. In fact, it was *America*'s hull design and new, superior sailcloth that had won the victory, and an inspection by Britain's preeminent yachtsman, the peg-legged Marquess of Anglesey, proved this point. After scrambling aboard the yacht, the marquis enlisted a crewman to hold his good leg as he peered over the stern to look for a propeller. He finally admitted the advantages of the design and declared, "I've been sailing my yacht stern foremost for the last twenty years."

In the decades that followed their win, the New York Yacht Club accepted a series of challenges from British yachtsmen who were willing to travel to a racecourse off New York and attempt to recapture the cup for the United Kingdom. Each challenge, which required the winner to prevail in three out of five heats, set off an expensive and complex campaign. Design, engineering, and craftsmanship were lavished on the vessels, while highly skilled crewmen—many of whom came from the humblest homes—were trained to work as devoted teammates. Great sums of money, and even greater amounts of ego and national pride, were invested in the cup races, which pitted the dominant maritime empire in history against a former colony and fast-rising competitor in world affairs. In short, yacht racing became a way for the American and British people to compete without shedding blood.

By the 1880s, the cup competition had become the biggest sporting event in the world, attracting front-page press attention and tens of thousands of spectators. In the days before scheduled races, steamships brought fans from Europe and remained to serve as oceangoing platforms for viewing. In the same period, trains, including some scheduled especially for the job, brought American enthusiasts from every corner of the country. They arrived in New York at a time of year—late summer—when conditions were generally ideal for both sailing and tourism. Clear skies, mild temperatures, and the steady wind made for perfect sailing. Since the event was a magnet for the rich and famous, out-of-towners who came to view the races also knew they would never have a better opportunity to glimpse a Gould, Morgan, or Vanderbilt on the streets, in a restaurant, or at the theater.

Oddly enough, the races themselves were almost impossible to follow with any certainty. Spectators who stood onshore could barely see any of the action and depended on reports shouted through megaphones by announcers who received updates from the course via carrier pigeons. Those who bought tickets to view the race from a vessel at sea rarely understood what they were looking at. Only an avid sailor could make sense of the maneuvers the boats made. And even when a boat crossed the finish line first, victory could be declared only after time allowances based on various arcane computations were factored into the result.

Nevertheless, the sight of the sleek boats with enormous full sails accompanied by scores of steamships and smaller vessels was more than enough to stir excitement among the onlookers. More reward came when the outcome of a heat was announced and the celebration (and commiseration) began in city saloons, taverns, hotels, and restaurants.

Year by year, as the New York Yacht Club defeated every challenger, the race crowds grew bigger. Newspapers nationwide reported everything about the cup challenges, from negotiations on the rules to selection of the captains. When the event arrived, it merited weeks of extensive front-page coverage. Although the nation celebrated American victories as proof of national prowess, the contestants seemed to be most concerned about who had the better manners. Victory and defeat were accepted with grace and good humor, and the race rose in stature to become a show of good sportsmanship, even as it was an emblem of national technological pride. However, as the decades passed and no British challenger ever won, negotiations over the rules and specifications for the boats became more intense. Gradually it became clear that the Americans enjoyed one great advantage: they could build stripped-down, ultra-sleek boats to meet only the demands of a few races. The challengers had to be heavy and strong enough to cross the Atlantic on their own with a full crew aboard.

In the mid-1890s, British frustration turned to acrimony. Before he even sailed to New York, the 1893 challenger issued a host of objections to the rules, among them the one requiring that he reveal the dimensions of his vessel in advance. No one who knew Windham Thomas Wyndham-Quin, the Earl of Dunraven, was surprised by his combative attitude. A lanky, severe-looking man with a twirled mustache, the earl was famously obstinate and temperamental.

The American defender, *Vigilant*, was built by the Herreshoff family shipyard in Bristol, Rhode Island, for a syndicate that included Edwin D. Morgan, Cornelius Vanderbilt, and August Belmont. Known as the "Wizard of Bristol," the designer Nathanael Herreshoff worked in secret and refused to let his clients make suggestions about the design of their own boats. (Ask once and you were refused. Ask twice and your order was likely to be canceled.) Nat wore a beard to save the time that would be spent shaving and demanded absolute silence at the dining table, even when guests were present. As his son eventually noted, he was "too busy" to be human.

The Herreshoff operation also included brothers James (the Boy Wonder) and John (the Blind Genius). Altogether the family was nick-named the Great Ones by locals, who gave them credit for the jobs, money, and acclaim they brought to Bristol, but who were also struck by Nat's cold eccentricity. No wonder some took pleasure in the family's occasional failures, like the time they set to work on a $140,000 steam yacht for a wealthy young New York banker, Howard W. Ream, who turned out to be neither rich nor a banker, but rather a pathological liar who just enjoyed placing orders for luxury items.

Ream may not have been who he claimed to be—indeed, even the name was fake—but he had excellent taste, as he ordered that his ship be built with the same expensive new materials being used to make the *Vigilant*. The actual *Vigilant* glided down the slipway in Bristol with so many technical advantages—bronze hull, steel frame, huge centerboard—that feisty Lord Dunraven was significantly behind before the boats ever approached the starting point.

Dunraven could do nothing about Herreshoff's superior design, but he did protest the size of the defender's crew—seventy compared to the forty on the *Valkyrie II*—on the grounds that they could serve as movable ballast that gave *Vigilant* the advantage of sitting lower in the water. His protest went for naught and he lost the series on a Friday the 13th when the wind ripped his boat's spinnaker. Afterward, Dunraven wondered aloud about sabotage of his sails and complained that his yacht had been bothered by spectator boats on the racecourse.

A man accustomed to getting his way, Dunraven soon made a second challenge, and appeared in New York late in the summer of 1895 with a new boat—*Valkyrie III*. He planned to face another great Herreshoff boat, called *Defender*, which was funded by a syndicate led by the banker C. Oliver Iselin, then the most prominent yachtsman in America. Dunraven arrived in New York already worried about cheating. On the evening before the first race he peered at *Defender* through binoculars and noted the position of various fittings. He also noticed that the crew seemed to be loading something onto the vessel. The next morning, as another boat lay next to *Defender*, Dunraven studied her again and became convinced she was four inches lower in the water, a sure sign that extra ballast had been secreted below her deck. He quietly lodged a complaint with race officials, but they did not act on it.

On the morning of the race the two yachts were towed to the course near Sandy Point, New Jersey. The sea was choked with steamships, pleasure boats, tugs, scows, and every other kind of floating conveyance.

It was the largest turnout in cup challenge history, and among the spectator vessels were many big steamers capable of carrying five hundred or more passengers, including the *General Slocum*, the *City of Lowell*, the *Richard Peck*—known as the "Flier of Long Island Sound"—and a new ship called *Yorktown*, which was the pride of the Old Dominion Line. The flotilla even included some oceangoing ships, such as the *Jane Moseley*, which carried 1,400 spectators. Among the private boats were A. V. Armour's *Ituna*, H. M. Flagler's *Alicia*, W. K. Vanderbilt's *Valiant*, and the famous *Corsair II*, J. P. Morgan's sleek black yacht. (Built on the power of blank checks, this 241-foot-long vessel was the world's largest pleasure craft. She rode low in the water and with her black hull and swept-back smokestack she could present an almost menacing sight, especially on a cloudy day.)

Run in light wind, which favored the sleeker American boat, the first heat of the 1895 challenge was uneventful and *Defender* won with ease. Boat whistles and bells greeted the American yacht's arrival. After the race, Dunraven reiterated his complaint about ballast, and the official "measurer," John Hyslop, dutifully conducted new inspections. He found that *both* boats were riding a fraction of an inch lower in the water. Not convinced, Dunraven continued to speculate aloud about cheating accomplished by night loading of ballast. That evening, as he considered his options, revelers toasted *Defender* and her crew. The celebrations were mostly peaceful, but along the Brooklyn waterfront the drinking led to brawling, and twenty-seven men wound up in the five cells at the Hamilton Avenue police precinct house.

The second heat in the best-of-five series was held on a day with more wind and nearly as many spectator boats in the water. Yacht races begin with a sort of race-before-the-race as captains maneuver for position behind the starting line. The main idea is to catch the wind at the perfect moment so that your boat hits the mark on time and at maximum speed without mishap. Expert sailors also try to use their sails to block and baffle the wind before it reaches an opponent. This way you handicap the other boat with "bad air." Every sailor understands the prestart competition and must play both "offense," to gain advantage, and "defense," to counter an opponent's feints, stunts, and aggression. In one-on-one contests the best start often involves hanging behind your opponent and then breaking ahead to steal his wind at the starting line. The games played to make this kind of start can be dangerous as captains chase each other in circles, risking collisions, damage to their vessels, and injuries to their crews. (Like car racing fans, decades later, many spectators at yacht races secretly hoped for exciting mishaps.)

On this day, as the two racers maneuvered on their approach to the starting line, the captains of dozens of spectator boats and ships also jostled for position. Suddenly, out of the tangle of bobbing vessels, the coastal steamer *Yorktown*—packed with spectators—drifted down the starting line. The people who lined her rail were no doubt pleased to get the best view. And since only the most knowledgeable observers actually understood what was happening on the course, few even understood that the *Yorktown* had suddenly become a disruptive part of the contest.

With quick moves, *Valkyrie III* managed to get past *Yorktown* at its bow and *Defender* passed along its stern. However, as they cleared the steamship, the two racers found themselves on a collision course. As the two crossed paths, *Valkyrie III*'s boom—or, to be precise, a shackle on the end of her boom—caught one of *Defender*'s sails and damaged her topmast. Though sailors scrambled up the mast to make repairs, the American boat was disabled and couldn't use its full load of canvas. The race proceeded and *Valkyrie III* crossed the finish line first, but *Defender* won on a protest. In the evening, rumors that an outraged Dunraven might quit the challenge circulated around the city.

The day of the third race dawned clear. A bright sun rose amid puffy white clouds. As the sunlight burned the mist off the harbor, conditions for racing were judged to be perfect. The captains of the spectator ships, aware of Dunraven's complaints, kept their distance. As the start time approached, *Valkyrie III* never set her sails for racing and soon after the gun sounded she turned about and headed back toward port. Dunraven had quit, allowing *Defender* to cover the course and keep the cup uncontested.

The gathered press and spectators were shocked to see a tugboat come alongside *Valkyrie III* and then tow her in. On the water, a boat loaded with newspapermen gave chase. Shouted questions were met by stony silence until one of Dunraven's men shouted, "You have been told not to come alongside. Now shove off!"

On the course, some of the excursion ships followed *Defender* while others sat becalmed by confusion. About an hour later she returned for the finish and was greeted by whistles, cheers, and brooms waved in the air to indicate a sweep of the races. In the evening Dunraven said something about an overcrowded course—in fact it had been clear—and declined to race anymore. After visiting friends at the mansion colony in Newport, he sailed for home, leaving behind a mess of confusion and anger.

Outrage boiled on both sides of the ocean. In Great Britain, Dunraven first got the benefit of the doubt, especially from yachtsmen who, tired of losing, could imagine that the defenders had indeed cheated. In the United States, racers, editorialists, and fans derided Dunraven as a quitter who had insulted the entire nation. Until this moment, the America's Cup had been a hallowed expression of fair play, manly competition, and British-American friendship. Dunraven had turned it into a petty fight, and, to make matters worse, would continue the squabble until two days after Christmas, when a committee of the New York Yacht Club—including J. P. Morgan and William C. Whitney—

conducted a closed-door hearing inside the Model Room of the club's headquarters on Madison Avenue. The committee had no power outside the confines of the club, but it was agreed, in the press, that if Dunraven proved his case, Iselin would be barred from the society of gentlemen forever.

The Model Room, which was lined floor-to-ceiling with carvings, paintings, sketches, and models of yachts, was cleared for a long table, covered in red cloth, where the five committee members sat. To their right a small table and chair were set to accommodate witnesses, and before it was placed another long table to serve lawyers and their aides.

The spectacle began when Lord Dunraven arrived accompanied by a bodyguard and his British barrister, George R. Asquith. After introductions, Dunraven made his accusations and was then subjected to a withering cross-examination by Joseph H. Choate, one of the most prominent attorneys in New York. This was followed by testimony from the bearded Wizard of Bristol, Nathanael Herreshoff, who appeared "sphinx-like as ever" according to *The New York Times*. He said Dunraven may have been fooled into believing that extra ballast had been loaded on *Defender*, because she was tipped to one side. Days of testimony followed, and then more than a month of deliberation, until the committee rejected Dunraven's claim. The verdict was read to a gathering at the clubhouse by J. P. Morgan and was met with great cheers.

Having challenged the dignity of the New York Yacht Club and the honesty of its members, and being found in error, an honorable man could face only one possible course of action—apology. The press in England said as much as it declared the verdict fair and demanded the conflict be ended. But Dunraven resisted. With one newspaper asking "What's He Waiting For?" he visited at Sandringham to consult with the Prince of Wales, who was commodore of the Royal Yacht Squadron. Prince Edward advised him to consider Anglo-American relations as he made his next move. Dunraven ignored the advice and wrote a letter to the New Yorkers that explained his actions, but offered no amends.

Iselin and his friends at the New York Yacht Club seethed and the press continued to play the controversy on the front pages. Finally, at the end of February, the New Yorkers met to consider expelling Dunraven, an honorary member, from their club. The proposal was approved, thirty-nine votes to one. A day later the lord's letter of resignation arrived. (Apparently he knew what was coming.) The dispute was over, but bad feelings persisted. Two British challengers who had previously announced they would compete in New York dropped their plans. The Americans suggested they might help finance an opponent, but even this offer went for naught. One year passed and then another. By early 1898 the relationship between the British and American sportsmen seemed frozen in mutual suspicion and resentment, and for the first time the future of the cup races was in doubt.

I n the United States, the Earl of Dunraven became the butt of endless jokes on the street and in the press, where he was called "Lord Quittingham." The cadets at West Point mocked him in their annual stage review, and *The New York Times* delighted in revealing he had been named among a group of prominent but secret adherents to Spiritualism, a faddish religion organized around séances and popular among the leisure class. In Great Britain the majority of editorialists found fault with Dunraven and the entire sailing community, which came to be seen, more and more, as a bunch of rich, spoiled, sore losers.

In early 1898, as the sorry state of Anglo-American yachting waited for the right man to fix things, Sir Thomas Lipton said nothing about boats and sailing but instead announced that his company would soon issue stock and become a public corporation. Lipton had been working in secret on the sale for more than a year with three key advisors. The first was Panmure Gordon, a former cavalry officer and a rather dashing London figure who was an established international financier. The second was the banker George Faudel-Phillips, who was a former lord mayor of London and linked by marriage to one of the nation's biggest press barons. The third was the same Marquess of Breadalbane (Gavin Campbell), who had brought Lipton into London society at the moment he won his royal warrant.

Investors had long admired Lipton's ever-expanding business and coveted his profits. Rumors of a stock sale had circulated for years. The news that he would actually take his firm public sent tremors of excitement through the country. One mail delivery—the largest ever made to date to a single address—brought Lipton eighteen thousand applications for reserved shares. Thousands of additional letters arrived, not with applications but with cash and signed checks. More than a hundred clerks were needed to handle the crush of correspondence. In every case Lipton turned down these requests for favored status, which only heightened public interest. Although some investors challenged widely held assumptions about the company's worth—even suggesting that the size of the firm had been deliberately exaggerated—Britons of almost every class and station eagerly awaited the issue.

On March 10, the day the stock became available at a London branch of the Bank of Scotland, people began crowding at the bank's door before it opened for business. As the cool but cloudless morning got brighter, more and more people hopped off horse trolleys or walked from the nearest railway stations to join the throng. By nine o'clock the street was filled with hundreds of men, and a few women, all clamoring to get inside to buy Lipton stock in person. London police came to clear a path for traffic and establish some order. By the close of business at four p.m., shares worth more than £20 million (equal to more than $3 billion in 2010) had been purchased.

The most successful offering in London history, the stock sale actually disrupted the overall equities market as it was flooded with 200,000 applications for Lipton shares. Banks were so burdened by withdrawals that the sale of bonds for the Chinese Imperial Railway had to be postponed. The event made Lipton much richer than he had been the day before. (His personal stake was worth the 2010 equivalent of $1.2 billion.) And thanks to the structure of the offering, he retained enough shares to maintain control of the firm. He even netted a bonus of $40 million (2010) from a special fee that Panmure Gordon had attached to one class of shares.

The hype and publicity around the sale drove critics to complain that Lipton didn't have quite as many stores as he said and that his tea estates were not nearly as vast as the company's advertisements suggested. Both of these charges were factually true. He was a habitual exaggerator, and the legal prospectus for the stock offering showed fewer stores and plantations than Lipton had previously claimed in the press. But in the aftermath of the sale, investors didn't seem to care about the disparities. Prices for the various types of Lipton Ltd. shares increased steadily after they were first issued, providing quick profits for those who were willing to sell. Lipton kept the rally going in the summer, when he won a big contract to feed 100,000 soldiers for the largest exercise of the British military since 1875. In September he would keep the stock balloon rising by announcing the purchase of a coffee plantation in Mexico.

At this time Lipton was richer than he had ever dreamed of becoming and was so well connected that he could make himself into an even bigger public person. He took a step in this direction by announcing his desire to fund a permanent charity that would replicate the Jubilee dinner for the poor every day all across Great Britain. To prove his sincerity, he enlisted the Princess of Wales in the project and gave her a check for £100,000—the equivalent of $15 million in 2010—to found a charity that would feed the poor every day of the year.

The fifty-four-year-old princess whirled around the room when Lipton told her of his plan. It called for funding charity dining rooms across the United Kingdom where subsidies would allow anyone to purchase a good meal for about a penny. A similar scheme had been tried in Gothenburg, Sweden, with some success, but Lipton's project quickly ran into an ongoing political conflict over poverty and its remedies. Critics, who said that charity bred dependence, opposed Lipton on moral grounds.

"Indiscriminate relief," was the term one writer used in a letter to the *Times* of London. "Desertion of wife and children, drink or any vice that has brought you low will be overlooked," added C. S. Loch of the Charity Organization Society. "Thousands of idle loafers [will be found] among the shelter folk."

The Lipton dining hall proposal also met with opposition from owners of regular cafés and restaurants—organized as the Eating House Keepers Association—who saw unfair competition in Lipton's project. They warned that Lipton's business might even profit from the enterprise because his own low-wage workers could avail themselves of cheap meals. Altogether, the opposition was strong enough to force Lipton to scale back his plan, but he didn't abandon it. He also agreed to put his start-up money into a new trust, bearing Alexandra's name. Restaurateurs who happily attacked Lipton wouldn't think of criticizing an antipoverty program offered under her name.

The fight against poverty had become a fashionable concern in late Victorian London as reports on hunger and new books by Charles

Booth and Henry George refuted the idea that the poor were lazy, wanton, and otherwise responsible for their plight. In aristocratic circles many women were beginning to think that something was wrong when a country awash with the riches of empire failed to feed its children. The Princess of Wales could not criticize the government directly, but she could lend her name to Lipton's proposal and help him obtain a royal charter. It was granted in August 1898, and in less than eighteen months the Alexandra Trust Dining Rooms would open in a large building on City Road, near Lipton's offices, where several tramlines used by area factory workers converged.

In keeping with Lipton's design, the four-story building was laid out with large dining rooms on the first three floors—each dining room seating five hundred—and a kitchen on the top floor. The kitchen was equipped with massive steam chests that could cook a ton of potatoes in half an hour. The roasting ovens were big enough to hold more than fifteen hundred pounds of ham per cooking, and the freestanding kettles held five hundred gallons of soup. Each day, cooks would prepare a menu that included roasted and boiled meats, stews, pickled fish, eggs, meat pies, sausages, vegetables, and cakes, and tea, coffee, and cocoa. The price for meals ranged from a half-penny for a porridge breakfast to four and a half pence for a dinner complete with dessert.

For decades to come, the trust would serve thousands of poor Britons at cost every day, and deliver free food to children at schools. The dining rooms were so successful that they became popular stops for wealthy tourists—especially Americans—who marveled at the volume of food efficiently bought, prepared, and served. Patrons got their meals at cafeteria-style counters, and sat comfortably at crowded tables while young women in black dresses, white aprons, and white caps kept order and whisked away dirty plates and cups. Altogether it was a ballet of kindness and consumption that alleviated both the hunger of poor Londoners and the guilt of the rich.

Having delighted the Princess of Wales with a very generous and public gift, Lipton then turned to help her husband, the prince. Owner of the world's most recognized yacht—*Britannia*—and commodore of the Royal Yacht Squadron, Edward, Prince of Wales, was, to a degree, personally responsible for the future of America's Cup challenges. As the third anniversary of Dunraven's ignoble retreat approached, none of the usual millionaire yachtsmen came forward to make a challenge on behalf of Great Britain. Lipton, meanwhile, allowed his name to be floated as a potential sponsor.

Although he had never owned a yacht or taken the helm of any vessel bigger than a twelve-foot catboat, Sir Thomas's lifelong love of the sea and ships was genuine, and he had the means to make a credible challenge. In June of 1898, with the news of his knighthood, charity, and stock sale widely appreciated in America, Lipton left for New York aboard the steamer *Campania*. As always, he eagerly anticipated the dynamism and energy of the country he considered an exhilarating second home. But he had never before visited America when she was at war, and he could not imagine the frenzy of patriotism and pride he would encounter in New York and across the country.

Four months earlier, the USS *Maine*, sent to protect American interests while Spanish rulers battled an independence movement in Cuba, had exploded and sunk in Havana Harbor. Two hundred sixty-six sailors were killed. Although the *Maine* may have been sunk by the spontaneous combustion of coal dust and ammunition, an official board of inquiry suggested a mine had set off the disaster. Given

America's support for the Cuban insurgency, the *Maine*'s destruction prompted calls for war against Spain. On April 20, President McKinley signed a declaration of war, and American forces then speeded up the preparations for battle.

Until this moment, America had not tangled with a European power since 1812, and the country had never engaged in a naval battle with modern steel-hulled steamships.

But as an emerging giant in world trade, the United States had been assembling a navy sufficient to protect its interests worldwide. This effort had been accelerated in the past decade with the launch of the nation's first modern battleships, among them the *Indiana*, the *Massachusetts*, and the *Oregon*. Just as America's yachting victories announced the nation's gains in design and technology, the rise of the U.S. Navy signaled to the world the emergence of a great new military power. With the destruction of the *Maine* in Havana Harbor, Spain, its own fleet aging and ill equipped, offered the Americans a chance to show their strength.

The first battle of the war came on May 1, as Commodore George Dewey's Asiatic Squadron entered Manila Bay and he famously told the captain of the cruiser *Olympia*, "You may fire when you are ready, Gridley." Six hours later the Americans had sunk or captured the eight Spanish ships that had occupied the bay. Gridley, who got out of his sickbed to help direct the battle, died weeks later from hemorrhagic fever. But in this decisive victory, not a single American was killed by enemy fire. A similar result was achieved weeks later in the Caribbean when an American flotilla led by the battleship *Texas* (the *Maine*'s sister ship) and the cruiser *Brooklyn* destroyed a Spanish squadron while losing just two sailors.

The U.S. Navy's power stunned Continental Europe, where Spain enjoyed broad support. Although the United Kingdom was officially neutral, she had quietly provided material aid to America. Even Lord

Dunraven spoke in favor of America's action against Spain, citing the Monroe Doctrine as justification. The relationship between Britain and the United States was based on a shared language, history, and moral outlook. With one rising and the other fearing decline, the countries did compete and measure themselves against each other; yet in most crises they came together. In late June, Lipton was a guest of honor for a banquet at London's Hotel Cecil, where the great hall was decorated with Union Jacks and the American flag and brotherhood was loudly and repeatedly proclaimed. Hours of toasts and cheers ensued, and an American officer got the tone just right when he declared, "We shall be joint ministers in the cause of civilization and progress."

Days later Lipton departed Liverpool for New York aboard the *Campania*, which was still the most luxurious ship afloat. During the crossing he joined in another celebration of Anglo-American solidarity that ended with everyone locking arms to sing "God Save the Queen" and "America" (also called "My Country 'Tis of Thee"). Lipton, in a burst of goodwill, then declared that he was certain an army of ten thousand British volunteers would respond if the United States called for aid. He also donated more than $10,000 to a fund for the care of Americans wounded in the fighting.

When he arrived in New York, Lipton was greeted as a genuine celebrity. Hailed in the press as "Jubilee Lipton" and "Sir Tea," he restated his love for America and made slyly cutting remarks about Spain. All girls are beautiful, he quipped, "except for Spanish girls."

Lipton was everything the Yanks hoped for in a wealthy British gentleman. He was tall and distinguished-looking—white hair, fine suits, strong build—and charming in a self-effacing way. Like so many Americans, he bore Irish and Scottish blood and he had dared to dream of rising above his birth. Best of all, he had achieved his dream and gave credit to what he had learned in America as a boy. Time and again he recalled that influence and made a favorable comparison between places like Chicago and New York and his native Glasgow.

Experience at home had prepared Lipton to play the role of self-made millionaire for the American press and public. His well-honed tale of childhood poverty was told without depressing references to the death and disease rampant in the Gorbals or violence beyond his scrap with Wullie, the butcher's boy. Instead, he spoke of his saintly mother, his Scottish thrift, and the wonders of doing business in an age of opportunity. However, his poor-boy-made-good routine didn't help him deal with a second role thrust upon him as he arrived—sex symbol. No other term serves as well to describe the Lipton who was announced to the country by the *New York World* when the *Campania* arrived. Under the main headline, "Bachelor Millionaire Lipton, Great New York Matrimonial Chances for an American Bride," the paper presented pictures and stories about four beautiful young women eager to meet him. Their street addresses were included in the article, which also explained how one had an "irresistible" mouth and another had been smitten after seeing Lipton's picture. "We four New York beauties love you for your success. We love you for your title," reported a caption under their photos.

A casual observer of Victorian America might be surprised by the way the *World* peddled "New York beauties," but this leering kind of publicity was common in the 1890s. Newspapers of the time were filled with suggestive personal ads placed by both men and women. Many papers published extensive and frequent reports on scandalous parties held in men's clubs and indecent entertainments in private dining rooms, and the *Herald* regularly printed highly suggestive photo spreads featuring underage girls. Compared with these displays, an illustrated article about the women who awaited Sir Thomas was really quite tame.

In this dawning of the age of mass media and photography, the wealthy and accomplished Lipton was a natural subject for writers and photographers. Tall, with a bushy white mustache and a perpetual twinkle in his eye, he possessed striking features, dressed impeccably, and moved with the square-shouldered bearing of a military man or athlete. Always smiling in public, he was exactly the man people imagined when they thought of a rich, kindly, playful British millionaire. Photographers loved to take his picture, and his image was so widely published that he was one of the most recognized men in the world. His friend, the whiskey millionaire Tom Dewar, tested Lipton's fame by dropping a postcard bearing a caricature of Lipton's face and the letters "U.S.A." into a mailbox. The card was delivered to Tea Tom at his hotel in New York.

Amusing as it might be, Lipton's popularity meant that he couldn't go anywhere without attracting attention. In train stations, hotels, and on the street, women flocked to him, and reporters begged for interviews. His rote answer for questions about romance began with a blunt message, "I am not looking for a wife," followed by admiring words for American women. These lines, and the addition of a few romantic feints, would carry the confirmed bachelor for the rest of his life. (Among the feints were a fanciful tale about a young Scottish woman who broke his heart in the 1880s and a baseless story about an engagement to the much younger daughter of his great ally George Faudel-Phillips. Since Faudel-Phillips's family owned newspapers, it's easy to imagine how a snippet about this "arrangement" was printed.)

If Lipton had to dissemble a bit to guard his personal life, he needed nothing but the truth to answer the rumors about a race for the America's Cup. He had already inquired with a shipbuilder and settled on the name *Shamrock* for his yacht. But as a showman, he appreciated the value of suspense. Yes, he told the American press, he was considering a challenge. But he had never actually owned a sailing vessel and he was not ready to make a formal bid. This pose had the effect of focusing even more attention on Lipton, as newspaper readers delighted in the prospect of a common man who loved America restoring the friendship that Dunraven had damaged.

Talk of Lipton and the cup continued as he went to Chicago on meatpacking business. While there he made a show of ordering that an extremely large American flag be draped from the roof and across the front of his packinghouse, where it would remain until the United States defeated Spain in Cuba and the Philippines. This gesture only increased his popularity when he returned to New York in early July. There he found a public enraptured by reports about the Rough Riders—a cavalry composed mainly of cowboys and Ivy Leaguers—and their victory at San Juan Hill. Their captivating commander, Theodore Roosevelt, was suddenly considered a viable candidate for governor of New York. Across the city, patriotic feeling ran high and no one passed up an opportunity to celebrate the nation or its allies. When the local chapter of the Sons of the American Revolution learned that Sir Thomas Lipton was about to depart for home, they gave him a farewell banquet awash in red-white-and-blue bunting and toasts.

The next day, the Sons were at the Cunard Line's Hudson River Pier 40, not far from the ratty rooming house where Lipton slept on his very first stay in New York, to bid their friend farewell. The delegation was led by the attorney Clifford W. Hartridge, who would become famous himself for representing the notorious murderer Harry Thaw, who killed the architect Stanford White. (Thanks to Hartridge's insanity defense, Thaw would never serve a day in prison.) At Pier 40, Hartridge gave Lipton a five-by-seven-foot silk American flag complete with a wooden pole topped by a gilt eagle. Rising to the ceremonial moment, Lipton announced in a voice loud enough for the reporters to hear, "I shall entwine this flag with the English Jack in my home." Good to his word, Lipton did add the Stars and Stripes to the decorations at Osidge Park, which was becoming so famous for its eccentric and varied decor that critics had taken to calling it "Sausage Park."

Lipton sailed home aboard the *Lucania*, sharing first class with William K. Vanderbilt. As co-owner of the 1895 America's Cup winner, *Defender*, Vanderbilt had been square in the middle of the Dunraven controversy. Lipton found friendship with him, and with the extended Vanderbilt clan, who would eventually welcome him to their mansions in Newport and Long Island. The Vanderbilt wealth, which came from railroads, shipping, and other businesses, far exceeded Lipton's resources. But both men had enough to invest whatever was required to produce the fastest yacht in the world.

Within days of arriving back in Great Britain, Lipton mapped out his challenge for the cup with all the care a playwright would apply to a new script. In a nod to the great Irish community in the States, he announced that the challenge would be sponsored by the Royal Ulster Yacht Club, which was based in the coastal town of Bangor, just outside Belfast. He also said he hoped the firm of Harland and Wolff would build the boat in Belfast, and that it would be manned by an all-Irish crew. Although the shipyard was renowned for its oceangoing steamships, it lacked the special expertise for yacht building and declined the job. Lipton then turned to Scottish designer William Fife, who agreed to design the challenger and would supervise its construction at the Thornycroft yard at Millwall on the Thames.

Fife was the son and grandson of yacht builders who had been more popular in the early part of the decade, when his designs were built in Europe and America. (His boats were popular at the New York Yacht Club.) In recent years he had been challenged for the top spot by fellow

Scotsman George Lennox Watson, who had designed both *Britannia* for the Prince of Wales and the *Valkyries II* and *III*. Lord Dunraven's defeat had dimmed Watson's star, and Lipton, who often said, "Never do business with an unsuccessful man," turned to Fife. The designer visited Osidge and with Lipton agreed the *Shamrock* would be a ninety-foot cutter similar to Lord Dunraven's *Valkyries*, though built along more graceful lines and out of a stronger but lighter combination of steel, aluminum, and bronze. They set a budget of £100,000 ($15 million in 2010), but both men understood the figure was just a guide.

To make certain that his team understood the conditions for the boat's design and the conduct of the races, Lipton added Fife to the entourage that traveled to New York to issue the formal challenge. At every point on the trip, including their midnight arrival by ship in Quebec, the Lipton emissaries were met by reporters, who filled the next day's papers with whatever they could glean. When the news was thin, they padded out their reports with descriptions of the magnificent Lipton and snippets of his biography. On the day that Lipton, Fife, and company departed by ship for New York, *The New York Times* ran a long article that allowed Lipton's men to claim that certain unnamed disgruntled British yachtsmen opposed his bid but that he was ignoring them. (In fact, the grocer/sportsman *was* the object of much sneering and joking in elite British sailing circles.) On the very next page of the newspaper, the editors reprinted a *London Chronicle* feature about how Lipton had taught the nation "a lesson in charity" with the food program of the Alexandra Trust. It explained the project in a way that made Lipton seem both a saint and a genius. The saintly part involved his huge donation and the pledge to double it if required. The genius part lay in the idea of charging a small fee for each meal so that the program would be self-perpetuating and less likely to promote dependence.

The publicity that showed Lipton to be a brilliant, generous, megarich sportsman who was so appealing that he drove women to distraction wasn't exactly free. Lipton had made big charitable donations, and the cup challenge was bound to be expensive. But no amount of money could have purchased the prime newspaper space devoted to him or the impact these stories had on the public. It's one thing to buy advertising to create an image, and quite another to have the press volunteer to make you into a hero and a heartthrob. When the Lipton delegation finally made it to the New York Yacht Club, they were greeted with such good-will that it took just ninety minutes for the conditions of the races to be set. Sir Thomas won an important concession when the New Yorkers agreed that *Shamrock* could be towed across the Atlantic. This meant she could be constructed out of lighter materials and without extensive crew quarters. The sides preserved the traditional best-of-five format and se-lected the usual thirty-mile course off Sandy Hook, New Jersey. They also sought to avoid any conflict over ballast, waterlines, and the size of crews. Captains would be allowed no more than three men for every five feet of their boat's length. All would have to be on board when waterline measurements were taken, and no weight could be added or subtracted once these figures were set down.

As he sketched his plan for *Shamrock*, Fife imagined a boat that would be 128 feet long, and almost 190 (the length of a short New York City block) when the boom and bowsprit were added. A steel mast of more than 130 feet would allow for a big spread of sails but also require innovative stays and rigging for safety. This design, built at an ultimate cost of more than $21 million (in 2010 dollars) pushed the limits of what was then known about the strength and flexibility of various met-als and the aerodynamics of racing sails.

As *Shamrock* was being framed, Lipton put $300,000 ($7.5 million in 2010) into the purchase of a luxurious steam yacht. Built for an Ital-ian count, the *Aegusa* was bigger and faster than the ship that had brought Lipton to America after the Civil War, and longer even than J. P. Morgan's newest *Corsair*. Painted a brilliant white, she was as sleek as a cutter and carried three masts to provide sail power to augment her steam engines. Lipton renamed her *Erin* and sent her to a shipyard for inspection and redecoration. The result was a 300-foot-long floating palace that included a music room equipped with a harp, a salon filled with antiques and Asian art, a formal dining room that occupied one entire deck, and a smaller starboard space that could accommodate seventy for lunch. Staterooms on the *Erin* were large and heavily decorated with lace and silk and furnished with gilt beds and cleverly designed washstands that with a flip became writing desks. Over time, as her owner constantly collected art and souvenirs, *Erin* would become overstuffed with vases, paintings, canaries, cabinets, and knickknacks. Thus converted into a traveling version of his comfy house, Osidge, she would serve as Lipton's personal transatlantic transport, a home during races, and a place to entertain crowds of a hundred or more.

In the spring of 1899, Lipton announced that he had hired a trio of officers to manage a crew of thirty sailors drafted from the Clydeside and several other English ports. Robert Wringe and Ben Parker would assist Captain Archibald Hogarth, a young yachtsman best known in America for commanding the Herreshoff-built *Isolde* on the day its owner, a German baron, was killed in a collision with the Kaiser's yacht *Meteor I*.

The *Isolde* tragedy did not diminish Hogarth's reputation. Physical risk was inherent to the sport, and yachtsmen understood that the dangers at sea increased along with advances in design and performance. In other words, great boats could become lethal beasts even with the best hands on the wheel. The beasts' power came from the enormous amounts of sail raised above their delicate hulls. The pressure the sails exerted was supposedly balanced by a bulb-shaped keel that might weigh eighty tons or more. But this balance was difficult to maintain. A helmsman must literally *feel* the tension in the sails of a yacht, gauge the stress placed on the rigging, and command the crew to make adjustments that produce maximum speed without a mechanical breakdown (such as a snapped mast). Hogarth remained one of a small number of men in the world able to sense a boat's performance and direct adjustments, while also keeping track of the wind, the water, the course, and his opponents.

With his officers and crew named, Lipton had everything in place except the boat. As anyone who ever built a cup challenger would expect, the Thornycroft yard had fallen behind schedule. At the end of March, Lipton confessed that the *Shamrock* wouldn't be ready until June. Tradition, as well as showmanship, required he stay mum about the details of the yacht's design, and the builder required everyone who came on the property to keep secret what they saw. Guards were posted twenty-four hours a day, and anyone who approached, whether on land or sea, was stopped and questioned.

The drama at the shipyard peaked on April Fools' Day, when two men were caught sneaking onto the Thornycroft property. Lipton's security guards found what seemed to be a drawing of a boat in one man's pocket and the police were called to make arrests. After much confusion, the men told the authorities that they were actually actors from the Alhambra Theater, a music hall on Leicester Square. They called themselves "spoof spies" and convinced people that even if they had caught sight of the secret vessel, they wouldn't have been able to grasp the significance of what they saw. As for the drawings? They were sketches of a lifeboat to be painted on theater scenery.

The story of the spies kept public attention on the Lipton challenge and he made sure the press was informed. Lipton did the same when three women in America sent a gold and green shamrock flag they had sewn for his yacht. The British public adored these stories because they adored Lipton and the idea of a commoner challenging for the cup and setting out to ease the discord Dunraven had caused. The press followed him to the Prince of Wales Horse Show, where he spent heavily on racers offered by Edward's stable, and to the Royal Opera House at Covent Garden, where he now kept a box. And if chance or the normal course of life didn't present a photo opportunity or press event, Lipton created one. The best of these was an invitation he proffered to the young Guglielmo Marconi to attempt the first transatlantic wireless transmissions during the cup races. (A year earlier, Marconi had visited Osidge and demonstrated his radio by sending messages from one side of the property to the other.)

Marconi was a young Irish-Italian whose mother came from the Jameson whiskey clan. Fluent in English, Marconi had been inspired by reports on early radios that he'd read in British journals. Before he was even twenty years old he began experiments at the family villa in Pontecchio, south of Bologna. By trial and error he refined various components—oscillator, receiver, antenna—and assembled them into a working device. (His key breakthrough was the use of tall, vertical antenna wires.) He then took his invention to Great Britain, which was still the world's capital of finance and industry.

Long interested in communications technology, the British Postal Service helped Marconi with a series of demonstrations in which he sent wireless signals over ever greater distances and in all kinds of weather. The chief engineer of the postal service, William Preece, made his success known in two public addresses. In March of 1899, just days before the April Fools' caper at the Thornycroft shipyard, Marconi became world-famous by sending a message across the English Channel. Skeptics doubted whether the technology would ever be used for ordinary communications. Marconi excited the public by predicting easy wireless communication between the United States and Europe. He also seized upon Lipton's invitation, winning headlines on both sides of the Atlantic as he agreed to transmit race results from New York to Europe.

News of the dashing young Marconi's impending visit—and his plans for reporting on the races—excited New Yorkers, who were starved for information about their own side's preparations for the big event. Indeed, as weeks and then months had passed, Americans learned far more about Lipton and *Shamrock* than they knew about the defending boat, which Herreshoff was constructing in Bristol for Iselin and others in his syndicate.

The silence was typical for Herreshoff, who appeared to leave all the prerace gamesmanship to Lipton. But then, at the end of May, he and Iselin began to play the publicity game, too. First they announced that a crew would be gathered from among fishermen in Deer Isle, Maine, a granite outcropping in Penobscot Bay. In 1895 the Deer Isle Boys, as they were called, had comprised the first all-American crew ever to defend the cup. (Previously sailors had been recruited from many countries.) Their performance was so impressive they were asked to return under a different captain, Charles Barr. The crew jobs paid so well—as much as $60 per month, plus $5 per race—that hundreds of boys applied for fewer than fifty spots.

In thirty-five-year-old Charlie Barr, Iselin had made a perfect choice of both a captain and a symbol. Barr was a full-blooded Scot from a town on the Firth of Clyde not twenty miles from Glasgow. He spoke with a thick burr and, like Thomas Lipton, had worked in a grocery as a young man. Introduced to sailing by his brother, Barr had been a member of the crew for the British cup challenge in 1887. He later commanded several of the world's greatest yachts, including the Clyde-built

Minerva, but then switched sides to help the Americans by commanding boats that tested the yacht that defended the cup against Dunraven.

In many ways Barr represented the dreams of all immigrants who succeed against the odds. Small and slightly built—five-foot-three and about 130 pounds—he could barely see above the wheel of a big yacht. (On land friends called him Wee Charlie.) And he had begun life as the son of a fisherman, which hardly assured him a connection to the elite world of yachting. Nevertheless, through intense study and countless hours at sea, he had developed an unmatched knowledge of the sailing art and an intensely commanding presence at the helm. Peering at the sea through eyes so dark they sometimes seemed blacker than ink, Barr would set a course to intimidate his opponents and order his men to add sail and speed to the point where they became terrified of a breakdown. Sometimes the Scot's risk-taking led to fouls and broken masts, but he always got the most out of a boat, and Nathanael Herreshoff considered him a genius on the water.

For months, Barr, Herreshoff, and the rest of the American group presented stony silence to the world, affirming the popular notion that they were grim souls focused solely on victory. But when they joined the publicity battle, Barr won the American public's love by announcing he would soon become a U.S. citizen. Then Herreshoff invited anyone who might care to attend to come to Bristol to view a big public launching that would show the world his beautiful, powerful, intimidating creation called *Columbia*.

The scene at the Bristol yard on the evening of June 10 was just short of mayhem. About five thousand people, many of whom arrived on a special train from Providence, crowded the shore where *Columbia* would slide from the shed where she was built, down a ramp and into the water. Hundreds more stood on the decks of boats and small ships that bobbed in the harbor. Among them was the previous cup champion

Defender. Clouds that had filled the sky began to break in the late afternoon, and as dusk arrived workmen switched on powerful calcium floodlights that had been brought to illuminate the event.

The doors to the construction shed were opened just before eight p.m., and shouts and applause echoed around the harbor. After some brief speeches, which few people could hear, Iselin's wife, Hope, broke a bottle of champagne on *Columbia*'s bow and she began to slide. Thanks to the lights, people onshore could look through the windows of the shed and see the radically sharp and sleek hull moving toward the water. The boat emerged, bow first, from the open doorway and slipped gracefully into the chop amid cheers, boat whistles, and the bright flashes of light from photographers using flaming magnesium to brighten the scene. In the commotion, hardly anyone in the crowd knew that one of these flashes was actually made by an explosion of magnesium that blew off the legs of a boy named Napoleon San Souci, who died soon after the accident.

Despite the tragedy, the big show and subsequent reports on the condition of *Columbia* put Lipton on notice. Slightly longer and capable of carrying even more sail—thanks to an innovative telescoping mast—the American boat was more extreme than *Shamrock*. In her first trial, which crowds witnessed from the shore in Newport, she proved better than *Defender*, which had previously been the fastest yacht in the world. As she cut swiftly between the warships anchored in the harbor, sailors aboard the battleship *Texas*, recently returned from Cuba, cheered loudly from the deck. Experts guessed that *Columbia* could complete the thirty-mile Sandy Hook course fifteen minutes faster than her predecessor.

In England, the reports from Newport added to the pressure felt by Fife, the boat builders, and Sir Thomas, who had now spent forty percent more on *Shamrock* than originally budgeted and would spend millions more racing her. Two weeks after the launch of *Columbia*, the Prince of Wales traveled to the Thornycroft shipyard and spent two hours inspecting the *Shamrock* and encouraging the hundreds of men who were rushing to finish her construction. The workers cheered Lipton's royal friend as he departed, and once again the newspapers devoted barrels of ink to the *Shamrock* and Lipton.

The publicity attached to the cup challenge was far more valuable than any he could purchase outright. Yet the investment was a matter of pride as well as promotion, because in the end Lipton truly wanted to win the cup. Indeed, if *Shamrock* was to be more than a vehicle for publicity, she would have to be a match for the Wizard of Bristol's design, and her crew and captain would have to outperform the Americans in unfamiliar waters.

As *Shamrock* neared completion, Lipton displayed his usual self-confidence. At first he announced that the yacht would be launched during a party for invited guests only, with reporters, cinematographers, and "Kodakers" excluded. This choice earned Lipton rare criticism from the newspapers. One noted that the list of attendees included titled men like "Lord Salisbury [a former prime minister] who are ignoramuses on the subject of yachting." Sir Tea promptly changed his mind and arranged for a formal luncheon at the Savoy Hotel, followed by a procession of coaches to Millwall, where a giant tent had been erected next to the shed where *Shamrock* was hidden. Hundreds of boats, barges, and small ships gathered in the river while crowds massed on the bank.

Once the bottle was broken on her prow, and the yacht was released, boat whistles, cheers, and bells created such a din that no one could hear the warning that *Shamrock* was going too fast. Emerging from the shed all decorated with British and American flags, the green-hulled boat with a gold-colored keel splashed violently into the Thames. Crewmen and shipwrights who had lined up on her deck scrambled for handholds as she promptly collided with a barge. The light hull of the *Shamrock* suffered minor damage, which would be repaired before she went to the southeast coast for test races.

Once she was equipped with sails and seen speeding in The Solent, rumors that *Shamrock* was a frail vessel were quickly dispelled. After a shakedown cruise, a member of the crew boasted that she might be the fastest boat in the world and would definitely win the cup. Lipton would say only that he was "satisfied with the spin." He continued to bar reporters from the boat and kept photographers so far away that they couldn't get a decent shot of her hull.

The mystery bred all sorts of rumors. *Shamrock* had a secret centerboard . . . Her keel was made of a special secret metal . . . Lipton had promised lifetime pensions to his crew if they won . . .

None of the tales were true, but no effort was made to dispel them, and by midsummer they had reached America and added to the sense that a great challenge was coming. *Shamrock* would sail to Scotland before being towed to New York by the steam yacht *Erin*. The only passenger aboard the *Erin* was the Chevalier de Martino, the queen's maritime painter, who would create *Shamrock's* formal portrait on the Atlantic crossing.

NINE

Never Fear!

og and drizzle worthy of the Firth of Clyde greeted the gleaming white *Erin* and the green-hulled *Shamrock* as they reached the Narrows on the morning of August 18, 1899. They passed between Staten Island and Brooklyn, and entered upper New York Bay at nine-thirty. Emerging from the mist, the *Shamrock* was immediately recognized by crews on nearby vessels who sounded their whistles. The tug *Robert E. Haddon* won the race to be the yacht's tow boat; after a line was tossed and secured she brought *Shamrock* to an anchorage where the crew had a clear view of the Statue of Liberty. Sculpted by Frédéric-Auguste Bartholdi and engineered by Alexandre-Gustave Eiffel, the 150-foot-tall goddess gazed down from a 154-foot-high pedestal that was at the time the biggest concrete structure in the Western Hemisphere.

Lipton's boat had made the Atlantic crossing in record time for a cup challenger. (The man himself would follow soon, aboard the liner *Campania*.) *Shamrock*'s arrival, which was days earlier than expected, surprised the city. As news spread, reporters hired boats to take them near but they were denied requests to board her and told to approach the crew of *Erin* with their questions.

Aboard *Erin*, the crew would say nothing about the design or construction of the cup challenger. However, they were happy to explain that the two Sinhalese servants who had sailed with their artist passenger were nicknamed "Erin" and "Shamrock." They also noted that both vessels had crossed the ocean carrying pots filled with live patches of four-leaf clovers. At the Custom House, where the collector gamely paid the port fees for *Erin* and *Shamrock* out of his own pocket, no amount of playful badgering could persuade Captain Archie Hogarth to talk about his racer. "A man doesn't show his hand," he said, "until the money is on the table."

Temporarily moored off Staten Island, the two Lipton vessels would attract a parade of ships and boats, each loaded with people who had paid to get a closer look. Steamers, sidewheelers, sailboats, fishing boats, tugs, and scows all circled, sometimes getting dangerously close. Shouts and whistles echoed from their decks and the bands on some of the larger ships played "God Save the Queen," "Britannia, the Pride of the Ocean," and Irish songs such as "Rory O'Moore" and "The Wearing of the Green." All this activity was a boon to anyone who owned a boat and was willing to carry paying passengers out to the mooring, and it turned the harbor into a churning riot of color, sound, and coal smoke.

Heavy tourist traffic would continue for days as the *Shamrock*'s crew removed braces that had been added to strengthen her for the ocean crossing and installed her racing mast and rigging. Everything the crew did—right down to washing their underpants and drying them on the boom—was fodder for the press. And every morning brought more speculation, including word from the captain of the *Robert E. Haddon*, who said he would wager hundreds of dollars on a *Shamrock* victory. All of New York seemed besotted with the green boat and the impending race. In Manhattan, a woman living on 159th Street composed a song— "The *Shamrock* and the *Columbia*"—which she dedicated to Lipton. In Brooklyn, Lipton's crew was mobbed by well-wishers when they visited Coney Island, where they could see belly dancers at an attraction called The Streets of Cairo and mechanical horses at the new Steeplechase Park.

The Coney Island crowds flocked to the visiting sailors because they were celebrity athletes in a time when such creatures were rare. No sporting event in the world was more prestigious than the America's Cup, and every challenge prompted excitement. And none had inspired the level of interest Lipton and *Shamrock* generated in the summer of 1899. Long before the races were to begin, bettors jammed the Maritime Exchange, where the *Columbia* was posted as the favorite. Tickets for the excursion boats that would sail to the course sold briskly at prices ranging from twenty-five cents for a spot on a crowded ferry to ten dollars for a stateroom on an oceangoing steamer and a catered lunch. Readers devoured every detail the papers could offer. True aficionados hired boats to sneak along the Brooklyn shore early in the morning in the hope of getting close to the *Shamrock* as the crew dressed her in sailcloth and tested her abilities. Few of these stalkers got close enough to see anything important before being shooed away.

What caused all the buzz? In part New Yorkers were responding to Lipton's persona and story. Also, it didn't hurt that Lipton stressed his Irish heritage and that a huge number of New Yorkers traced their lineage to the old sod. Even the names of his boats—*Erin* and *Shamrock*—echoed pleasantly when compared with the stuffy monikers—*Valkyrie, Galatea, Cambria*, and others—borne by previous British challengers. Finally, many people just liked the *idea* of Lipton and his brightly colored

Shamrock better than the arrogant Nathanael Herreshoff and his creation, *Columbia*. They were tired of this peculiar, self-impressed, and
dictatorial man, and somewhat bored with his success.

Public interest in the cup, and in marine technology, were also
driven by postwar national pride and by a growing sense that the United
States was becoming a global power. With the defeat of Spain—the
terms of the peace treaty had taken effect in April—America had gained
authority over the Philippines, Guam, Puerto Rico, and Cuba. This instant empire discomfited some, including Andrew Carnegie and Mark
Twain, who helped found the American Anti-Imperialist League to
oppose their country's colonial impulse. But these critics were a tiny
minority in a nation that now looked to the oceans with confidence,
imagining a mighty fleet flying the Stars and Stripes. Great ships still
represented the ultimate in technology, and with its stunning victories
the U.S. Navy had declared America's new rank. Some even dared to
believe that the United States could challenge mother Britain for su-
premacy on the seas.

By the summer of 1899 the press had made the hero of the war with
Spain, Admiral George Dewey, into a godlike figure. Harper and Brothers
issued an instant biography by the war correspondent John Barrett, and
Washington began to layer Dewey with honors. (He would be the only
man ever given the special rank of Admiral of the Navy.) Lipton, ever
eager to connect himself with important people and events, sent several
hundred packages of tea—four pounds for each sailor and officer—to
the admiral's flagship. Cities around the country competed to host his
welcome home with a victory celebration.

Dewey accepted an invitation from New York City, and in Manhattan various committees set to work planning two days of celebration
that would include parades on the water and on land. The admiral's
cruiser *Olympia* reached the Mediterranean in midsummer and would

depart for New York in September. During this time the press was filled with reports on the plans for the two-day victory celebration, which would begin with the biggest parade of ships in American history.

Combined, Dewey's impending arrival and the prospect of the cup challenge created a public sensation. The name Dewey became popular for newborn boys, and donations poured into a fund established to give the admiral a new home. In New York, Bloomingdale's and Macy's did a huge business in flags, bunting, and framed Dewey portraits for the home. (The largest measured three by four feet and fetched seventy-five cents.) While the general public overdosed on flags, bunting, and pictures, New York's rich and powerful traded favors and called in markers to win a spot at one of the many events where they might meet the hero in person.

On the night of September 1, Thomas J. Lipton sailed right into this great and happy furor aboard the massive and glamorous ocean liner *Campania*. With pennants flapping, cabin lights glowing, and smoke belching from its two red, raked-back smokestacks, the ship's appearance in the harbor sent a wave of excitement across the city. Several welcoming vessels, including the revenue cutter *Calumet* and the SS *State of New York* raced to meet her because Sir Tea was on the passenger list. As they neared, Lipton, dressed in a dark blue yachting jacket, white pants, and cap, walked onto the promenade deck and began waving. Tall, ruddy-faced, and perfectly costumed, no one struck the pose of "yachtsman" with more precision and flair. The greeters responded with whistles and cheers as their smaller vessels drew alongside the big steamer and a gangway was lowered to allow them to board.

Dozens of state officials, local yachtsmen, city leaders, and reporters risked a plunge in the harbor as they scampered up a boarding ramp and onto the *Campania*. They were quickly ushered into the richly paneled and upholstered first-class salon. Lipton received them with a beaming smile and hearty voice. He laughed about the huge amount of money he had spent on his racer and gamely declared, "I am here to win if possible."

Lipton deferred technical questions to his companion, the designer William Fife. Round, bald, and heavily mustached, Fife was coming down with an unspecified ailment and would not be able to help in the cup challenge. (Instead, he would be confined to his hotel.) He mentioned none of this to the reporters, but chose instead to brush them off with the gruff declaration that he had "come to work, not to talk."

Fife's silence couldn't dampen the mood in the salon as Lipton entertained the welcoming party and journalists with stories and quips, including the playful promise that he would hit up J. P. Morgan for a loan if he needed more cash to support his challenge. "He has plenty," he noted.

When the *Campania* finally reached its berth on the west side of Manhattan, a large crowd had gathered on the pier. New York City police officers boarded to escort Lipton down the gangway. As he descended, cheers and shouts arose.

"We like you, Sir Thomas!"

"I'm glad to hear it, by Jove," he replied. "I rather think I will be sorry to take that cup after all."

"We will give you a good run for your money!"

"I don't doubt it. You have always done that. You are a jolly crowd. That is what you are!"

When he stepped onto the pier, Lipton arrived in a country that was bursting with energy and wealth. Steel production had tripled in ten years, and the country had surpassed Great Britain to become the world leader in industrial output. The U.S. population was about to top seventy-eight million—twice that of the United Kingdom—and the country had risen to third behind New Zealand and Great Britain in

per capita wealth. Of course vast inequalities prevailed, as the most
ruthless capitalists built monopolies and syndicates on the backs of
workers. And yet, as Lipton and anyone else could see, wealth was still
distributed more evenly in America than it was in Britain. The country
had a much bigger middle class and far more people could afford proper
food, housing, and niceties like Lipton's tea.

Before he could get lost in the bustle of greeters, Lipton was hustled
to a horse-drawn carriage—automobiles were just beginning to appear
in New York—and driven to the posh Fifth Avenue Hotel. In the days to
come he would observe *Shamrock*'s outfitting and tests of her handling
and speed. He attended receptions, parties, and banquets in Manhattan
and entertained daily aboard *Erin*. Always accompanied by reporters and
photographers, he posed patiently and lingered to answer every last
question with as much wit as possible. A writer who pressed him for
information about his romantic life then reported to her readers:

> "Was I ever in love? Never!" Sir Thomas's blue eyes twin-
> kled with not so much as the shadow of disappointment
> in them.
> "Come now, there must have been one . . ."
> "Bless you, one? A hundred!" cried he. "I can tell you
> I'm daft on them. Blonde, brunette, redhead—there's a
> special charm in every one."

In denying a true love, but claiming to be "daft on" women, Lipton
echoed perfectly the coded and dualistic way that many Victorian men
approached sex and romance. In general, they were supposed to regard
women as emotionally and intellectually indecipherable and, possibly,
not worthy of the effort. At the same time, they were expected to be satyrs
of a sort, perpetually energized by the pursuit of women as objects,

whether blonde, brunette, or redheaded. In Lipton's case, denying love for one woman but expressing lust for them all explained his bachelor status and identified him as red-blooded. With this tidy explanation he was also able to avoid personal specifics, and move on to more comfortable questions about the upcoming races.

Everywhere he went, Lipton hyped the cup challenge and proclaimed his *Shamrock* ready to win. If, for some reason, he wasn't available with a comment, the press could count on David Barrie, Lipton's "personal representative" in America, or Lipton's personal secretary, John Westwood. But they hardly needed to make much effort to get attention because Lipton was one of the most skillful men in the world when it came to publicity. How else to explain the fact that *Shamrock* and *Erin* (with Lipton standing on the bridge) were the first vessels to hail the steamship *Oceanic* when she reached New York Harbor on her maiden voyage? The largest ship in the world, at more than 700 feet, the monster of the White Star Line had been eagerly awaited by New Yorkers, who had been reading about her for months. Lipton's name was the first one mentioned in the *New York Times* report on her arrival. He had nothing to do with the ship's construction or operation, but there he was on the front page, waving his cap from the deck of the *Erin* while the great liner, breathtakingly beautiful and enormous, blasted a basso profundo greeting.

In quiet little Bristol, Rhode Island, where the Wizard and his men put finishing touches on *Columbia*, they regarded Lipton as ignorant, misinformed, and more interested in publicity than sailing. The tea merchant may have boasted that *Shamrock* was ready to win, but no one can be sure how a new boat will fare in real competition, and trial runs always turn up unexpected difficulties.

The Iselin/Herreshoff team had experienced a few problems of its own earlier in the summer. The most dramatic of these incidents involved the failure of the boat's towering mast, which at 175 feet was too tall to pass under the Brooklyn Bridge. On the day it was raised, Nat himself predicted it would fail. The first time wind was allowed to fill *Columbia*'s sails, it snapped right in the middle.

After the mast broke, the Deer Isle Boys turned against skipper Charlie Barr and even threatened to strike, insisting they didn't trust a "foreigner" with the dangerous task of wrangling a super-fast ocean racer. Some members of the New York Yacht Club also raised doubts about the captain, but the mutiny was stopped, the mast was replaced, and, as trials continued, Barr proved to be an almost perfect helmsman. In all sorts of conditions he maintained precise control despite the huge amount of power generated by *Columbia*'s massive sails and the delicate balance required to keep her stable in steady winds and safe in heavy traffic.

The Americans knew that their boat was considerably faster than the previous winner, *Defender*, and the information they had on *Shamrock* suggested that she wasn't up to the challenge. In fact, they were certain that their design was once again "one boat ahead" of the British vessel, which was far better than any of Dunraven's yachts, but not good enough.

The difference between the *Shamrock* and *Columbia* was mainly a matter of weight and shape. The American boat was sleeker, lighter, and better balanced. As word of her performance spread, local bettors in Rhode Island rushed to put their money on *Columbia*. At the New York Yacht Club one member who had received reports from the trial races told the press that *Shamrock* would have to be "a wonder" if she was to win.

As the days passed and *Columbia*'s captain and crew learned to work together, they thrashed their sparring partner, *Defender*, in one race after another. At the same time, tugboat captains in New York reported that *Shamrock* was sailing at a swift thirteen knots. Of course, their estimates were based on their own claims to speeds as high as twelve knots, and every sailor in the city knew that only a handful of the tugs in the harbor could actually go that fast. Besides, Dunraven's last boat, *Valkyrie III*, had supposedly posted intimidating speeds during trials, but turned out to be what sailors called a "ten-knot sloop" when it came time to race.

For the general public, claims and counterclaims about the two racers made for lively conversation and debate in saloons, cafés, clubs, and oyster houses. Some thought *Shamrock* a better "flyer" in strong winds. Others insisted that *Columbia* was more versatile and better able to make speed when the breeze was light. But anyone who sought the truest measure of expert opinion only had to check with the oddsmakers. And, no matter what the tugboat captains said as they returned from observing the *Shamrock* at work, bettors continued to favor her opponent.

Across the ocean, British gamblers read the signals from America and wagered against their own man. But those who worried about higher things—like Anglo-American relations—applauded Lipton's efforts. The editors and writers at the *Pall Mall Gazette* examined the great volume of reports coming from New York and saw that Lipton was winning America's heart. Even a casual review of the press coverage would show that every move Lipton made was given fawning attention, and his name was mentioned far more often than that of anyone else connected with the cup races. "He is a most excellent man of the hour," concluded the *Gazette*.

The feeling was shared by New Yorkers of every station, but the rich fell over themselves to make the man they called "the Irish Knight" feel at home. On one day a cannon salute welcomed him and the *Erin* for a visit at the New York Yacht Club's dock at the foot of East Twenty-sixth Street. On another day J. P. Morgan sailed his *Corsair* to meet Sir Thomas on the Long Island Sound, near New Rochelle. One of the most powerful bankers in the world, Morgan was notoriously blunt, blustery, and generally uneasy in public. He was afflicted with rosacea, which turned his nose into a swollen red knob, and made him avoid photographers at all costs. The combination of his appearance and personality meant that the papers and the public rarely had anything nice to say about Morgan. By contrast, Lipton's handsome figure and jolly demeanor made him the most likable millionaire anyone could imagine. Altogether, Sir Tea and his beautiful boats had scored a great victory even before the first challenge race was held. Only one man of the sea— Admiral Dewey—could have been more popular, and soon Lipton would manage to join their names.

The racecourse for the America's Cup began at a lightship off Sandy Hook, New Jersey. Formed by sand deposited by ocean currents and the Shrewsbury and Navesink rivers, the seven-mile-long "hook" points northward from the Jersey coast like an index finger extended from a fist. Fort Hancock, at the tip of the finger, protected the town, and a lighthouse warned away ships. In 1868 a lightship was posted three miles off the Hook to mark the wreck of the *Scotland*. For the next fifty-six years, through storms, collisions, and repeated overhauls, the lightship kept mariners safe and attracted the world's attention whenever the America's Cup was in play.

Inside the Hook, little coves and bays offered shelter for smaller ships and yachts, as well as flotillas of sea turtles that nested on the warm beaches. Though just ten miles from Manhattan, these places were as quiet and serene as any desert isle. In the days before the 1899 cup races were to begin, Lipton moved the *Erin* and the *Shamrock* to one of these spots, a sun-washed inlet called Horseshoe Cove, so that final preparations could be made without the distraction of the city and the interference of uninvited guests. Here *Shamrock*'s three officers could plot strategy and make easy visits to the course to observe the wind and the currents.

Sandy Hook was also the ideal place to watch for New York–bound ships entering the harbor from the southeast, and an observer at a light-house on the spit kept constant watch for approaching vessels. The biggest and newest steamships were awaited with great interest, as were vessels carrying important passengers (like Lipton aboard the *Campania*), and news of their arrival was quickly telegraphed to the city. Of course, the vagaries of the weather, the sea, men, and machines made this ship-spotting more difficult than you might imagine. Many ships arrived hours or days late and some appeared earlier than expected. A few even slipped past the Hook under cover of night, or fog, and caught the city completely by surprise.

Shrouded in mist and drizzle, and two days early, Admiral Dewey's cruiser *Olympia* approached the Hook before the sun rose on Tuesday, September 26. When observers at the lighthouse first caught sight of her, they thought she was the USS *Chicago*, an older ship that was, like *Olympia*, painted a brilliant wedding-cake white. (The *Chicago* was due in from a cruise in the South Atlantic.) In short order the spotters recognized Dewey's four stars on the ship's flag and realized their mistake. By five-thirty a.m., telegraphs in newspaper offices across Manhattan tapped out the report that Dewey had arrived. Hours would pass while editors located reporters and photographers and roused them to action.

Having arrived so early, Dewey requested that a pilot boat guide *Olympia* around Sandy Hook to Horseshoe Cove, where crews would be able to touch up her paint prior to entering the harbor. The anchor was dropped less than a thousand yards away from *Shamrock* and *Erin.* A cannon salute rang across the water from Fort Hancock—the first ever fired by a battery there—and *Olympia* responded with a few shots of her own. Roused from sleep and alert to the opportunity, Sir Tea immediately gathered every newspaper on his yacht, hopped into a steam launch that was tethered to the *Erin*, and putt-putted over to the great warship. The *Olympia*'s crew lowered a gangway so that Lipton could come aboard with his gifts. The admiral, dressed in his stiff white uniform with its high collar and gold buttons, clambered down to greet him.

"I suppose you have come for the tea," said Dewey, recalling Lipton's gift.

"No, you are welcomed to it if anyone can drink it," answered Lipton, flashing a smile.

Dewey invited Lipton to breakfast, and Sir Thomas followed the admiral to his stateroom, where they spent the better part of an hour. Ten years older than Lipton, Dewey was of medium height and build. He had deep-set, dark eyes, gray hair, and a white mustache that contrasted sharply with his weathered brown skin. Although the newspapers preferred to describe him as vigorous and strong, he was a bit stooped by age, and, like Lipton, he was developing a paunch. Dewey's forehead was creased and deep lines gave his eyes a weary look. He had been ill during his Mediterranean cruise and the effects still showed.

A lucky anchorage had made Lipton the first man to shake the hero admiral's hand upon his return to America. This mere fact was the most important thing about the encounter, which may explain why Lipton says so little about it in his memoir. He reports that "Admiral Dewey was tremendously interested in the forthcoming races and we had a lot to talk about." Just what that was, he leaves to the imagination. However, he does recall that as he departed, some of the crewmen on the deck waved their tea boxes at him, offering their thanks for the gift.

Fortunately for Lipton, Dewey seized upon the task of promoting his new acquaintance and the upcoming races. Without being prompted by a question, he asked the reporters who soon arrived what they thought about the upcoming contest. "Is the *Shamrock* going to beat the *Columbia*?" he asked in all earnestness. "Tell me something about the two boats. The *Columbia* is a fine light weather boat, they say. How is that?"

Suddenly pressed into the admiral's service, the writers offered their opinions. Then the admiral added his. Speaking of Lipton he said, "That man means business, but I hope we have the better boat. I would very much like to see one of the cup races, but that is looking too far ahead."

In their effort to tell their readers everything, pressmen gave much ink to the admiral's sea-weary dog—a bushy-haired Chow named Bob—and to an account of his Chinese servant's happy reply to the news that he would be permitted ashore. (According to *The New York Times*, he said, "Me likey velly, velly much.") Of course it was Lipton who received ongoing publicity as the admiral visited *Erin* for dinner on his first night home, and the huge Lipton yacht was picked to lead the contingent of civilian vessels that would follow the warships in the upcoming naval parade.

The parade, like everything about Dewey's return, was planned to be both enormous and extravagant. Two days of almost nonstop celebration—banquets, concerts, fireworks displays, and oratory—were scheduled, and people who were determined to take part had been flocking to New York from all over the country. Hundreds of thousands of visitors had already descended on the city and filled every hotel room and boardinghouse.

Days before the official events were to begin, New York was already gripped by Dewey fever. False reports of his arrival at this hotel or that café caused near riots in the streets as people rushed to glimpse a man who—lucky for him—wasn't there. Police were overwhelmed by a rash of street crimes and the needs of "timid women" in distress. The entire city seemed to be in a constant state of celebration as saloons never emptied and fireworks filled the night sky. In public squares street performers worked magic tricks and mounted bright displays of "red fire," a kind of pyrotechnic produced with strontium nitrate.

The epicenter of all this excitement was at Madison Square, where sculptors, masons, and carpenters had built a triumphal arch more than eight stories tall and sixty feet wide. Modeled after Rome's Arch of Titus, the Dewey monument was decorated with figures of sailors and flanked by huge winged angels on pedestals. It was topped by a quadriga—a team of four horses, harnessed abreast—pulling a ship as if it were a chariot. Colonnades of white pillars lined the roadway leading to the arch and would funnel marchers and carriages through the opening. Illuminated by hundreds of electric lights, the entire gleaming display—arch, angels, colonnade—glowed both day and night with the luster of white marble. It was not made of concrete or stone, however, but rather out of a material like plaster of Paris that was intended to impress the crowds on the moment when Dewey's great triumph would be hailed. Left unprotected, it would deteriorate and crumble in a few years.

When the first day of formal Dewey celebrations arrived, a crowd estimated at one million people lined both the Manhattan and New Jersey shores to watch fireboats, their hoses spraying water high into the air, usher *Olympia* and seven other warships past the Statue of Liberty and Governors Island—which themselves were crowded with people—and then up the Hudson River. Temporary grandstands at the Battery held thousands who cheered as the admiral's big white cruiser passed. Farther up the Hudson, *Olympia* drew so near to the docks that, as one writer put it, "a biscuit might have been tossed from pierhead to quarterdeck." People on rooftops and in the windows of buildings waved flags and set off firecrackers. Kites launched from Manhattan flew over the river and disappeared over New Jersey.

As the flagship moved slowly upriver, hundreds of vessels of every sort jostled to give paying customers a view. The paddle wheeler *General Slocum*, five years away from a disastrous fire that would claim a thousand lives, carried almost three thousand passengers who had paid two dollars each to get close to the admiral. Tugs loaded with photographers and fishing boats filled with families darted between the bigger ships and bobbed in their wakes.

The parading men-o'-war were followed by more than seventy yachts and two hundred ships of various sizes, strung out along a twenty-mile stretch of water. This huge flotilla was led by Lipton's *Erin*, which was decorated in American flags and red-white-and-blue bunting. She carried a full crew, including Lipton's Sinhalese servants, and scores of passengers from around the world. Included among Lipton's guests were prominent British jurists, millionaire industrialists, officers of the Royal Ulster Yacht Club, two Belgian princes, and Lord Charles Beresford, an admiral, member of Parliament, and friend of the Prince of Wales.

With Sir Thomas waving from the bridge, the great yacht was met by an almost continuous din of bells, boat whistles, and music from shipboard bands. When the *Erin* passed the New York Central Railroad's yard at Pier 65, engineers on six locomotives sounded their whistles in unison. A half-mile farther upriver, a little tugboat named *Charm* pulled close enough for Lipton and his party to hear a chorus of twenty beautiful young women serenade them with Irish songs. No ship in the parade, other than *Olympia*, was greeted with more noise and excitement.

The public's affection for Lipton was so strong and constant that it merited eight paragraphs and two subheads in *The New York Times*'s front-page account of the Dewey celebration. Morgans, Goulds, Roosevelts, and others received barely a mention, but Lipton was lavished with attention and encouraged to comment at length. "I expected something very fine, but I never dreamed there would be a demonstration such as this," he said, adding that the parade was more impressive than Queen Victoria's Jubilee celebration. "It is a fitting tribute to one of the greatest naval fighters the world has ever known," added Lipton. "I have never in the whole course of my life seen such an outburst of enthusiasm."

In fact, the Dewey naval parade was only the beginning. In the evening, while fireworks shot into the air from a dozen spots on both sides of the Hudson, the warships and private vessels that had paraded in the morning put on a glittering show of electric lights and Chinese lanterns. The *Olympia* displayed her name in white lights, while the USS *Texas* declared herself in red, white, and blue. Lipton's crew marked out the word *Erin* with hundreds of lightbulbs that had been painted green and suspended between her two masts. The message was framed by more than two thousand additional white lights, which ran along the rails of the vessel and outlined her cabins.

The night was set ablaze as more fireworks were launched from barges in the middle of the river and, on the New Jersey side, ground displays spelled out "Dewey" and "Victory" in fire. On Governors Island the pyrotechnics included a giant sparking portrait of the admiral. In Manhattan, where bars offered "Dewey cocktails" for eight cents and vendors sold unbreakable Dewey plates for a nickel, the commotion lasted until midnight, when rain showers drove people to shelter. Dawn found the shoreline littered with abandoned crates and folding chairs and the streets of Chinatown carpeted red with the shredded wrappings of discharged firecrackers.

On the second day of celebration Dewey attended ceremonies at the Battery, City Hall, and Madison Square, where he reviewed a seven-mile-long parade. The crowd that lined the route was estimated to be two million strong, double the number that had witnessed the naval exhibition the day before. At every turn in a day filled with honors and pageantry, Dewey was accompanied by New York mayor Robert Van Wyck, federal officials, governors of various states, military officers, and his new friend Thomas Lipton.

In the great press of well-wishers and publicity-seekers, Dewey used Lipton as a shield, deflecting attention his way and joking about how "that man has become very popular." Lipton wasn't far from Dewey as he occupied a stand near his victory arch to review a parade that was led by New York governor Teddy Roosevelt astride a horse and West Point cadets in their shakos. Thirty thousand soldiers, sailors, and other marchers followed along with twenty-five thousand horses and eighty-six marching bands. A bewildered Dewey watched in wonder as so many bouquets were thrown at his feet that the pile grew waist high.

In the evening, the exhausted admiral retired to allow his sailors the spotlight at the Waldorf-Astoria, where the "Jack Tars" of the *Olympia* were showered with gifts—including tobacco pipes with Dewey's face on the bowl—and treated to a banquet and vaudeville show. The entertainment began with Oscar Hammerstein taking the stage to shout, "Boys, I've got my best talent for you." Clouds of pipe smoke and howls of appreciation wafted toward the ceiling as a brass band began to play. The big hits of the night were scored by the boxer James J. "Gentleman Jim" Corbett and the full-figured Marie Dressler, a Broadway star who appeared in a sailor suit and hat.

Looking down from a balcony he shared with Mayor Van Wyck and the Irish-born Tammany Hall boss Richard Croker, Lipton marveled at the spectacle of ordinary sailors being treated as honored guests. When the sailors shouted for him to speak, Lipton rose and addressed them. "I mean to try and get a little American property here myself," he said, then added, "I hope that when that little engagement comes off, you won't squash it up like you did the Spanish fleet in Manila."

From the beginning of the celebration to the very end, Lipton had managed to associate himself with Dewey in the most positive way. Content and even eager to serve as a jolly sideshow, the man became a living symbol of maritime strength, elegance, and excitement. He succeeded at this with extraordinary timing and the most effective kind of self-promotion. In the absence of any other likable foreign dignitary, people simply gave Lipton the role of America's best friend. The goodwill reverberated all the way back to London, where, as the Dewey celebration ended, the press reported that when he returned, Sir Thomas might be asked to stand for Parliament as a Liberal Party candidate.

On the day after the celebrations ended—a Sunday—Admiral Dewey visited a doctor for a "tonic" to cure his fatigue and prepared to depart for Washington. Although many of the out-of-towners who had come to New York for the victory celebration crowded train stations and steamship docks, a significant number remained to watch the America's Cup competition.

Lipton's challenger, *Shamrock*, and the defender, *Columbia*, were scheduled to begin their races on Tuesday. The great contest would offer spectators the chance to see a real battle on the seas, which was an irresistible prospect for those who had come to celebrate great ships, great men, and great conflicts. The managers of New York's better hotels reported to the newspapers that they were seeing even more demand for rooms than they had seen for the Dewey days. Suites at the Waldorf-Astoria were packed with cots, but so many guests continued to arrive that proprietor George Boldt opened his own home for some, and found rooms in other mansions for others.

Accommodated in luxury aboard *Erin*, Lipton and his friends were able to socialize in Manhattan with their peers but retreat to serenity in the evenings. *Erin* also allowed them to skirt the heavy traffic on the streets and railroads. On Sunday they steamed to Oyster Bay, Long Island, for dinner with Governor Roosevelt at his Sagamore Hill estate. In place of Dewey, Lipton was now the man of the hour, with the city of Chicago sending an invitation for him to help lay the cornerstone of a new federal building, and New York state inmates featuring him in their monthly magazine, *The Prison Forum*. In Lowell, Massachusetts, a pair of wealthy industrialists pledged to spend a fortune to challenge Lipton if *Shamrock* won the cup. From London came hints that with a victory in the cup races, Sir Tea would be admitted to the Royal Yacht Squadron. (Despite his being sponsored by the Prince of Wales, Lipton had so far been denied membership because he was a common grocer.)

Although the races were an ocean away, London was captivated by the coming contest. The *Daily Mail* had placed searchlights on top of London's Harmsworth Tower that would signal the results of the races with beams visible for many miles. (A cipher for the color code was published in the paper.) The *Evening News* had gone a step further, setting up a huge blue canvas as the background for two carved hulls representing the racers. One carried a green light to represent *Shamrock*. The other carried a red one to indicate *Columbia*. The screen faced the north bank of the Thames, and in the evening hours the lights would be bright enough for onlookers to see where the boats stood in relation to each other. The positions of the models would be changed every ten minutes as Marconi—aboard the excursion steamer *Ponce*—radioed reports from ship to shore and then telegraphers tapped the news out with their index fingers. (Marconi's dream of wireless transatlantic communication had not yet been realized.)

British enthusiasm for the races exceeded anything the country had ever seen. On the evening of Tuesday, October 3, 1899, more than twenty-five thousand people filled the few square blocks of Fleet Street where local, national, and international newspapers kept offices. Stage plays were presented to half-empty houses as young men and women waited for the drama of the race to be shouted from upper stories and posted in display windows. Fleet Street hadn't seen this much excitement since Prime Minister Gladstone's Home Rule proposal for Ireland was defeated by the House of Lords in 1893. Although Irish pride was in play during both events, the real difference between the Home Rule vote and the first cup race—besides the obvious fact that one involved a sport and the other a nation's future—was the certainty of a result. When the lords began deliberation, they were bound to reach a conclusion. In the case of the *Shamrock* and the *Columbia*, nothing, not even the completion of the race, was guaranteed.

On the first race day a pair of tugboats huffed into Horseshoe Cove at about eight-thirty a.m. In light, cool winds one tug cozied up to *Shamrock* while the other sidled over to *Columbia*. Lines were tossed and made secure, and sometime after nine o'clock the crews held tight as the slack was taken up and the two yachts began moving, like little wagons pulled by schoolboys, north to the tip of Sandy Hook and then due east, toward the lightship.

As they passed the Hook, thousands of people, dressed in winter clothes to protect themselves from the chill, shouted and cheered from the beaches. In the open water, the two boats were met by hundreds of spectator ships and boats of all different sizes. Each one of these vessels was decked out in flags, and some flew banners showing their support for one yacht or the other. (Among the honored guests on various ships were governors from around the country and foreign officials from throughout the United Kingdom.) The bands on the larger ships played as loud as they could and produced competing brassy melodies—"The Star-Spangled Banner," "The Wearing of the Green," "Columbia, the Gem of the Ocean"—that together sounded like a military marching band crashing into a circus calliope.

To the relief of the racing crews, a squadron of revenue cutters and Navy torpedo boats steamed into this mess from the north. Fast and menacing, the government boats were under the command of a grizzled old Navy man, Robert "Fighting Bob" Evans. The patrol boats buzzed the spectator vessels, and their officers barked through megaphones to order them away from the competitors. Some of these guardians then accompanied *Shamrock* and *Columbia* toward the starting line. Others cruised southward to take up positions along the course. They would patrol for the rest of the day and with a few exceptions—

three passenger steamers and a British yacht called *Whyte Ladye* intruded onto the course—would succeed in keeping the path clear.

With the vast stage set and tens of thousands of spectators gathered in bobbing excitement, J. P. Morgan's steam yacht *Corsair* arrived and took up a position opposite the lightship. The starting point for the race would be an imaginary line between these two vessels. Captains Barr and Hogarth played their game-before-the-game behind the starting line, feinting and turning their boats with the hope of gaining an advantage when the starting gun was fired. Hogarth won this contest and when the shot was heard at 11:15, the *Shamrock* crossed the line first with her towering sails filled with wind. Most of the spectators weren't quite certain what had happened, but when they caught on, great cheers echoed over the sea.

Blessed with a strong wind, the two captains set their big ballooning spinnakers—*Columbia*'s was yellow, *Shamrock*'s gray—and they swelled to look like giant shields. With his boat to the east of Barr's, Hogarth held the lead as the yachts raced southeastward, along the Jersey shore, toward a point fifteen miles from the start. Hogarth was able to keep *Shamrock*'s sails filled with wind and increased her lead as Barr moved westward toward land and saw his own sails fall slack. A quick change of canvas for *Columbia* (the spinnaker came down) gave her more speed at the precise moment that Hogarth was suddenly becalmed. In less than fifteen minutes *Columbia* was able to reach the challenger and then pass her.

While all of this was going on, the steamship *Ponce* stalked the racers, and men on board shouted reports on the action to the radioman Marconi, who turned their words into dots and dashes for wireless transmissions through an antenna attached to a mast. A receiver at a telegraph station in the village of Navesink caught the messages and relayed them to the offices of the *New York Herald*, which then transmitted them to London, where the position of the boats was hollered along Fleet Street and flashed upon the great screen posted along the Thames by the *Evening News.*

Competitors to the *New York Herald* relied on an established routine for their race reports. Some used telegraphers in a securely moored boat, the steamer *Mackay-Bennett*, who listened to reports made by men with binoculars and spyglasses and relayed the positions of *Shamrock* and *Columbia* via eight cables that ran to a station onshore. Other papers hired fast boats that would dash from the course to the beach, where a runner would catch a canister thrown from the water. The message inside would be delivered to land-based telegraph stations and translated into Morse code.

However they got the news, the New York papers posted it immediately on their street-level bulletin boards for people gathered in the streets. Thousands filled the blocks outside newspaper offices, and souvenir sellers worked the crowds offering choice items like a three-leaf clover pin that showed Sir Thomas, the America's Cup, and his yacht, each occupying one leaf.

For the news watchers, and the few who could see what was happening on the course and understand it, the first hour of the race proved both puzzling and exciting. Knowledgeable American sailors would criticize Barr's early handling of his boat, especially his decision to run close to shore where the ocean currents, the same currents that had heaped up the sand over the millennia to make the Hook, worked against him.

The experts also gave credit to Hogarth for his well-timed start. And *Shamrock*, they could see, was the best challenger ever to come across the Atlantic.

As the afternoon progressed, the two boats seemed quite evenly matched, and after almost three hours they were bow-to-bow on the

Famous, in part, for being famous, Lipton was depicted in newspapers and magazines all over the world. This portrait appeared in *Vanity Fair* in 1904. (COURTESY THE AUTHOR)

All Lipton stores were modeled after Lipton's first shop, which he opened in Glasgow after returning from America. At its height, the chain had approximately three hundred stores, which were credited with bringing high-quality food to the masses at low prices. (BOB THOMAS/POPPERFOTO/GETTY IMAGES)

When his tea plantations in Ceylon (modern Sri Lanka) were at peak production, Lipton
employed as many as five thousand workers, who picked each leaf by hand. (LIBRARY OF
CONGRESS, PRINTS & PHOTOGRAPHS DIVISION, LC-DIG-GGBAIN-0255)

Postcards, often provided free in packaged
goods, were a popular form of advertising
in the late nineteenth and early twentieth centuries. (HOBOKEN HISTORICAL
MUSEUM)

Above Left: William K. Vanderbilt was co-owner of *Defender*, which defeated *Valkyrie III* in the 1895 America's Cup race. He became the leading member of the great railroad family after his brother Cornelius died in 1899. (LIBRARY OF CONGRESS, PRINTS & PHOTOGRAPHS DIVISION, LC-DIG-GGBAIN-05942)

Above Right: A Beaux-Arts creation of the architect Whitney Warren, who also participated in the design of Grand Central Terminal, the New York Yacht Club building that opened in 1904 on West Forty-fourth Street in Manhattan became an instant landmark. (COURTESY LIBRARY OF CONGRESS, LC-USZ62-74404)

The model room of the New York Yacht Club holds one of the most extensive collections in the world, including more than 450 fully rigged models and 1,200 half-hull replicas used by builders. (COURTESY LIBRARY OF CONGRESS, LC-USZ62-80595)

Left: J. P. Morgan was a prominent figure in New York yachting circles and owned a series of steam-powered yachts, each named *Corsair,* renowned for their size and technological advances. He befriended Lipton on a transatlantic crossing. (COURTESY LIBRARY OF CONGRESS, LC-USZ62-94488)

Below: Morgan often lived aboard his yacht *Corsair,* which was anchored in New York Harbor, and commuted on his launch *Mermaid.* Here, at center, he arrives at a dock on the West Side of Manhattan. (COURTESY LIBRARY OF CONGRESS, LC-USZ62-104532)

Above: Shamrock IV was sheltered in a cove near Sandy Hook, New Jersey, as she awaited her races against *Resolute* in Lipton's 1920 America's Cup challenge. (© MYSTIC SEAPORT, ROSENFELD COLLECTION, MYSTIC, CONNECTICUT, Nº 4438F)

Left: Always dressed for the occasion, Lipton wore nautical outfits, including a captain's cap, whenever aboard his yacht *Erin.* (LIBRARY OF CONGRESS, PRINTS & PHOTOGRAPHS DIVISION, LC-DIG-GGBAIN-00634)

"The Wizard of Bristol," Nathanael Herreshoff designed four of the five boats that defeated Lipton's *Shamrocks*. (HERRESHOFF MARINE MUSEUM)

Shamrock IV and *Resolute* sail in the fifth and final race of Lipton's 1920 challenge, which had been delayed by World War I. Lipton came closest to winning this time, but *Resolute* prevailed by a score of 3 to 2. (© MYSTIC SEAPORT, ROSENFELD COLLECTION, MYSTIC, CONNECTICUT, № 44284)

Sobered by reports of civilian casualties in Serbia during World War I, Lipton turned his yacht *Erin* into a hospital ship and brought a medical team to aid the wounded. Ever the stylish host, he is shown here at a picnic with British nurses. (HULTON ARCHIVE/TOPICAL PRESS AGENCY/GETTY IMAGES)

As soon as automobiles were reliable enough to compete, the wealthy used them for races. Here Lipton watches from the grandstand as cars whiz down a private parkway built by William K. Vanderbilt.
(DETROIT PUBLIC LIBRARY)

Plants and animals, including dogs, rabbits, and in this case even a baboon, were offered to Lipton as tokens of good luck. This primate in a sailor suit, shown on the deck of the yacht *Erin*, was named Tim Lipton. (HERRESHOFF MARINE MUSEUM)

Equipped with a spyglass, Lipton followed the America's Cup action from the deck of the *Erin.* In the early races he needed expert interpretation to understand what was happening on the water, but by 1903, when this photo was taken, he was able to follow and understand all the maneuvers he witnessed. (COURTESY LIBRARY OF CONGRESS, LC-USZ62-43728)

return home. But as they labored against each other, the crews also struggled with the wind, which began to die out. Tacking continuously, the skippers did everything possible to capture energy from the light and ever-changing breezes. In one moment Barr would prevail and move ahead. In the next, Hogarth would get the advantage and draw even.

And then, with *Columbia* ahead, a terrible fate struck the two racers at the same moment—they ran out of time. At 4:45 p.m., with the competitors still four miles from the finish, a shot was fired from a tug dispatched by the race committee. All five and a half hours allotted for the race had been consumed. There would be no winner today.

On Fleet Street in London, the crowd that had lingered until almost ten p.m. with hopes for a *Shamrock* victory greeted the nonresult with disappointment but took pleasure in the way Lipton's boat and crew had held their own. In the morning the *Pall Mall Gazette* would hail the chivalry, determination, and fair play of "Anglo-Saxons" on both sides. (No matter the event or the moment, the theme of Anglo-Saxon superiority was a staple of the press and politicians on both sides of the ocean.) On "newspaper row" in Manhattan (Park Row, opposite City Hall), race fans who had hoped to celebrate drifted off into the evening.

In the waters off the Hook, the *Columbia* and *Shamrock* yachts turned westward, toward the land, and lowered their sails. Within minutes their tugs arrived and they were towed back to their moorings in the shelter of Horseshoe Cove. Exhausted crews rested on their decks. Passengers on the spectator boats, tired from a full cold day on the ocean, warmed themselves with tea, coffee, and whiskey during the return trip to Manhattan.

With no winner, reporters were left to ask various experts to analyze the day's events. Here they got the kind of comments one expects from political partisans interviewed after the polls close but before ballots are counted. Americans seemed to believe that *Columbia* had showed herself superior in light and tricky winds. *Shamrock*'s supporters noted her fast start and her greater spread of canvas and predicted she would trounce the defender under normal conditions.

"Wait till it comes on to blow and we'll knock 'ell out of *Columbia*," boasted one of Hogarth's men as he left the boat for the night. All around him, English and Scottish mates roared with laughter.

Amid the posturing and analysis, Thomas Lipton steered a politically correct course, praising the officials who kept the ocean clear for the two racers and noting that *Columbia* and *Shamrock* seemed very well matched. Lipton met the press wearing his blue jacket, white pants and shoes, and a jaunty yachting cap. Lilies of the valley were pinned to his lapel.

"I can only say," he declared, "that either boat may win."

New Yorkers and visitors from around the country cheered Lipton's sportsmanship. This was no dour Dunraven but rather a cheerful and generous sportsman. At the Church of the Divine Paternity, on the corner of Central Park West and Seventy-sixth Street, the pastor preached a sermon about Lipton's great character. A packed church heard him praise Lipton as an example of modern manhood who heeded Saint Paul's admonition to "run with patience the race set before you."

For a nonevent, the first race produced an astounding amount of publicity for the emperor of tea. The slow-motion drama in the waters off New Jersey put Lipton's name and photo in newspapers worldwide. In the United States and Great Britain, his two biggest markets, most editors gave the yacht race the front page. The effect of this marketing coup in America was most important to Sir Thomas because, as he had taken his company public through the sale of stock in London, he kept possession of Thomas J. Lipton, Inc., in the United States.

With a day of rest scheduled between each event and rules requiring at least three races be completed to determine a winner, every cup challenge was guaranteed to produce at least a week of fierce preparations and sailing. The expense of maintaining boats and crews in this time was considerable. Lipton hired a ship to house his men in the cove where his racer was sheltered and he paid to berth and entertain dozens of guests aboard the *Erin*. The American syndicate bore identical expenses for their boat and crew, while the New York Yacht Club covered the cost of conducting the races. Add the money spent by tens of thousands of people visiting to watch the event, and the entire enterprise required that great sums be spent every day on everything from fuel for patrol boats to ice cream for spectators on steamers. But of all the wealthy men who were part of the race, the only one who stood to gain anything but bragging rights and a trophy was Lipton, whose fame and status as a tea merchant grew with every day that the contest continued.

Because he was winning so much acclaim, Lipton wasn't much perturbed when the boats again sailed out to the lightship, answered the starting gun, and failed to finish before time ran out. A strange weather pattern had settled over the region. Early on the morning of the second race day, warm humid air from the south produced heavy fog that refused to be burned off until around eleven o'clock. With the clearing, boaters saw an almost glassy sea with hardly a breeze to create a ripple. Conditions were terrible for sailing, but Lipton found them perfect for entertaining a special guest, Thomas Edison, who had accepted an invitation to see his first yacht race from the deck of the beautiful *Erin*. Lipton had greeted the inventor with some overblown sentiment about the glory he had brought to the day, in response to which Edison mumbled something self-deprecating. Although he wouldn't see much sailing,

Edison was treated to hours of feasting and impromptu entertaining—including songs from a Sinhalese houseman—to make up for another suspended race.

So it went for another full week as, every other day, the yachts went forth to float and drift in seas so calm that a hard-paddling duck might have made faster progress on the thirty-mile course. Although crews rigged sails to capture whatever wind could be found, the *Columbia* and *Shamrock* were often so still that they looked like a pair of fantastic lighthouses rising out of the water. Excursion captains gave up on the wind sooner each day, returning their paying customers to the docks. Those who were alert did get to see one good contest, however, as the superrich owners of the steam yachts *Amphitrite* and *Josephine* wagered a friendly $3,000 on a fifteen-mile sprint from the lightship to the New York Yacht Club dock at East Twenty-sixth Street. *Amphitrite*, owned by Oliver H. Payne, won by a big margin.

More excitement occurred aboard the spectator ship *Georgeanna*, an iron side-wheeler that left the Battery in lower Manhattan at 9:30 a.m. on the second race day carrying a combustible mix of tourists, yachting fans, gamblers, and prostitutes. The working women began soliciting customers as the boat left its dock. When they weren't busy inside private cabins, they wandered to the ship's bar to demand free drinks. The gamblers set up poker tables, roulette wheels, and dice games in the main cabin and before the ship had passed the Statue of Liberty the wheels were spinning and cards were being shuffled.

The excursion customers who had paid to see the races quickly realized that the ship had actually been chartered by a criminal mob. When the crew announced that mechanical problems would keep the *Georgeanna* away from the racecourse, these upright citizens convened what one reporter called "an indignation meeting." As they gathered on deck, some of the gamblers' touts circled and shouted warnings. In other parts of the ship thieves confronted passengers and relieved them of cash, rings, and watches.

Out of the group of indignant men emerged a leader. A one-armed veteran of the Civil War, C. A. Norton had achieved the rank of captain while fighting with the First Maine Infantry. Hoping to avoid a brawl, he first tried to persuade the ship's captain, Alphonse Sterck, to establish order on the *Georgeanna* and return her to Manhattan. When Sterck refused, noting that the crooks had chartered the ship, Captain Norton organized an attack on the makeshift casino. He led dozens of men who entered the main cabin, confronted the gamblers, seized the card tables and roulette wheels, carried them onto the deck, and heaved them overboard.

Bottles and glasses flew through the air, and the chief of the gambling syndicate, a New Yorker named Charles Berry, growled for one of his men to "stick a knife" into Norton. However, in the melee that ensued only one man, who was hit with a stool, suffered serious injuries. Greatly outnumbered, the gamblers, thieves, and prostitutes hurled more threats and curses than punches. Once they were confined to the bar area, Norton went looking for Captain Sterck, who was found hiding in the pilothouse. As Sterck agreed to steer the boat back to its berth, one of the day-trippers went to the stern of the ship and turned the American flag that flew there upside down to signal distress. When other boats approached, responding to the signal, *Georgeanna's* law-abiding passengers shouted their reports of what had gone on. Word spread across the harbor, and by the time the embattled ship reached Pier 6, dozens of police officers awaited.

At dockside, passengers who rushed to leave the ship were pushed back by a squad of police officers wielding clubs. On the other side of the ship several gamblers jumped into the river, only to be pulled into waiting boats. Inspectors and deputy police chiefs began sorting out the criminals and the excursionists. Dozens of men, including Captain Sterck and the gambler Berry, were dragged off to municipal court to face charges. The passengers who had found themselves caught on a ship of sin missed seeing the *Shamrock* and the *Columbia* but were far more entertained than anyone else who took to the water that day.

But for the saga of the *Georgeanna*, and a few other incidents— the pesky English yacht *Whyte Ladye* actually collided with Fighting Bob's revenue cutter *Manning*—people following the races would have had nothing to talk about for eleven straight days. In this time, from October 3 through October 13, the cup racers tried five times to complete one heat and failed for lack of wind every single time. Sir Thomas tried to maintain public interest with anecdotes about racing the royal yacht *Britannia* and a little cheerful taunting of his opponents.

"It seems a pity that we have really no opportunity to show what *Shamrock* is to *Columbia*," he said, before adding that with a good breeze Captain Hogarth would give the Americans a view of *Shamrock*'s backside "if they have a good pair of glasses on board."

Despite Lipton's efforts, by the time the yachts made their seventh failed attempt at a race, many of the less wealthy visitors and excursionists had given up and left town. In London, people stopped gathering on Fleet Street and the Thames embankment for reports from the course and contented themselves with news in the morning papers. Britons still believed that *Shamrock* was the best challenger yet and continued to admire Lipton, but they lost enthusiasm for the spectacle.

On the morning of the eighth try, just a dozen spectator boats left New York for the course. Lipton, fogbound aboard the *Erin*, sent a message warning his many supporters to stay in the city because conditions were so poor. Nevertheless, he directed his steam yacht to follow Hogarth and Barr as they set out for the lightship under a solid bank of clouds and mist that was almost rain. They were met by a light easterly wind that was just strong enough to fill their damp sails. As the gun sounded the Lipton boat crossed the starting line three seconds ahead of the defender. Lipton, watching from the *Erin's* bridge, gave a little cheer.

In minutes the giant sails of the boats became, first, indistinct white blobs, and then entirely invisible as the mist swallowed them whole. *Erin* gave chase and caught the racers in time to see *Columbia* tack twice and press past *Shamrock*. The American racer added to her lead so quickly that by the time she reached the halfway mark and turned for home, the result was certain. Only an act of God—lightning? a whale strike?— would change the inevitable outcome, but God did not intervene. To the surprise of many onshore, the boats returned to the line in time to make the race official. *Columbia* finished with a lead of two miles and just over ten minutes.

With the weather spell broken, an eleven-knot breeze prevailed as the boats set out for the next heat. *Erin* followed *Shamrock* and arrived at the starting line with her deck crowded with women in brightly colored dresses and men wearing green ties. Lipton, in his yachting uniform, practically glowed with happiness as the sun bathed the deck in warm light.

This race was crucial for the *Shamrock*, and as he maneuvered prior to the gun, Captain Hogarth ordered his crew to raise a sizable topsail. It swelled with air as the boat—heeling to the port side with her rail slicing the water—crossed the starting line slightly ahead of the American yacht. Five minutes later the pressure created by this sail, combined with the action of a large swell, snapped *Shamrock's* topmast. As the piece of mast, topsail, and spars crashed to the starboard side of the boat, Hogarth was finished. He turned off the course and headed for Sandy Hook. Barr steered *Columbia* onward.

After making sure that no one on *Shamrock* was hurt, Lipton went to his guests. With newspapermen gathered, his choice of words would matter more, in a commercial sense, than the outcome of the cup challenge. He blamed the break on "a loose bolt or a broken backstay" and stressed that Hogarth had put the *Shamrock* in a position to win before the disaster struck. Repairs would be made in time for the next race. When one of his friends wondered aloud about the chance that the wind would die before *Columbia* finished, Lipton refused to hear it.

"I wish for nothing of the kind!" he almost shouted. He then added that the rules allowing *Columbia* to finish alone were fair and that despite the disappointment "I am not discouraged."

A few excursion boats stayed with *Erin* and the damaged *Shamrock* and followed them to the Sandy Hook anchorage. The band on one of these ships, a steamer called the *Joanna*, played a few Irish songs to lighten the mood. Lunch was served aboard *Erin*, and before four p.m. the great sportsman got his wish as *Columbia*, with the wiry Barr at the helm, finished the course in only three hours and thirty-seven minutes. In a short time a small steam-driven tender, *Blackbird*, pulled up to the *Erin* to collect Lipton's city-bound guests. After they were loaded, they gathered to offer three cheers for their host.

"Never fear!" he replied. "I've been in much tighter holes than this and came out on top!"

Undoubtedly Lipton never met Nathanael Herreshoff and Charlie Barr in any of the holes he had dug himself prior to the cup race, because if he had, he would have been trapped forever. Skilled and profoundly determined, Herreshoff and Barr had made *Columbia* into an unbeatable boat. In Britain people seemed to grasp this fact as the press declared that the Yanks were winning fair and square and *Shamrock* was simply outclassed. The newspapers still lauded Lipton for his sportsmanship, but interest in the outcome of the races all but evaporated. One small paper published in the north of England reported that the great soap maker William Lever, founder of the industrial town of Port Sunlight, near Liverpool, was already considering a future bid for the cup. (A true Victorian eccentric, Lever was so devoted to a fresh-air craze that he habitually slept in the open air, exposed to rain and snow.)

In New York, people were in no rush to replace Sir Thomas with another challenger. As the sun set on the *Shamrock*'s second loss and the western sky turned a brilliant purple, Lipton sat on the deck of the *Erin*, a sheaf of telegrams in his hand. Every one expressed some version of the sentiment in one that he read aloud, "Don't be disheartened: *Shamrock* may lose but Sir Thomas wins the respect and goodwill of millions of Americans." In response, Lipton declared that his experience in recent weeks had proven to his own countrymen that America was a land of "generous hearts . . . willing hands . . . honest men."

After another day ruined by calm winds, the boats finally left Sandy Hook for the final contest on October 20, after more than two weeks of stuttering competition. *Shamrock* carried roughly three thousand pounds of additional ballast, ordered by designer Fife, who had followed events from his sickbed in a luxury hotel. (Fife's absence from the racecourse had certainly handicapped the *Shamrock* team.) Early cloud cover had broken, and the wind was so brisk that as soon as the boats cleared Fort Hancock they encountered a lively chop in the water. The wind, blowing at twenty to thirty miles per hour, sliced some of the little waves into whitecaps and promised more than enough energy to push the racers along. The course would again require the boats to race to a point fifteen miles southeast of the lightship, turn, and come home.

With many people expecting the cup's fate to be settled this day, the spectator fleet that crowded the starting line was bigger than it had been earlier in the week. Thousands of people braved the cold and the wind because they were certain to see history. The race began with *Shamrock* jumping the gun—she would be penalized for the time advantage—and Charlie Barr deploying *Columbia*'s massive spinnaker despite the danger posed by gusting winds.

Barr used the spinnaker to catch up with *Shamrock*, pass her, and then momentarily block the wind. This strategy worked and *Columbia* surged ahead to a comfortable lead. As the skippers strained for advantage, they often let their boats lean into the water. Great plumes of spray rose as top rails caught the sea, and in certain moments, as they shot from the crest of a swell, the sleek boats looked like dolphins skimming the waves. Crewmen threw themselves onto the deck, lining up like sardines in a can and clinging to the opposite rail. Here, at last, was the beautiful excitement that owners, captains, crews, and spectators had come to see.

When *Columbia* took the lead early in the race, Hogarth's men raised the extra sail that had snapped *Shamrock*'s topmast on the day of her second defeat. This time the mast held, and when a little extra wind suddenly rushed in from the north the green boat began to close on her opponent. Conditions were nearly perfect. As Fighting Bob Evans put it, "Any yachtsman who wishes for more wind than this is a hog."

Hog or not, Hogarth didn't get quite enough power to overcome *Columbia*'s speed—or his own minor errors, which sometimes buried his boat's rail too deeply in the sea. Aboard the *Erin*, Lipton watched through binoculars and listened as more experienced yachtsmen analyzed what was happening. By one p.m. he concluded that the cause was lost. Turning to his guests, he said, "Nothing but an accident to the *Columbia* would give us the race and I would not have that happen for the world. Let us all go below and have luncheon."

Though disappointed, Lipton was nevertheless proud of his boat and his team. In the time between her conception and the final day of racing, *Shamrock* had taken up residence in Lipton's heart and in the hearts of many racing fans. Her jaunty Irish name, green paint, and fine figure appealed to sentimentalists and those who had an eye for nautical beauty. Her story, as the brainchild of an eccentric self-made millionaire sent to compete and heal a wounded friendship, inspired a happy kind of hope. She was, in many ways, the closest Lipton would ever come to having a real child of his own. Noting the absence of designer Fife, who had been confined due to illness since arriving in New York, Lipton wondered if *Shamrock's* best had been shown. "If Mr. Fife had been there," he added, "there would have been no doubt."

Out on the course, Nathanael Herreshoff allowed himself to feel some relief. (In the evening he would even celebrate with a drink, the first and only taste of alcohol he would ever know.) Herreshoff had recognized a true threat in *Shamrock*, but after three straight wins, no one could have questioned *Columbia's* superiority. The American yacht reached the turning point more than a minute ahead of Lipton's boat. She put even more distance between her and the challenger on the run home, and crossed the finish line more than four minutes ahead of *Shamrock*. The victory was won at 2:40 p.m., and by 2:50, on Lipton's command, crewmen raised a pair of American flags to the top of *Erin's* twin masts. "The better boat has won," said Sir Thomas as he raised his glass before his guests, "but I have it in mind to challenge again unless some other Englishman should wish to do so."

Despite the rumbling about William Lever's interest, no other Englishman wanted to match Lipton's effort. He had spent the 2010 equivalent of $25 million on his cup challenge, and if he hoped to win he might have to make a bigger investment the next time. Among the more prominent British yachtsmen, few if any possessed the fortune required, and fewer still had anything to gain, commercially, from the publicity bonanza that accompanied a challenge. Lipton had something to sell—his name and the products that bore it—to both the Americans and the citizens of the United Kingdom. This meant that with every cup challenge he could win, even while losing.

The cup defenders could not claim the same status. The men who formed the syndicates that funded the American yachts were not merchants or manufacturers of consumer goods. Though famous, these financiers, railroad men, steelmakers, and investors were hardly popular. This was most obvious when Lipton visited the *Corsair* to concede defeat and was embraced by the New York Yacht Club's commodore, J. P. Morgan. Publicity-shy and brusque with the press, Morgan was, in sum, the utter opposite of Sir Thomas. And when he declared, "You have won the love and respect of every living man and woman in America," he described perfectly the reason why Lipton would return for another go at the cup.

While Herreshoff and Barr quickly departed New York, Lipton lingered to be honored and even roasted at banquets and parties. At one of these events, a New York senator said that Lipton was so popular, the idea that he might become an American citizen worried every politician in the country. He got a roar out of the crowd by saying Lipton could claim anything he wanted, and then, after a pause, asked sotto voce, "Where *is* she?" One sympathetic woman told Lipton she had heard that the American side had "put something in the water" to prevent him from winning. Lipton said she was correct. They had "put the *Columbia* in the water for just that very purpose."

After a tour of his American business interests and some interviews in which he committed to another cup challenge in two years' time, Lipton finally booked passage home on the steamer *St. Louis* on November 1. His departure was a long, drawn-out affair that began with a crowd and a brass band meeting him on the sidewalk in front of the Fifth Avenue Hotel. As his carriage made its way to the pier, people stopped on the sidewalk and cheered him, and once he reached the ship he was hailed by hundreds of well-wishers, another band, and dignitaries intent on making speeches. He received a silver cup, sent by a committee that included Thomas Edison, and a display of flowers shaped like the *Shamrock*. He waved from the deck as the *St. Louis* pulled away and then, as it passed Sandy Hook, sent messages ashore via carrier pigeon. One, addressed to the New York Press Club, said, "Give all the boys my kind love."

TEN

Celebrity

On his return to London, the papers began to refer to Sir Thomas Lipton not as a manufacturer, merchant, or sportsman, but as a celebrity. When he attended the next Mayor's Banquet, which was the most exclusive event of the season, he was announced with the same trumpet fanfare as the visiting Maharajah of Kapurthala and the new secretary of state for war. Having been named an honorary lieutenant by the mayor, Lipton appeared in a uniform heavy with stiff epaulets and gold brocade and completed by a white-plumed officer's parade hat. He wore it as well as any man who had actually served.

Other wealthy businessmen enjoyed notoriety and honors, but only a few—Tom Dewar, for example—shared their names with a consumer product, and fewer still were so well-known around the world. And not one of them could say that his face was instantly recognized by millions of people across the United States and throughout the British Empire. People didn't know what the bean-and-ketchup man named Heinz looked like, for example, nor did they care. But during his America's Cup challenge the world press had made Lipton—striking a pose on the deck of a ship, his bright blue eyes staring out from under a commander's cap—into the iconic image of the modern sportsman and an all-around role model for spirited entrepreneurs.

Lipton received this kind of acclaim because his life story, honed over decades of telling and retelling, had been shaped to fit perfectly into the master plot many writers followed to tell a Gilded Age tale of success. Presented as antidotes to muckraking reports on robber barons, swindlers, and industrial scoundrels, these stories always connected achievement to hard work and fair play, and their subjects were paragons of virtue who loved their mothers and resisted all vices. Newspapers and magazines presented these fables to assure readers that old-fashioned virtues survived. In this way, Lipton the good millionaire served as a sort of social safety valve, easing the pressure of class resentments, which seethed in many quarters throughout the Gilded Age.

International publicity served individuals in powerful ways, too. It amplified the might of political leaders like Teddy Roosevelt and affirmed the genius of an Edison or a Bell. Performers like Sarah Bernhardt and William F. "Buffalo Bill" Cody cashed in on their fame through the sale of tickets to their shows. (Cody, who transfixed all of Europe with his pageant of the American West, was one of the richest performers in history.) But given the limits of time and place, performers could only squeeze so much value out of their names and likenesses. Lipton was able to depend on a vast network of retail stores and wholesale operations that offered dozens of different products under his name in markets where more than two hundred million people could respond with a purchase every single day. In this way his fame was converted into increased sales and profits that could be counted in the millions of dollars annually.

Although Lipton still commanded regular valuable attention from the press, the country had far more serious preoccupations. While Sir

Tea had been bobbing around Sandy Hook in 1899, Britain had gone to war with the Boers of southern Africa, whose independent states harbored some of the richest gold and diamond deposits in the world. The pretexts for this war included the philosophy behind Rudyard Kipling's "White Man's Burden," which referred to the empire's supposed duty to bring Western civilization to the world, and concern about the treatment of prospectors from the United Kingdom, whose numbers had overwhelmed Boer authorities. Britain's true purpose was to extend the empire one last time, but the going at the outset was rough. When Lipton returned from his cup challenge, reports from Africa noted that hundreds of British troops had been killed and thousands captured in various battles. A pall had fallen over London. Lipton offered the British military his yacht *Erin* for use as a hospital ship. When this gift was declined he gave £10,000 to the Alexandra Trust for its programs to aid wounded soldiers.

Lipton used the waning months of 1899 to catch up with business at his City Road office. Although fully infected with "cup fever"—he was already obsessing about the next challenge—he remained the head of the company and was determined, despite the presence of a new board of directors, to make it run according to his standards. His handling of a conflict over dividends illustrated his approach. The directors wanted to pay more than the usual twelve percent, and revenue would have permitted it. However, Lipton felt the firm needed cash reserves and fought the increase. He prevailed with both his business sense and personal checks distributed to the directors to compensate for the earnings they would have realized with a higher dividend.

The dividend decision came as the kind of corporate duty that the founder would continue to carry out as the head of his now public company. However he no longer took responsibility for the intimate, day-to-day management of the far-flung Lipton enterprise. With stockyards, plantations, distribution centers, manufacturing plants, retails shops, and a vast transportation network, the company was just too big for one man. Besides, Sir Thomas was having far too much fun in his new and exceedingly rewarding role as a sportsman and icon. He spent thousands of dollars on silver Lipton cups, which he sent to various yacht clubs in Great Britain and America, where they would serve as trophies for annual races. And he quietly cultivated his budding friendship with Albert Edward, Prince of Wales.

Called Bertie by family and Edward in the press, Albert Edward was, in 1900, a fifty-nine-year-old king-in-waiting who had spent his life in the smothering shadow of his mother, Queen Victoria. Widowed for nearly four decades, the eighty-one-year-old Victoria was both the longest-serving monarch in British history and the world's most famous grieving woman. After Albert's death she wore black for the rest of her life. Every evening she had her husband's clothes laid out for the next day, and every morning she had water placed in his washbasin.

Victoria's name was given to an era known for its exquisitely fussy art and design, stunning industrial growth, and overly mannered approach to all of human affairs, but most especially to sex. She regarded her son as inadequate in almost every way and kept him out of national affairs. He didn't even have access to information about the inner workings of the monarchy until he was fifty.

Inevitably, Edward had thrown himself into the spaces left open to him, namely diversions and indulgences. He drank and ate prodigiously and spent evenings in a cloud of cigar smoke and perfume. Vain and eager to cover his many physical flaws, the short, rotund prince was devoted to fashion and dressed as a "heavy swell," which meant he always wore the most expensive fabrics, every imaginable accessory, and ornate costumes for special occasions. Like Lipton, he loved wearing the uniforms that came with honorary titles. His, of course, indicated he was a colonel or admiral—not a lieutenant—and they carried so many decorations that his entire chest was practically bulletproof.

Bertie shared other interests and attitudes with Sir Tea. He adored America, which he first visited in 1860 as a nineteen-year-old, and entertained a steady stream of visitors from the States. Although he struggled with idle chitchat, he was outwardly warm to almost everyone and cultivated a casual mood with his friends, who came from an exceedingly wide cross section of society. He especially enjoyed investors and bankers, who could help him with his money, and he defied the anti-Semites in his circle to make the financiers Reuben Sassoon and Ernest Cassel his confidants and advisors. (Edward was the first member of the royal family to attend services in a synagogue.)

While Cassel and Sassoon helped satisfy the prince's need for income and assets, confident, self-made millionaires like Lipton provided jolly company. Well traveled, well spoken, and full of stories gathered on adventures around the world, Lipton was a perfect companion for the prince. As one social columnist noted, Lipton had "a very funny way of relating funny things." When Edward talked about a royal order for Lipton—meaning a ceremonial award—Sir Thomas fell into his grocer role and volunteered to send a price list "at once." On another social occasion, Lipton playfully dropped some keys down the neck of Bertie's shirt.

A man who could drop keys down Edward's shirt and get away with it possessed extraordinary social gifts. Lipton put these skills to use as a regular guest in the prince's homes, where he met and formed relationships with the kings of Spain and Italy, Eugénie, the last empress of France, and many other men and women of title. Like Edward's other rich friends, Lipton was generous and useful. These men kept the prince's secrets as he entertained countless sexual partners, some professional, in various hideaways, palaces, hotels, and seedy private clubs. (Nothing excited Edward more than to visit the sin districts of major cities while posing as a gentleman named "Baron Renfrew.") His days-long parties at country estates involved so much Marx Brothers–style room swapping that bells were rung in the hallways to signal when morning had come and it was time for people to return to their assigned chambers. This behavior appalled the more conservative members of society, who at one point complained to the Archbishop of Canterbury about the "Marlborough set," which was what they called the crowd who gathered at the prince's house. The protest didn't do them any good.

Though his friends and even the press colluded to keep the prince's most scandalous escapades secret, the identities of his truly beloved mistresses were widely known. Before Lipton came along with his checks for the Alexandra Trust and his America's Cup challenge, the prince's heart was invested in the affections of the actress Lillie Langtry, a woman of middling stock who had been able to enter London society thanks in part to the effort the prince had made to break down old barriers. Once admitted to the best parties and banquets, she met artists who, taken by her pale skin, square features, and voluptuous body, made her famous with their portraits, which were sold as prints by the thousands. After she was introduced to the prince by an Arctic explorer, Lillie became his mistress and confidante, and grew so famous that when items were chosen to be buried in the foundation for an Egyptian obelisk brought to London, her picture was included.

Lillie was followed in the role of Edward's mistress by Frances "Daisy" Greville, Countess of Warwick, who had once been the queen's choice for marriage to Prince Leopold, Bertie's younger brother. Daisy's first serious extramarital affair had been with Admiral Lord Charles Beresford, whom she loved with terrific intensity until the admiral renewed his commitment to his wife. When she turned to Prince Edward for consolation he responded with devotion. But though he loved her and called her his "Daisy wife," the relationship ended when Edward's actual wife, Princess Alexandra, learned that a pamphlet detailing the relationship was circulating in society. Generally tolerant of her husband's appetites, she couldn't abide public humiliation, and her indignation, joined with other threats of exposure, forced an end to the affair.

The final and greatest love of Albert Edward's life arrived in early 1899, while Lillie Langtry was in America starring in a play titled *The Degenerates*, which revolved around a female character who had been cast out of society's highest circle. Twenty-nine-year-old Alice Keppel was a small, lively woman who captivated men with her husky voice and large blue-green eyes. Though hardly Langtry's dramatic equal, and not as classically beautiful as Daisy, Alice was the kind of intelligent and stylish woman the prince adored. (He called her "La Favorita" and allowed her to call him "Kingy.") She was also, like the others, a married woman, and this was where Sir Thomas entered the picture.

Married women from wealthy households made good Victorian mistresses because they were, in general, well cared for and unlikely to make demands or behave indiscreetly. The problem, in Mrs. Keppel's case, was financial insecurity. Although her husband, George Keppel, was the son of the seventh Earl of Albemarle, he was a man of modest means. An affair with the heir to the throne required a woman to come with enough money to let her dress well and move about freely. For this her husband required a real income. Sir Thomas Lipton stepped in with the offer of a job at his Buyers' Association, which sold an amazing array of goods—groceries, bedding, even Siddeley motorcars—at wholesale prices to its members.

Six feet, four inches tall and unfailingly kind and generous—he

never complained about his wife's affairs—George Keppel fit perfectly
in the job and even used his wife's connections to solicit customers.
After less than a year in this post he was transferred to Lipton's offices
in New York, where he would live alone for several years. There, at least,
he would escape encounters with those who both admired his reticence
and pitied him as a cuckold.

In taking care of George Keppel, Lipton served the Prince of Wales
in a way that was necessarily discreet but also evident to people who
mattered. Every summer, as the rich and powerful fled London for
Cowes on the Isle of Wight, he put *Erin* at the prince's disposal, and the
great yacht served both as a banquet hall and as a hideaway where royals
and others could be entertained, above deck or below.

Social life at Cowes revolved around the activities of the Royal Yacht
Squadron, which the prince served as its commodore. The most exclusive
yachting organization in the world—and one of the most prestigious
social clubs—the RYS was founded in 1815 to promote yachting and
the development of new vessels. Limited to 250 members, it occupied a
sixteenth-century castle overlooking The Solent, the body of water separating the island from the English mainland ten miles away.

At the dawn of the twentieth century, the RYS was in its golden age,
and its regattas attracted the greatest yachts of Europe and America,
including the German emperor's *Meteor*. By day, The Solent was filled
with sails as the rich and the famous and the titled endured the swells
and sea spray to watch the races arranged by the squadron. By night,
hundreds of the world's most important people arranged themselves in
houses, apartments, and staterooms, where they re-created the social
dramas that would otherwise be conducted in London or at country
estates.

Lipton wanted to be a member of the yacht squadron. His status as
Edward's friend helped his chances, and when he made the America's

Cup challenge some in the press speculated that a victory would have made him a shoo-in. However, the club was a stuffy and hidebound institution. After Lipton lost his challenge it became clear that Prince Edward's sponsorship would not be enough to get him in. Sir Thomas was blackballed by members who preferred not to socialize with a man "in trade." When the prince asked, "Can't it be done?" a gentleman of the membership committee replied, "It can sire, but if it is the RYS will have but two members, you and Sir Thomas."

In the dance of manners that governed Victorian society, Lipton never complained about being excluded. He even threatened legal action against any journalist who reported that he had been blackballed. But the rejection was a symbol of the enduring power of class at a time when the Prince of Wales sought to break down social barriers. Lipton's outsider status during the Cowe's season was an annual reminder of British class boundaries. Yet he never showed that he felt hurt. Every year he camped aboard *Erin* in The Solent and hosted lavish parties. His sailing yachts often prevailed in the most-watched races. And with the ready support of the Royal Ulster Yacht Club in Northern Ireland, he was always assured of a sponsor for another run at the Americans.

Lipton had spoken of a second cup challenge from the moment of *Shamrock*'s third and deciding defeat off Sandy Hook. He wanted more of the valuable publicity realized in his first challenge, and no doubt he longed for more of the ego boost he had received in New York. He believed that the America's Cup was the holy grail of sport and that with a little more effort he could seize it.

In order to maintain suspense, and keep the Americans guessing, Lipton pretended to be uncertain about who might build his *Shamrock II* and just when he might issue the formal challenge. In fact, he had decided soon after coming home—at the start of 1900—that W. G. Jameson, captain of the royal yacht *Britannia*, would organize and oversee a more expensive and ambitious challenge than the first. Lipton also decided that the new *Shamrock* would be designed by the world-famous naval architect George Lennox Watson. Watson, the founder of the first full-time professional yacht-design firm in Britain, had already drawn and completed more than three hundred vessels. In a letter he wrote at the Cap-Martin Hotel on the Riviera in February 1901, Lipton revealed that Watson had been working for him, in secret, for nearly a year. He told the Marquess of Dufferin, commodore of the Royal Ulster Yacht Club:

> I have a feeling that *Shamrock II* will be successful. . . . Since the beginning of last year Mr. Watson has been working and experimenting all the time in preparation of the challenge.
>
> In confidence, he has made some wonderful discoveries in his tank experiments. In fact, at one time he said to me that the results of his tests made him feel as if he had known little about yacht building up until now.

A pool eight feet deep, twenty-three feet wide, and more than three hundred feet long, Watson's test tank was located at the William Denny & Brothers shipyard, which was on the Firth of Clyde, ten miles east of Glasgow. (The yard had produced many important ships, including the last of the great tea clippers, the *Cutty Sark*.) The tank allowed Watson to observe the way water flowed over wax models of hulls he designed with mathematical precision. He had used it to finalize the plan for *Britannia*, and the prince's cutter had proved its value when it beat Nat Herreshoff's *Navahoe* and his *Vigilant*, which had won the

America's Cup in 1893. For Lipton's boat, Watson tested twelve different wax models and made more than fifty modifications before settling on a final design.

By the time Lipton sent his letter from the Riviera, *Shamrock II* was framed and Watson had ordered the metal for her hull. Since Lipton had, in Watson's words, "planked down the money and said, 'Go ahead,'" the designer was free to choose the most advanced and exotic materials. Steel was substituted for timber. Aluminum supplanted bronze. To accommodate the inevitable breakdowns caused by the forces of air and water, everything would be ordered in duplicate, and, in some cases, triplicate, so that repairs could be made quickly. Naturally, the spare-no-expense effort meant that *Shamrock II* would cost substantially more than her predecessor. The open checkbook also allowed Watson to keep to an accelerated schedule, so the boat could get into the water for testing as soon as possible.

"From what I have heard said," Lipton told Lord Dufferin, "the Americans think that we will launch the boat about May, but we intend to have her launched about the third week of March and hope to have her ready for sailing in the Solent from the 5th to the 8th of April and we intend to sail her with *Shamrock I*, testing her for six weeks so that she will be properly tuned up before going across." The original *Shamrock* would be commanded by Robert Wringe. For his new boat, Lipton chose Captain Edward Sycamore, who had skippered Dunraven's last challenger, *Valkyrie III*. A legend in yachting on both sides of the Atlantic, Sycamore had competed often in American waters. His crew for the cup challenge would be selected from the best on the two boats.

Like most big yachts, *Shamrock II* was born a little tardy. With her manganese bottom polished to a brilliant gleam, she absorbed the

christening blow from a champagne bottle—swung by Lady Dufferin—
and slid into the Clyde on April 20. Optimism ran high under a cloudless
Scottish sky and the boat was declared nearly perfect. Her lightweight
hull, heavy keel, and big overhangs would support fourteen thousand
square feet of sail, the biggest spread of canvas for an America's Cup
yacht in more than twenty years. Designer Watson hoped this big ex-
panse of canvas would give the boat power under all conditions.

At the postlaunch banquet, Lipton glowed with confidence and predicted his new yacht would win the challenge. Archibald Denny, one of
the shipyard owners, answered a flowery toast honoring his firm with
praise for other great yachts and the excited claim that his company was
at work on a "flying machine." Flight was all the rage, and in fact the
shipyard *was* working on an experimental helicopter. However, it would
not hop off the ground until 1909, by which time the Wright brothers
and others had soared in fixed-wing aircraft. Soon after it was completed, the Denny machine was wrecked by a storm, and the project was
abandoned.

On the day of the launch, the Denny flying machine received little
notice, but *Shamrock II*, painted green and gold, was attended by a full
press corps and a gaping public as she left Scotland and sailed to The
Solent for testing. When her older sister beat her in a trial race, the
papers in New York reported the results and doubt swept the Lipton
team. Watson called for platers and riveters to rework her hull. A week
later, as the improved boat prevailed in a second race, Sir Thomas's
optimism was restored.

Test races gave the Lipton group a chance to discover if Watson had
actually produced a superior design for all the money that had been
"planked down" and to see how the boat and her crew responded to
different kinds of conditions. Spring in The Solent brought change-
able winds, including sudden squalls, which added to the excitement as

Lipton's most royal friend arrived to witness a match involving both *Shamrock*s and another Watson-designed yacht, the *Sybarita*, which was owned by a flamboyant mining magnate named Whitaker Wright. (Under investigation for financial irregularities, in three years' time Wright would respond to his conviction by committing suicide—a dose of cyanide—in the Royal Courts Building.)

Edward arrived at the seaside not as Prince of Wales but as King of the United Kingdom and Emperor of India. His mother, Victoria, had taken ill during her traditional Christmas visit to Osborne House, the family residence on the Isle of Wight. She had died in the evening of January 22, 1901, with her son at her bedside and a portrait of her husband in view. Her passing brought immediate speculation about Edward's social circle. "Will it entirely revolutionize his way of life?" wondered a young Winston Churchill. "Will he sell his horses and scatter his Jews or will Reuben Sassoon be enshrined among the crown jewels and other regalia? . . . Will the Keppel be appointed the 1st Lady of the Bedchamber?"

Mrs. Keppel received no formal appointment, but she remained La Favorita, and the king held on to other friends, including Sir Thomas. Four months to the day after his mother's death, Edward VII arrived at Southampton to watch *Shamrock II* in her trials. He traveled quietly with a small retinue—including Alice Keppel and W. G. Jameson's wife—and, except for a few extra policemen at the train station, no one knew anyone special was in town.

The monarch intended to sail aboard the new boat so that he could experience her speed and conformation firsthand. But at the pier, where he was met by Lipton, he was convinced that the race might be too dangerous and he agreed to observe from the *Erin*. Then, as the steam yacht entered The Solent, the king changed his mind. He really did want to feel the new boat catch the wind, and taste the salt spray. At his insistence the entire party—Lipton, the king, Mrs. Keppel, and a few others—were transferred to the new *Shamrock*.

The captains of the two *Shamrock*s, mindful of the king's request, prepared to put on as much speed as they could. As they headed for the starting line, near a spot marked by Brambles Buoy, both added club topsails. The king and his group, seated on the deck, held on to the rails as *Shamrock II* heeled at a forty-five-degree angle.

As the boats gained speed, the wind suddenly grew much stronger and clouds swept in from the west. A squall struck so suddenly that Captain Sycamore and his crew were unable to respond to it. As the king and the other observers moved to get belowdecks, *Shamrock II*'s steel boom swung from starboard to port, barely missing Edward's head. A moment later the topmast snapped. Heavy with sail, it fell over to the port side and its force immediately pulled down the rest of the one-ton mast.

With canvas, steel, wire, and other gear crashing down, Lipton, the king, and their companions ducked. On the deck, the crew rushed to stabilize the boat and prevent her from being swamped. Nearby, the captain of *Shamrock I* swung his boat around to offer aid but another big gust of wind hit her and toppled her topmast, making it impossible for him to maneuver. After a few tense minutes on *Shamrock II*, the squall began to subside and the king poked his head up to ask, "Is anyone hurt?"

Miraculously, the tons of debris that came down with the mast had fallen so that not one of the dozens of people aboard was struck. As nearby vessels raced to help, the king, reassured that all was well, lit a fresh cigar. Dinghies were dispatched from a press tug as well as from a Royal Navy torpedo boat that had been patrolling nearby. Edward, Alice Keppel, Mrs. Jameson, and Sir Thomas were ferried to *Erin*, where they clambered aboard. (Reporters on the tug went ashore to send telegrams reporting the accident and noting that all were safe.) Back at the scene of the disaster, the crew of *Shamrock II* recognized immediately that the wreckage would have to be cut away and sent to the bottom. They worked furiously to complete the job before sunset, and, after the spot was marked with a buoy, the yacht was towed to shelter near the seaside town of Hythe.

Safe aboard the *Erin*, the king and his group relived their adventure as they dined with Lipton. *Erin* cruised The Solent and finally turned toward Southampton. At about ten p.m., the big white yacht reached the dock, where the city's mayor waited with his wife. The train brought Edward VII to London at midnight. A small crowd, alerted to the accident by evening papers, cheered him when he arrived at Marlborough House. Inside waited stacks of telegrams hailing his safe return. It had been a most exciting day.

Telegrams also awaited Thomas J. Lipton, who was forced by the accident to request more time to prepare for his cup challenge. The request was granted by the Americans, who had their own troubles to sort out. Ten days after the *Shamrock II* was dismasted, the Herreshoffs' new boat, *Constitution*, suffered a similar disaster in Narragansett Bay. Racing along with its three lower sails set, some piece of the rigging failed and in a cascade of slow-motion breakdowns the yacht's mast collapsed. One member of the crew was swept overboard, but quick action by his mates brought him back on deck.

Constitution had been built at a cost twenty percent higher than the outlay for *Columbia*, a fact that irritated certain members of the New York Yacht Club, who believed they were caught in a war of dollars because Lipton was trying to spend his way to a victory. (They hoped that if he lost, Sir Tea would leave them alone for a few years.) Thanks to advanced materials, the new boat's hull was much lighter than *Columbia*'s. The reduced hull weight allowed for a heavier lead keel to balance more sail. The accident affirmed the fears of many who believed that designers on both sides of the Atlantic were pushing too hard. "The *Shamrock*s and *Constitution* are dangerous monstrosities," said the London *Daily Graphic*. In New York, the *Times* said the boats were not fit for the ocean, and warned of a "disaster in which human life will be lost."

If the *Shamrock*s and *Constitution* were "monstrosities," then the critics were left without an adequate term to use for *Independence*, a Boston-built yacht that had been given an even more extreme design. Technically a scow, this boat was 140 feet long. She carried a fin keel instead of a lead bulb, and could raise an even larger mountain of white sail than her competitors. Her owner was the financier and mining giant Thomas W. Lawson, whom the newspapers called "The Copper King." Lawson had recently joined with William Rockefeller to form a trust that would eventually take control of the Anaconda mining company. His fanciful estate, located outside Boston and called Dreamworld, was filled with art treasures and marked by a round stone tower inspired by German castles and constructed, at great expense, to cover up a water company standpipe that his wife found unsightly.

Mistaking the New York Yacht Club's trophy—the America's Cup, which was named for a boat—for a prize honoring the nation, Lawson had demanded that his yacht be considered for the defense against Lipton. The club's members resisted him at first, noting that he would have to join their organization in order to participate. An outraged Lawson protested, and after a negotiation his boat was permitted to race against *Constitution* and *Columbia*, which had been refurbished for pre-cup trials off Newport, Rhode Island. The races would be billed as exhibitions, not qualifying heats, but Lawson harbored the hope that if his radical boat prevailed, public acclaim would force the New Yorkers to let the *Independence* defend against the British challenger. From across the sea Lipton gamely sent word that he would let *Shamrock II* race against just about anyone's boat, as long as the New York club approved.

Plagued by leaks and faulty steering—at one point her rudder was jammed and she turned in circles—*Independence* was almost sunk by a storm as she traveled from Boston to Newport for the trials. When told that proper repairs would take weeks, Lawson ordered his captain, Henry Haff, to get the boat to the starting line on time, even if she wouldn't survive the course. Haff did as he was told, but *Independence* was in such bad shape that she moved, according to one report, "like a sleep walker." Aided by a pump, she performed a little better in the rest of the heats but never won a race against *Columbia* and *Constitution*. She would return to Boston and be dismantled before the end of the year. (Lawson would withdraw from yacht racing but return to seafaring fame in 1902 as the namesake for a freakishly large steel-hulled schooner that bore his name. Nearly five hundred feet long, the *Thomas W. Lawson* was the only ship in modern history to carry seven masts and twenty-five sails. She hauled coal and oil on the Eastern Seaboard and then sank before completing her first transatlantic voyage.)

Independence was a flop; however, the trials she joined did produce a surprise for the public. In one race after another, the old warhorse *Columbia*, sailed by Captain Charlie Barr, proved better than the newer *Constitution*. Nat Herreshoff would argue that *Columbia* prevailed because of the skill shown by Barr and his crew. The cup challenge committee met for two hours and decided the difference really was in the boat. For the first time ever it seemed the Wizard of Bristol had failed to achieve a real improvement with a new design. *Columbia* would once again defend against Lipton, who had the advantage of taking a new *Shamrock*, built to compensate for the flaws in her sibling, into the fight.

The British invasion for the 1901 cup challenge began on July 28 as *Erin* and *Shamrock II* left the Inverclyde town of Gourock for New York. They were followed in early August by an emissary representing several London sporting clubs and carrying $150,000 to be wagered on Lipton's boat. At roughly the same time, after a visit to Buckingham Palace for the king's encouragement, Thomas J. Lipton began his trip to America at a London train station. Recognized by people on the platform, he drew a big crowd of well-wishers who sang "For He's a Jolly Good Fellow." Not one to let a center-stage moment pass too quickly, Sir Thomas lingered as the train lurched forward and slowly moved along the platform. He shouted a few words about sportsmanship and his gratitude for the public's support and then broke from the crowd to hop onto the moving train as they cheered him.

Dramatic exits and entrances were now a reflex for Lipton. He arrived in New York bowing and waving from the bridge of the White Star Line steamer *Teutonic* as every ship and boat in the harbor whistled a welcome. Decked out in a dark suit, white canvas shoes, and a blue sailing cap, he was perfectly costumed for the reporters and dignitaries who, unable to wait at the dock, rushed to the *Teutonic* aboard tugboats and climbed up a gangway. (They were led by David Barrie, Lipton's indefatigable representative in America.) Sir Tea made sure they knew that the king would be following the races while he traveled on the Continent and that his interest had only increased public support for the *Shamrock II*.

From the way the papers reported on them, New Yorkers could be forgiven if they believed that half the lords and ladies of the United Kingdom had already arrived for the races. Dukes and duchesses filled the city's hotels and practically overran the so-called cottages at Newport. And in almost every newspaper column about social affairs and the gowns women wore, Mrs. Keppel occupied a visible position. One day she was at Sherry's for luncheon wearing a blue frock with a black and white hat. (No mention was made of the recent scandal involving a private room at Sherry's, an exotic dancer named Little Egypt, and a number of gentlemen whom the police found less than fully dressed.) The next evening Mrs. Keppel was at a banquet with the Astors and the Drexels.

True to the code of the era, no one actually said that Mrs. Keppel mattered because she was the king's mistress. Instead, observers simply compared her directly to Edward VII's previous paramours. Just prior to the races the *Times* sneered that while Alice Keppel was graceful, dignified, and one of the best-dressed women in England, she could not approach the beauty of "Mrs. Langtry" or the "Countess of Warwick." Having thus established her in the ranks of the concubines, the paper then tweaked the American elite by adding that Mrs. Keppel could nevertheless provide them with entrée to London society "if such should be desired in the near future."

Most of the wealthy and powerful Americans who flocked to Alice Keppel also sought an audience with Sir Thomas, who seized every opportunity to be seen by the press in the company of the right people. He attended banquets in Newport, lunched with Vice President Theodore Roosevelt, and entertained half the membership of the New York Yacht Club aboard the *Erin*. Three-o'clock tea on Lipton's yacht, which sometimes involved a hundred invitees, was a lavish event, worthy of Miss Cranston. Each guest's cup was delivered on an individual silver tray that also carried a slice of lemon, two lumps of sugar, and a dragon's-head milk pitcher. Broiled fowl and pastries would be accompanied by champagne, and each guest received a small present at the end of the meal.

Although the tokens given aboard the *Erin* varied depending on the guest and the occasion, when he went out in public Lipton often carried a pocketful of enameled green-and-gold Shamrock pins, which became little treasures for the people he happened to meet. Chorus girls who entered a beauty contest he was to judge received them, as did the children he met on the street.

Playfulness was Lipton's hallmark and whenever possible he praised America and emphasized the strong bonds between the United Kingdom and the United States. The Anglo-American relationship had become strained by the Boer War. Many Americans sympathized with the underdog Boers—most were farmers armed with hunting rifles—and were appalled by British tactics, which included the destruction of communities, execution of prisoners, and detention camps for civilians. With his dogged generosity and a constant smile, Lipton offered Americans an alternative image of the British man abroad. Energetic and optimistic, he wanted nothing more than to be a happy challenger, the fellow who would do his best to win, fair and square.

For the cannier, Lipton also represented a British version of the Barnum-style self-promoter. A bit of a rascal, this type of character amused those who could see how he maneuvered for attention, popping up anywhere and everywhere a reporter might be present. Lipton even managed to have his name mentioned when he wasn't present for a newsmaking event. For example, when a young Arctic explorer named Mark Otis arrived at the port, he was met by *Shamrock II's* Captain Sycamore and David Barrie, Lipton's American representatives. They managed to get the boss's name into the paper, right above the exciting paragraphs describing Otis's hunts for polar bears and walruses.

Otis had returned to America on a steamship filled with people eager to see the cup races. Many also intended to visit the Pan-American Exposition, a huge world's fair under way in Buffalo. Their plans, and the great exhibition, were disrupted when an armed assassin emerged from the crowd at the fair's Temple of Music, stepped in front of President William McKinley, and shot him twice at point-blank range. As bodyguards threw anarchist Leon Czolgosz to the ground and wrestled the pistol out of his hand, the collapsed president said, "Be careful how you tell my wife."

Czolgosz, who had suffered a nervous breakdown in 1898, sympathized with a small American anarchist movement that saw irredeemable corruption in the political and economic systems of the Gilded Age. He had been inspired to violence by the assassination of the Italian king Umberto I the previous year. After he was arrested, Czolgosz was beaten so badly by security officers that the Buffalo police feared he might die in their custody. Though Czolgosz soon recovered, McKinley, who was taken to the home of the exposition's head director, John Milburn, struggled for life. Surgery would confirm that one bullet had been deflected by the president's breastbone but the other had penetrated his abdomen and damaged his stomach.

In New York, news of the shooting stunned the crowds at theaters, who listened to announcements at intermission, and those who heard paperboys shouting bulletins on the street. Authorities across the country and much of Europe reacted to the assassination attempt with investigations targeting supposed anarchists, and with debates about the best way to handle the threat. U.S. Secret Service officers rushed to Paterson, New Jersey, to question the editor of an anarchist journal. Scotland Yard reported a "nest of anarchy" among foreigners settled in the Soho district of London. Newspapers in Germany called for a global strategy to prevent further anarchist attacks.

The furor over the anarchist threat quieted as the president's doctors, equipped with an X-ray machine sent by Thomas Edison, removed lead from his abdomen and stitched his wounds. Hundreds of people

k

who had gathered behind police barriers set up to protect the Milburn residence were elated to hear that McKinley was gaining strength. A week after the shooting, newspaper readers around the world learned that he was talking, eating, and conducting the country's business from his bed. The president's condition was so good on September 10 that his wife, his brother Abner, and many others who had stood vigil left the Milburn house. As Vice President Roosevelt departed for a hunting trip in the Adirondack Mountains, Roswell Park, McKinley's doctor, predicted a full recovery within a month. Edward VII sent a telegram expressing his relief. The directors of the Pan-American Exposition planned for a day of thanksgiving.

The joy lasted for about a day. On September 12, McKinley suffered what doctors called "a sinking spell." Obviously stricken by infection, his body temperature rose, his pulse became weak, and he complained of profound fatigue. Family, cabinet members, and old friends arrived in a rush of automobiles and horse-drawn carriages. In the Adirondacks, messengers were sent up Mount Marcy, where Theodore Roosevelt was hunting. Just before midnight he learned the president's death was imminent and began a long journey to reach the nearest train depot, thirty-five miles away. With rain pouring down, the vice president rode through mud and muck on a relay of horses supplied by members of a local hunting club.

As the vice president rode through the night, the crowd outside the Milburn home swelled to thousands. When visitors left the house, onlookers could see the course of events in the expressions on their faces. Those standing at the north side of the house watched as the lights in the room where the president lay were raised and dimmed as physicians went in and out. The president died just before three a.m. Two hours later, Roosevelt learned the news as he reached the terminus of the Adirondack Railroad in a village called North Creek. A waiting train would take him to Albany for transfer to an express bound for Buffalo. Twelve hours after McKinley's death, tearful members of the cabinet gathered at a private residence in Buffalo to witness Roosevelt taking the oath of office before a federal judge. In his first public statements, Roosevelt would pledge to continue his predecessor's policies.

America would need less than two weeks to bury President McKinley and also arraign, try, and convict his killer. During this time people stopped going to the Pan-American Exposition, college football games were canceled, and the America's Cup races were postponed. Reporters scrambling for an angle on the assassination visited Lipton's little fleet—*Shamrock II, Erin*, a tug named *James J. Laurence*, and a steamer-turned-dormitory named *Porto Rico*—to get his reaction. They discovered each of the vessels flying the Stars and Stripes at half-mast and Lipton ready to offer condolences on behalf of himself and all British people. Then, as so often was the case, Lipton revealed he had a personal connection to the big events of the day.

"I am very much pained and grieved at the sad news regarding the President's death," he said, "all the more so as I had a most cheering telegram from his brother on the 10th saying he was happy to inform me that the doctors looked to a speedy recovery. His death is a loss to the whole world and it will be felt no where more than among the British people." America's favorite Briton, Lipton would retreat until the unofficial mourning—ten days, according to yachting officials—had passed. Then he would join the sporting world as it focused its attention on the course off Sandy Hook.

After one failed attempt, when the boats were defeated by an indifferent breeze, the racers set out for another try on Saturday, September 27. A gloomy overcast hung about Manhattan and discouraged many excursion ticket holders who saw the clouds and decided to stay home. At eight a.m., as the fleet of spectator boats and ships began to depart Manhattan, they carried only the optimists. They were rewarded as they passed through the Narrows and saw patches of blue sky in the distance. Somewhere around Swinburne Island (a quarantine station off Staten Island) the breeze quickened, and the clouds parted like stage curtains. At Sandy Hook the sunlight glinted off the nearly still surface of the water and a mild, eight-knot wind blew from the east.

Already out on the course with the *Erin*, Thomas Lipton hoped that the breeze would quicken so that *Shamrock II* could prove her abilities. Experience had made Sir Tea a more knowledgeable observer, if not an actual sailor, and he understood the strengths and weaknesses in the two boats. His racer had been designed to fly in moderate seas and a steady wind. *Columbia* seemed a better all-weather boat, and with Charlie Barr's skills and experience off Sandy Hook, she was probably unbeatable in a breeze of ten knots or below. Though still hobbled by a fall he had suffered the previous week, Lipton would spend the entire day on the bridge of the *Erin* as she chased the racers.

When a cannon shot announced the start of the race, the mild conditions favored *Columbia* but Lipton's skipper, Edward Sycamore, managed to outfox Charlie Barr and block the breeze with his sails. With the crew all shifted to the leeward (lower) side, *Shamrock II* heeled sharply and scooted ahead. Sycamore maintained a slight lead as the boats knifed into deeper waters, spray flying off their bows. Barr tried repeatedly to get ahead of *Shamrock II* but he didn't have enough speed to clear the challenger's bow.

With the aid of expert sailors who called out the progress of the race, spectators along the course understood that an exceptional battle was unfolding. Though *Shamrock II* never gave up the lead on the outward leg, *Columbia* stayed within three hundred yards. As they rounded the outer mark and turned for home, *Shamrock II* led by forty-one seconds. More than an hour of racing remained and Sir Thomas, still on the bridge, called to his guests on the deck, urging them to go below for lunch. Most of them, including Mrs. Keppel, stayed put. Even the least experienced spectator could see that the boats and crews were engaged in a close battle and no one wanted to turn away.

As Barr chased Sycamore, the racers headed closer and closer to the spectator fleet and the patrol boats hustled to clear a path. The revenue cutter *Gresham*, its horn tooting, pushed several steamers away and then turned to loop behind the flotilla. As the *Gresham*'s commander, Thomas D. Walker, would later recall, the *Erin* made a sudden turn, and though he called for reversed engines, he was unable to slow his fast-moving ship. In the distance he could hear happy passengers on the *Erin* singing "Britannia Rules the Waves." Walker sounded his whistle again and crewmen shouted a warning across the water. Sailors aboard the *Erin* rushed to steady her passengers as her captain called for full speed and threw the wheel of the yacht to starboard.

The quick action avoided a direct hit, but the ships did collide. The *Gresham*'s starboard torpedo tube dragged along the port side of Lipton's great white yacht. Several of the *Erin*'s passengers, including Mrs. Keppel, were thrown to the deck. Three women passengers on the cutter, all guests of the Collector of the Port, fainted.

After the accident the *Gresham*, which came to a dead stop, quickly reversed to clear the *Erin* and reveal a crease in her steel flank. Commander Walker was relieved to see the damage was not severe, and he brought the cutter close to the yacht.

"I am very sorry, Sir Thomas, it was an accident," he shouted from bridge to bridge.

"You are all right, Captain Walker, and I know you would not have done it if it could have been avoided."

Once Mrs. Keppel was righted and the unconscious ladies were revived, officers on both ships confirmed that no one had been injured.
In general, sailors on the two boats agreed that *Erin* had been turned
abruptly so that her passengers could catch sight of the *Shamrock II* as
she passed with *Columbia* giving chase. The sight of the green boat leading in the homeward leg of the race was a rare and exciting vision for
Sir Thomas and his supporters, who were jubilant about the challenger's
performance. In the excitement, *Erin*'s captain had probably lost track
of the revenue cutter's position.

In fact, at the moment of the accident, *Shamrock II* was performing
at her best in less than optimum conditions. The wind was still only
moderate, and Captain Sycamore needed all of his boat's extra sail—she
carried roughly one thousand square feet more than *Columbia*—and
every trick he could imagine to stay ahead. The lead he held as he passed
Erin on the way home was small and in a matter of minutes *Columbia*
closed the gap and passed. For a moment, thousands of spectators wondered if an important turning point had been reached and the white
defender might spring away. Instead, *Shamrock II* fell in behind her, like
a hound chasing a fox, and never lost the scent.

For fifteen miles the challenger chased the defender and twin armadas
of spectator vessels—one on each side of the course—tracked along. Lipton, rooted to the bridge of his yacht *Erin*, peered through binoculars and
questioned the men who stood by as advisors. As they approached the
lightship and the finish line, the spectator ships gathered like a herd of
cows at a gate. In the last minute of the race, whistles and horns and
cheers rang across the water. *Shamrock II* gained a few yards but *Columbia* prevailed, crossing the line about two boat-lengths ahead. A cannon
shot, fired from the deck of the committee boat, *Navigator*, signaled the
victory for *Columbia*.

On the steamboat *Chapin*, which was packed with members of the

New York Yacht Club, rich men hugged and swung their wives around with such wild abandon that hats were crushed and binoculars flew in the air. On an upper deck, a group of young men joined hands and danced in a circle. In the dining room a startled waiter dumped a bowl of chowder down a passenger's back.

Not far from the *Chapin*, Thomas Lipton still occupied the bridge of the *Erin*, where he had stood for the entire race. From the look on his face, his guests might have imagined that *Shamrock II* had won.

"Wasn't it a beauty," he said as he descended to the main deck. "I never expect to see a greater yacht race in my life." Satisfied that his boat and his men had sailed as well as they possibly could, Lipton insisted that with just a little more breeze, his challenger would prevail. "Give us a twelve-knot wind or more and the *Shamrock* will win."

The race had been the third-closest in cup history and one of the best ever sailed in American waters. It so excited the spectators that many of the steamers and tugs engaged in a race back to the port. Across the Atlantic, British fans took heart from *Shamrock II*'s performance, and they grew even more enthusiastic when the next heat was called, for lack of time, with Lipton's boat in the lead. The hope would not last. In the next race, under brisk conditions that were supposed to be perfect for the challenger, *Columbia* trounced *Shamrock II*, crossing the finish a full three and a half minutes ahead. The New Yorkers aboard the *Chapin* concluded, and rightly so, that Lipton and his racer could not beat *Columbia*. But the victory was not met with complete joy, as they had been traumatized when a crewman fell off a nearby vessel and drowned before their eyes.

Columbia completed the sweep the very next day. (Although *Shamrock II* crossed the finish first, she had been penalized for an early start.) Most of the credit went to Captain Barr, who, in the words of the yachting expert W. P. Stephens, "took chances that would have been dangerous in the extreme for an average good skipper." One member of the New York Yacht Club who had hoped for Lipton to win one race—"for he is such a good fellow"—blamed Sycamore for failing to "understand the vagaries of this American breeze."

In the wake of defeat a few of the people aboard *Erin* raised doubts about the timekeepers, suggesting that perhaps the finish had been misjudged. Lipton refused to hear it. He turned to the many members of the New York Yacht Club who were aboard the *Erin* and said, "I have a feeling in my heart that if there was an error of judgment it would be in my favor. I have an idea those fellows would give me a race if there was the slightest closeness."

Instead of lodging a protest, Lipton ordered his crew to fly an American flag and steer *Erin* toward the *Columbia*. When the two vessels were close, he took a megaphone to the bridge and shouted, "*Columbia* ahoy! Three cheers for the *Columbia!*" He then turned to his guests and led them in three hurrahs. The large crew on the winning boat, fifty-odd men in white and a handful of officers in blue, answered with cheers for Lipton.

When he returned to the main cabin of the *Erin*, Lipton finally allowed his disappointment to show. The huge cost of *Shamrock II*'s design and construction and the expense of the race—$2,000 per day for more than a month's time—had been just part of his investment in the pursuit of the cup. But he had also poured his heart into the effort. Yes, he loved America, and New York was a second home. And yes, the races had put his name, and therefore his products, on the front pages for millions to see day after day. Nevertheless, he wanted to win, and every one of the half a million spectators who had attended the competition knew this was true.

"I would have liked to win one race as a kind of consolation and relief," he confessed. "It is a hard thing to see your boat, after racing for

nearly forty miles of water, beaten at the last by a few beats of a pulse. . . .
This has been a severe strain. I won't deny it. I felt it because I worked
so hard to win." Lipton's voice cracked, and he was unable to speak. In
the silence, one of the New Yorkers said he believed "that if a vote were
taken among the members of the New York Yacht Club they would give
you the cup."

Another member of the club, a banker, recalled the bitter feelings
caused by Lord Dunraven and reminded the crowd that Lipton had
"won our hearts" and "the hearts of the American common people." He
had done more to improve diplomatic relations "than any other man in
England or America," said banker Samuel Jarvis. "No greater sportsman
has ever been born, and he is a greater diplomat than sportsman."

An emotional Lipton grasped the hands of the men around him.
The crowd grew quiet, and more than a few of his American friends
considered the man in the yachting outfit, his shoulders slumped and
his face downcast, and quietly concluded that Sir Tea had made his last
challenge.

ELEVEN

Injured by a Tea Rose

New York next saw a trophy-obsessed Sir Thomas on July 4, 1902. This time his yacht was called *Hibernia* and in a shocking turn of events the cup challenge was disrupted by a plot to sabotage the American defender. The character behind the scheme was an Englishman named Ivory D. Queers who worked for a British betting syndicate. The crime was averted by a plucky New York heiress and her young suitor who had come to America as a member of *Hibernia*'s crew. The episode cast a harsh light on elite society and the world of high-stakes yacht racing. And if it hadn't occurred on the stage of the Herald Square Theatre, it might have damaged Anglo-American relations more than Lord Dunraven's temper.

Billed as a "nautico-musical," the play, called *The Defender*, starred Harry Davenport in the role of Sir Thomas Ceylon Teaton. Scion of a grand old theater family, Davenport was a master of makeup who made himself look, sound, and move like the real Lipton. The play attracted many prominent patrons, including two Boer generals on a post-surrender tour, and it entertained big crowds—thanks in part to a booming economy—until it closed to make way for the autumn offerings

at the theater. Harry Davenport would perform in plays and films—
including *Gone With the Wind*—for nearly fifty more years.

The appearance of Sir Teaton on the boards at the Herald Square
Theatre confirmed the degree to which Lipton had been embraced by
America as a popular personality. After the second cup challenge, he
received similar attention in Great Britain, where newspapers and magazines competed to tell his story. A writer for *Windsor* magazine followed him around his City Road office and then visited Osidge, where
he discovered tea being served in the tree house. He listened patiently
as Lipton repeated his recipe for success—hard work, perseverance,
honesty, advertising, good humor—and dutifully reported that Sir Tea
was a great "self-made" man who had thrived in a fair but cruel world
that rewarded only the fittest of the species.

The article in *Windsor* reflected the general view of Lipton as a happy
merchant prince with a remarkable slum-to-society biography. Talk of
additional royal honors circulated in London and once again Fleet
Street speculated on the possibility that King Edward might press for
his nomination to the Royal Yacht Squadron. The RYS would remain
out of reach. (Some members threatened to resign and form a new club
if the king pressed the matter.) But Lipton would find acceptance
among many in the Edwardian elite. One society columnist wrote:

> For about the thousandth time I have heard the complaint
> "What a pity that the King should take up with a grocer
> like Lipton simply because he has made money." But the
> fact is that Lipton is not merely a man who has made
> money. He is a clever man, has traveled much, has seen
> men and manners in many countries. . . . He conducts
> himself as one sure of his equality with everyone without

ever putting off his respect for the Crown. That is a rare
gift and . . . an infallible passport to bored royalties.

Anyone who would be the often bored king's friend faced the difficult challenge of the man's temperament. Edward was perhaps the most
open-minded monarch in British history. He was interested in all sorts
of people and pursued life's physical pleasures—sex, food, drink, sport—
with an earthy kind of gusto and in defiance of those who disapproved,
including his own son, George. He was, as much as a king could be, a
man of the people. He sought to improve the welfare of his subjects and
believed that democracy would soon make the Crown obsolete.

However, as informal as he might be, Edward could and did exploit
his rank in his personal relationships. Alexandra, adored by the public
for her beauty and charity, had no choice but to accept his philander-
ing. And in a similar way, certain friends were required to accept a bit
of humiliation if they wanted to remain in his circle. One of Edward's
abusive habits surely stemmed from his own childhood experience with
a schoolhouse bully who had dumped red ink on his head. As king,
Edward played the tormentor's role by occasionally pouring brandy
down a wealthy friend's neck. The man, a member of Parliament named
Christopher Sykes, would accept the embarrassment and say, "As your
Royal Highness pleases." The little scene, repeated from time to time,
was funny to some, but it was also pathetic.

Sykes, who squandered his fortune playing host to the king during
lavish weekends at his country estate, was just one of a number of social
friends whom he treated as well-polished buffoons. Lipton fit into a second category of crony, which was comprised of charming but accomplished men of wealth and power whom the king treated with steady
respect. Since Edward would often summon his playmates on short

notice, these friendships could be demanding in their own way. Lipton was able to respond more readily because he was unattached. Whether the day called for a hunt, the races, or a weekend at Balmoral, Lipton was generally available.

When Edward's coronation approached, in the late spring of 1902, Lipton was trusted with managing a banquet for half a million poor and working-class Britons. The United Kingdom's victory in the Boer War, which resulted in new colonies in southern Africa, heightened the sense of excitement in London, but plans were set aside when the king was stricken with appendicitis. Lipton was at Buckingham Palace on the day Edward underwent a dangerous surgery that would turn out well. The very next day his name was included in the list of those granted coronation honors. Sir Thomas had been made a peer, albeit one with the low rank of a baronetcy. His award was announced along with those granted to the scientist Lord Kelvin, the writer Arthur Conan Doyle, and one of Edward's surgeons, Lord Lister, who revolutionized medicine with his promotion of antiseptics.

When Edward was formally crowned, on August 9, Lipton attended the ceremony at Westminster Abbey along with such other special guests as Sarah Bernhardt and Mrs. George Keppel. Money made it possible for Lipton to keep up with the Marlborough set, and this included matching the king's interests—horse racing, yachting, and the new craze of motoring. By 1902, sputtering, gasoline-powered automobiles were slowly replacing horses on the streets of London, and the trend was led by Lipton's rich and titled friends. On weekends, Edward roared around the countryside in his Coventry-built Daimler, shouting, "Faster! Faster!" as his driver dodged horses, dogs, and the rocks thrown by boys who surely didn't know just who occupied the car.

Sir Thomas bought his own Daimler in July 1902 and began driving it on his commute from Osidge to City Road. In August he joined the fashionable elite who made headlines when they wrecked their cars. He was speeding to the office with his assistant, John Westwood, and another employee when the car's tires slipped on streetcar rails in the district of Wood Green. The Daimler was destroyed, along with portions of the iron railing that it hit, but no one was injured. Lipton immediately bought another car and resumed a career of reckless driving that earned him countless fines and, once, a short stay in a French jail.

France was the cradle of automobile racing, which started in Paris but quickly spread to Great Britain, where the gentry competed on tracks cleared on their estates. Many rich Americans, including Albert Bostwick and William K. Vanderbilt, traveled to Europe to buy and race cars that they later brought to the States. By 1902 the *Washington Post* considered the rapid growth in auto races and declared that no sport "has ever enlisted so much power and money." These contests of endurance and speed spurred the development of better vehicles in the same way that races on the water had played a role in the development of maritime technology. Although early car races stoked class resentment, dropping prices meant cars and trucks clearly represented the future for all kinds of transport, and both business and government rushed to put them to use.

And, just like steel and steam power, the rise of the automobile changed the way people imagined the modern world. Within days of Lipton's crash in Wood Green, an American tourist named Dudley H. Fanning drove a car into the courtyard of London's Hotel Cecil, which was then the largest anywhere. He parked the car abruptly, hopped out, and announced he was Jesus Christ newly arrived from heaven thanks to his fancy machine. He toured the court and the lobby, shaking hands with everyone he met. Fanning, who also claimed to own all the yachts in the world, wound up before the city's Lunacy Commission.

D. H. Fanning may have been a lunatic—no official diagnosis was ever published—but his fixation on automobiles and yachts showed he was attuned to his time. Science and technology were moving forward, and the changes they wrought were seen first in the upper classes. Rich men were turning toward motor power and, though they still loved their boats, away from sails. Like so many emblems of class and conspicuous consumption (a term coined by social critic Thorstein Veblen) that marked the Gilded Age, the appeal of the great yacht races that had once transfixed the world was beginning to fade.

Appearing in 1899, Veblen's book *The Theory of the Leisure Class* had finally named and explained the economic and social dynamics that began with the Industrial Revolution and reached a peak in the 1890s. In these years, which coincided with Lipton's lifetime, roughly half the wealth in America, and an even greater proportion in Great Britain, had been concentrated in the hands of one percent of the population. The very rich came to control far more money than they could possibly spend in any reasonable way, so they indulged in outrageous luxuries, including yachts built with no purpose other than to win a single race and cars that could be smashed to pieces and replaced the next day.

Veblen's analysis intrigued intellectuals but years would pass before resentment for monopolists, robber barons, and other extreme capitalists would force the rich to be more restrained and discreet. Seen as one of their own, Lipton would never face the scorn of the working class. He was free to surprise the New York Yacht Club with yet another challenge for the America's Cup. As he renewed his quest he told the New Yorkers he hoped they wouldn't consider him "unduly covetous of the precious trophy"; he was, however, still quite obsessed with taking it from them.

Some members of the New York Yacht Club *did* think that Lipton was "overly covetous." His continual challenges had forced them into a hugely expensive competition that might benefit the business of a tea merchant—every Lipton boat was a giant advertisement—but brought absolutely no financial reward to them. To make matters worse, every time he crossed the Atlantic, Lipton's popularity increased as he made everyone else, by comparison, look somehow less gracious. In the shadow of his personality, men like C. Oliver Iselin, who would once again manage the defense, all but disappeared from view.

Few men could have been more different from Lipton than Iselin. Born the heir of an enormous family fortune, he had increased his wealth not through labor but through marriage. He was an intensely private person who avoided the press and bristled at criticism. Iselin found Lipton an annoyance, and he wanted to thrash Sir Tea so thoroughly that he would go away for a good long while. This could be accomplished, he believed, with a reinstatement of the rule that required that a challenger's vessel be sturdy enough to survive an ocean crossing under tow. This simple requirement would make it almost impossible for a designer to match the speed of the American defender, which could be built for the sole purpose of skimming across the summer sea off Sandy Hook in a handful of races.

Iselin began his campaign with an appeal to his club's members— investors, steel men, oilmen, railroad men, and bankers—who immediately contributed $300,000 (nearly $7.5 million in 2010) just to get a boat started. These men understood that more money would be needed later, and were prepared to give it. The managing partner then contacted the Herreshoff company to arrange for design and construction. To Iselin's surprise, Captain Nat declined.

After observing that he had been in the America's Cup business for almost ten years and had reached the age of fifty-four—"quite a little older than you are"—Nathanael Herreshoff told Iselin that he was sure that his "best years for such work have passed." He suggested that younger hands and minds take up the task and closed his reply with the words: "Believe me. Most Sincerely Yours."

Herreshoff had plenty of reasons, besides age, to reject the commission. His ego had been bruised during the previous cup defense when his new boat *Constitution* was unceremoniously sidelined by *Columbia*. His shop was overwhelmed with orders. His wife was not well, and he fought his own daily battle with rheumatism. Iselin knew all this and yet believed he could change the Wizard's mind. The job would require months of correspondence, but by the time Lipton's formal challenge came, via the Royal Ulster Yacht Club, Iselin succeeded. Herreshoff agreed to again battle Lipton.

Once Herreshoff made the commitment, he threw himself into the task of building the most extreme yacht he could imagine. The defender would be a true Bristol craft, a descendant of all the great boats that had been launched at the yard. But Herreshoff had learned a few things from Lawson's big scow *Independence*, which had been sent from Boston to challenge him in 1901. He had also developed some new insights into materials and hydrodynamics. This new racer, to be called *Reliance*, would be bigger than any previous cup entry and carry a huge amount of sail. He hoped that under full sail she would practically leap out of the sea.

The plan for *Reliance* excited members of the New York Yacht Club and gave them hope that Iselin might succeed in his pursuit of a decisive sweep of the races. After such a victory, noted club secretary George Cormack, "I am sure we will be left in peace and quiet for some time."

Having failed first with William Fife and then with George Lennox Watson, Lipton involved both of his country's greatest yacht designers in his third challenger, and relied again on the Denny yard in

Dumbarton to build her. As Fife took the lead in developing the plans, Watson returned to the testing tank and labored to find mathematical answers to every flaw he observed as the water flowed over his wax models. Together he and Fife came up with a vessel that looked like a sleek traditional British yacht but borrowed bits of American technology to save weight and improve performance. The most notable among these insinuations was an actual wheel for steering. Although Americans had relied on wheels for decades, every previous British challenger had been steered with an old-fashioned tiller.

When *Shamrock III* was launched in March 1903, Lipton confessed she might be his "last shot at lifting the America's Cup." He added, "The *Reliance* may beat us but it will not be because I have not got the best boat British brains and workmen can produce. If the cup stays in America it will stay there because of the extraordinary genius of the American boat builder. If he can produce a still further improvement in his art, I shall begin to think he is a bit more than human."

A few weeks later in New York, rich men who hoped this challenge would be Sir Thomas's last departed for Bristol, where they would witness the launch of *Reliance*. The yacht that they saw glide down the ways was a beautiful giant with a shiny bronze hull that glowed with the luster of gold. Like *Shamrock III*, *Reliance* would ride at her mooring on a waterline—the length of the hull actually in contact with the water—within the ninety-foot limit set by the rules. But thanks to Herreshoff's design, big overhangs gave her a total length of more than 143 feet. Her mast reached almost two hundred feet, and her boom, which would swing across the deck with every major tack, was even longer.

In all, the monster *Reliance* could spread more than sixteen thousand square feet of sail, which was considerably more than any modern cup racer had deployed. After she was launched she won eight out of nine trial races against *Columbia* and *Constitution* and proved to be superior in every sort of sea. Although she suffered a few malfunctions, the tests showed she was the most intimidating defender that had ever been built for the America's Cup contest.

While the Americans tuned up *Reliance*, the cup challenger, *Shamrock III*, was raced against the original *Shamrock* in the waters off Weymouth, in southeast England. Under the command of Captain Robert Wringe the new yacht reeled off three quick wins. Further trials produced more mixed results when the older boat was given time allowances. In one contest, when *Shamrock I* prevailed, the experts decided it was due to fluky winds. In the very next heat Lipton went aboard *Shamrock III* for the race, taking a position on the deck where he would not interfere with the crew.

A strong cold wind accompanied the sun on the morning of April 17. *Shamrock III* crossed the starting line flying a jib and foresail. The hull rose and fell on the swells of the sea, and the speeding yacht's bow occasionally dipped into the water, sending spray raining onto the deck. As Wringe shouted orders, Lipton sent a crewman named William Collier below to fetch some binoculars. When Collier returned, he handed the glasses to Lipton and moved to take a position on deck. With the boat heeling to port and water covering the deck on that side, the captain directed a tack to starboard. Suddenly a gust of wind shocked the sails and the mast overhead seemed to explode at a point just seven feet above the deck.

For a moment the sound, like a bomb going off, seemed to freeze the crew and even the yacht itself. The illusion was broken as the steel mast, blocks, cables, and sails crashed down. As crewmen dodged the debris, Lipton's hand was struck by something that left him with a bruising injury. The blow sent him tumbling down the hatch and he thought that his yacht was sinking. Billie Collier was swept off the deck, and a fellow crewman who saw him in the water dove in to try to save him.

As soon as the boat was stabilized, everyone aboard checked for casualties. Besides Lipton, whose hand was not broken, the wounded included a man with a head laceration and another with a leg injury. Rescue dinghies were lowered from *Erin* but a thorough search of the water around *Shamrock III* failed to turn up Collier. Sir Thomas, shaken by the catastrophe, stayed on the yacht as barges arrived to recover the mast and other equipment. He remained until the work, some of which required divers to plunge into the cold sea, was finished. He reached the shore in late afternoon and told reporters about the accident—a failed wire splice was to blame—and about Billie Collier, who was Captain Wringe's brother-in-law and a veteran of the two previous cup challenges. A distraught Lipton said his only "lasting regret" would be "the loss of the man."

King Edward sent condolences to William Collier's widow and child and to his friend Lipton, who compensated the family financially. (Billie's body would not be found until May 24, when it was discovered off the Isle of Portland.) Repairs to *Shamrock III* would cost about $25,000 but she was quickly readied to cross the Atlantic. She began the journey, towed by the *Erin*, on May 28. Her sparring partner, *Shamrock I*, also made the trip. She was pulled along by an oceangoing tug. In all, the flotilla required 170 crewmen. Lipton, accompanied by his secretary and press agent, John Westwood, followed on the White Star Line's steam-powered palace, *Oceanic*.

In Lipton's departing wake, the magazine *Punch* honored him with a playful report titled "The Bart.'s Progress, or Lipton Day by Day," ("Bart." being the standard abbreviation for "Baronet"). Written to suggest that it was a record of his activities in America, the piece began by noting that when he arrived in New York, Lipton was welcomed with a torchlight procession and then presided over a parade of carriages covered with flowers. Final entry for the day: "Sir Thomas injured by tea rose."

On his second day in America, according to *Punch*, Lipton won a walking race from Wall Street to Washington, where he dined with the president and painted the White House red. After these achievements, Lipton drove a locomotive to Chicago, saved a few lives, was kissed by twenty ladies, invented a "skirt for yachtswomen," and lent his name to a new Sousa march.

Amid all this activity, the magazine reported, poor *Shamrock III* sank at her mooring, rose like Lazarus, and was stolen in the dark of night. Sherlock Holmes, the New York police, and Pinkerton detectives all searched before the yacht was found in a dry dock. In response, a much-relieved Sir Thomas Lipton "gives a champagne lunch on the *Erin* and receives cable of congratulations from the German Emperor. Preliminaries to race concluded."

With this gentle satire, the editors at *Punch* placed Lipton the sportsman, millionaire, and socialite in a new category: charming eccentric. In a time when the rich and powerful—including the royal family—were under increasing scrutiny from social critics and politicians, this treatment was a boon to Lipton. In general, Britons reserved a safe place in their hearts for oddballs and self-promoters who could amuse and sometimes serve their fellow citizens. As long as Sir Thomas qualified for this kind of gentle ribbing, his positive public image was secure.

O n the morning of June 24, 1903, the *Oceanic* entered New York harbor flying Thomas Lipton's yachting flag—a green shamrock on a field of gold—from its mizzenmast. The usual Lipton welcoming committee of dignitaries, magnates, and yachtsmen was augmented by President Roosevelt's adjutant general, Henry Corbin, who had traveled from Washington the previous day. Joined by a gaggle of reporters and photographers, they sailed out to meet the ship while it was held for quarantine.

The liner rode so high in the water that the greeters and the pressmen were out of breath when they finished climbing up to the main deck. Still tall and broad-shouldered at age fifty-five, Thomas Lipton met the "boys," as he called them, with his typical exuberance. When he removed his yachting cap he revealed a bit less hair than he sported on previous visits. But his eyes still twinkled, and his voice, with its Scotch-Irish brogue, was still strong.

After greeting Lipton a few of the journalists split from the group to look for J. P. Morgan, who had also crossed on the *Oceanic*. Morgan recoiled when the newsmen found him. He refused to be interviewed and grew angry at photographers who pestered him like mosquitoes. Eventually the ship's purser intervened and got the newsmen to leave with a threat to ban all cameras from the ship.

While Morgan and the purser batted away photographers, the Lipton welcoming committee convened in *Oceanic*'s saloon. An exhausted General Corbin wiped his brow, declared, "This is worse than automobiling," and then invited Lipton to lunch at the White House. During the toasting and singing that followed, Sir Thomas was declared "a typical American" and a "great big, whole-souled, good-hearted fellow." The applause, as he stood to speak, lasted for more than two minutes.

After a night's sleep, Lipton and his designer Fife traveled by train to Washington. At one p.m. on June 26 they arrived at the White House and were ushered into the state dining room, where a single large table was set for ten—a group including General Corbin, a New York Yacht Club official, and the powerful United States senator from Ohio, Mark Hanna.

Since the men had all met before, they required no introductions, and the casual nature of the event meant no formal speeches were given. When the meal was served, the president was flanked by Lipton on his right and William Fife on his left. Just what transpired between the men is lost to history. No official record of the encounter was issued; however, Roosevelt and Lipton came from such different backgrounds and perspectives that it's not hard to imagine awkward moments.

Roosevelt was, after all, the product of great wealth, privilege, and formal education. He considered himself a man of great character who was skeptical of extreme capitalism and devoted to the ideal of a public good. He was also an exuberant polymath who feasted on history, current events, and literature. By contrast, Lipton was a son of the Gorbals with limited schooling who could tell great stories of personal adventure but almost never spoke about politics or world affairs. Although he was quietly engaged with a limited number of political issues—the cause of Ireland and the care of his nation's poor—he didn't dwell on these matters. Instead, he came across as a merely sociable Gilded Age man of manners, and as future events suggest, this airy quality may well have tried the president's patience.

When his White House visit was over, Lipton would report only that the reception was warm and the lunch included ices shaped like sailboats and decorated with the flags of the United States and Great Britain. The meeting went well enough that the president invited Lipton to join him on the USS *Mayflower*, the Clyde-built presidential yacht, during a prerace naval review in Oyster Bay. In the weeks between, Lipton raced around the country in an imitation of the "Bart." whose progress was described by *Punch*. Lipton's British aide, John Westwood, who accompanied him always, kept the press informed as his boss engaged in an endless variety of stunts intended to burnish his fame.

Although most of his efforts at self-promotion were focused on New York and the cup race, Lipton made time for a whistle-stop tour from the Lehigh Valley to the Canadian border. Wherever crowds gathered at a station, Lipton hopped onto the locomotive as it slowed on its approach. Always there was a small speech and a joke. He tossed carnations in Bethlehem and kissed babies in Buffalo. Many of those who didn't get a kiss or a flower received one of the aluminum rivets that Lipton had brought from the Denny shipyard to give away as souvenirs.

In New York, Westwood and Barrie made sure reporters knew their boss would attend the new smash play *The Wizard of Oz* at the Majestic Theatre. A big press contingent accompanied him that night and saw that Lipton was met by such a mob of well-wishers that the police were called to rescue him in time for the curtain. The play, which featured Munchkins, brilliant scenery, and a scarecrow come to life, was the talk of the city. Every night the ingénue Lotta Faust—playing the wizard's girlfriend, Trixie Tryfle—provoked roars of laughter by singing the most popular tune in the production, a highly suggestive love song called "Sammy," while staring at the shyest man in the audience. When he attended, Lipton found himself in the "Sammy seat," and Faust adapted the lyrics for the moment.

> *Tommy, Oh! Oh! Oh! Tommy*
> *When you come wooing*
> *There's something doing*
> *Around my heart.*

"Lipton! Lipton!" shouted people in the audience as Sir Thomas turned red and beamed a smile. After the performance ended, Lipton lingered with the "boys" of the press as the audience departed. The reporters and photographers followed him to the stage, where the cast awaited. Lipton playfully demanded the newsmen "take a back row now, for I'm interested in the women." A moment later more than twenty showgirls lined up to kiss him, one by one. When the bussing was over, Lipton met the Cowardly Lion and the Tin Man. His night ended with a quick tour of the new subway station at nearby Columbus Circle, which was nearing completion. (The city's first underground transit line, running from City Hall toward the Bronx, would open the following year.)

With the subway nearly completed and many other great projects under way, including the Flatiron Building and the Williamsburg Bridge, New York was fast becoming the most exciting city in the world. Only London had more people, but with immigrants arriving daily, New York was clearly destined to reach the top spot. As usual, the approach of the America's Cup races added to the energy in the city. Thousands of tourists arrived by train from around the country and more came by ship from overseas. In the last days before the first race a dozen revenue cutters, enlisted to patrol the course, assembled in the harbor along with scores of excursion ships that would ferry spectators to the course.

On Long Island, the presidential yacht, *Mayflower*, was anchored in Oyster Bay, where Theodore Roosevelt would host a party to review a parade of the North Atlantic Fleet. Thomas Lipton was in the party, which also included Admiral Dewey and naval attachés from Great Britain, Germany, Russia, and Japan. (Soon the Japanese would commence a war on Russian outposts in the Far East, which Roosevelt would help end through negotiations that would win him the Nobel Peace Prize.)

The Oyster Bay review of modern warships was bigger and more impressive than the parade that had welcomed Dewey home in 1899 and clearly demonstrated America's naval power. (Although the United States had not yet matched the British Empire as a global leader, it was quickly approaching parity when it came to military and industrial might.) The maneuvers in Oyster Bay ended with a carefully planned display by five destroyers that gathered outside the bay and then sped, in close formation, directly toward the president's yacht. Black smoke poured out of the stacks of the destroyers as they reached a speed of twenty-two knots and held to a wedge formation with just a few feet of open water between them.

Roosevelt's guests watched with some excitement as the destroyers, which rode low in the water, bore down on them. Then, as the ships reached a point roughly one mile away, a mechanical problem caused a collision. A few of the women on the *Mayflower* screamed as the destroyer *Dale* struck her sister ship, *Decatur*. Fast thinking and sharp orders prevented an even bigger disaster, and the spectators were relieved to see the speeding warships separate successfully. Neither the *Dale* nor the *Decatur* was disabled, and no injuries were reported. The president said, "Good, good, well done!" Lipton, overlooking the mishap, praised the U.S. Navy and said the fleet seemed ready to fight.

Coming after a dramatic naval accident, a Broadway spectacular, and a seemingly infinite number of toasts and songs, the actual racing was a terrible anticlimax. An August heat wave descended on the region, sending temperatures into the nineties and stifling everything that might move, including the wind. Although conditions suggested the race would be canceled, Lipton went ahead with his usual race-day celebration. Roughly two hundred guests dressed in summer finery were received aboard the *Erin*. He was attired in his usual sailing costume—blazer, white pants, floppy spotted bow tie, and captain's cap. Everyone had a splendid time even though this first attempt at a race was canceled.

The next day, a Saturday, brought huge crowds to the docks and piers from New Jersey to New York and Long Island. They came wearing Shamrock pins and waving little American flags and carrying baskets of food and drink. Everyone wanted to see the race, and excursion tickets offered at prices from $3 to $5 became so scarce that scalpers began selling them at several times their face value. City and state inspectors monitored the loading, and protests arose when they decided a ship had reached its capacity and closed a gangway.

But even the disappointed were in high spirits. When the gangway to the *City of Savannah* was closed, one out-of-town gentleman aboard told the crew that a woman he was supposed to escort had not yet arrived. The captain, W. H. Daggett, agreed to wait for fifteen minutes. Soon people on board and many remaining on the dock learned why the ship had not cast off her lines. "Look out for a woman in white!" came the call from the deck, and when she finally huffed and puffed into view she was greeted by so much applause that her cheeks turned red.

Slower ships began to depart for the racecourse at eight a.m., and by nine o'clock the Buttermilk Channel was so crowded it looked like a man could reach Brooklyn from Governors Island by simply walking from deck to deck. The flotilla included deep-water liners, coastal steamers, riverboats, tugboats, barges, fishing boats, and every type of private vessel imaginable. Among the holiday excursion boats, which accommodated 1,500 or more passengers apiece, were many from distant points. Most flew extra flags and pennants. The *Manhattan*, operated by the Maine Steamship Company, was practically covered in red-white-and-blue bunting.

In all, more than fifty thousand people—the largest oceangoing crowd ever assembled for a race—witnessed the first battle of *Reliance* and *Shamrock III*. Captain Barr scored a decisive victory, finishing more than seven minutes ahead of the *Shamrock III*. The second completed race was closer, but *Reliance* still prevailed and made Lipton's ultimate defeat a foregone conclusion. The real excitement of the day came after the finish, as crews secured the racers and excursion ships steamed for their berths.

For more than a week locals and visitors who had sweltered in the awful heat and humidity had prayed for the relief of a cool front that would bring showers, or perhaps some thunderstorms, followed by fresh air. After the second completed race their prayers seemed to be answered when black clouds appeared on the western horizon at about three o'clock. But as the next hour passed and the storm front reached the coast, hope turned to fear.

This was no ordinary wave of thunderstorms. It was a menacing black cloudbank that obliterated the sun as it passed. In Manhattan retail shops, clerks rushed to turn on lights as patrons were cast into darkness. In office buildings, secretaries and errand boys went to the windows to see what was happening. Men on the street ran for shelter from a roaring wind that filled streets and alleys with dust, litter, and shingles torn from buildings. Teamsters struggled to tether horses that suddenly thrashed in their harnesses. Drivers parked their clattering cars and trucks and scrambled for shelter. As they joined others who cowered in saloons and cafés, they gaped in wonder as the driving rain arrived in sheets so thick and black that a man standing at a window couldn't see the building across the street.

For some, escape was impossible. When the heaviest wind and rain arrived, nine ironworkers were trapped at the top of a 180-foot derrick that had been built on a pier to lift and place steel girders for a new railroad bridge across Newark Bay. The workers clung to the timbers and rods of the spindly structure as it swayed violently and men below ran for their lives along the trestle. Those who didn't make it to shore threw themselves down on the tracks and held on tight. Above them, the derrick workers moved to a ladder and began to descend. The crane swayed one last time and then began to topple over. As it fell, five of the men on the ladder were able to let go and throw themselves free and land in the water. The other four went down with the debris and were either killed by blows from pieces of the derrick or drowned.

Meanwhile, out in New York Harbor, yacht-race spectators huddled in steamship cabins and clung to the railings of smaller vessels. Two sisters died when the small sailboat they were in capsized. Other day sailors were rescued from overturned boats as police and revenue service crews responded to distress calls. In the supposed shelter of Sandy Hook, vicious winds tossed big yachts like they were toys in a tub. Two steamers, including one where Captain Barr had sought shelter, dragged their anchors and collided with a coal barge. Determined to prevent further collisions, Barr went out on deck in the howling gale. As his vessel, *Sunbeam*, drifted perilously close to *Shamrock III* he screamed a warning to Lipton's crew. The British racer was spared when the storm suddenly passed.

After the storm, the idea of spending a day on the water lost much of its appeal. On the day of the final race, fewer than a dozen spectator vessels waited at the starting line when the gun was fired. After a clean start, a freshening breeze carried the boats to the outer mark fifteen miles away. *Reliance* made the turn first, with *Shamrock III* a full mile astern. Then a fog bank rolled in and swallowed the yachts whole. As the crews struggled to keep to the course, the excursion boat captains turned their vessels toward the finish line. Crewmen sounded horns and called out in the fog until the steamers reached the lightship, where they then dropped anchor and waited. Lipton, aboard the *Erin*, hoped for a victory but did not expect one. Yachts, like racehorses, rarely improve much from one bout to the next, and Captain Wringe had already convinced Lipton that *Reliance* was the better horse by far. "Barr in *Shamrock III*," he had told Sir Thomas, "could no more beat me in the *Reliance* than I could beat him."

More than two hours passed as the fog grew thicker and visibility dropped below a hundred yards. The few thousand people who remained at the line waiting to see the finish strained to see an oncoming sail. When it arrived, they actually heard it first, flapping with the gusting wind. Then, out of the white mist came *Reliance*, squarely on course and speeding along. She crossed the line four and a half hours after the start. Once the celebration was over, the winner's crew joined the others to await the challenger. After half an hour she came into view, but so far off course that she didn't actually hit the finish line. Discouraged and defeated, skipper Wringe and his men offered their congratulations and turned for Sandy Hook and the tug that would tow their yacht to a mooring.

The Americans had so thoroughly defeated Lipton with Herreshoff's superyacht that the irritated millionaires who had resented the expense of his challenges could hope that he would stay away for a good long time. For his part, Lipton acknowledged the superior performance of the *Reliance*, and of the American effort overall. Britain's two best designers—Fife and Watson—had worked together to create the fastest and most beautiful racer ever sent to challenge for the cup. But still Herreshoff and Barr had prevailed. "I would challenge tomorrow if I thought I had a chance of winning," said Lipton, "but who could design a boat for me?"

After his defeat, Lipton received, once again, more loving attention than the men who had won. Indeed, in the month after his boat won the cup races, Nathanael Herreshoff's name was not mentioned once in *The New York Times*. The managing partner for the cup's defense, C. Oliver Iselin, got a bit more ink, but most of it was for his business dealings and social appearances. His connection to the *Reliance* was noted just four times. By contrast, Lipton made news every single day for almost three weeks running and got his name in the paper a total of forty-three times. Mark Twain, who had watched the races from the yacht of his friend Henry Rogers (the philanthropist who paid for Helen Keller's college education), published a lengthy spoof in the *Herald* in which he analyzed Lipton's failure. Two minutes were lost in one race while a crewman wound his watch, noted Twain. He blamed another defeat on the fact that an anchor had been left at the Waldorf-Astoria.

Even when he was supposedly off duty and relaxing as a regular tourist in New York, Lipton attracted attention. On one such day he managed a quiet morning tour of the fort at Governors Island but was then met by a crowd of five hundred people at the New York Aquarium at Battery Park. Much of this crowd followed as he went inside to inspect moray eels, salmon, angelfish, and a giant turtle. He and the pressing crowd spent extra time at the new manatee exhibit, where the whiskers on the creature inside the tank fairly resembled the drooping mustache on the man outside.

From the aquarium it was on to a Manhattan firehouse, where Lipton admired the equipment and visited the upstairs dormitory. The brass pole which firefighters used to slide down to the ground floor caught Lipton's attention and one of the men quickly demonstrated.

"That looks easy," said Lipton.

"Try it," responded his tour guide, a captain.

Lipton accepted the challenge and managed to glide down after the captain and was applauded on the ground floor.

As Sir Thomas exited the firehouse, he found that the crowd that had followed him from the aquarium was now even bigger. By the time he reached his next stop, the police boat tied up at Pier A on the Hudson River, more than three thousand people were gathered on the dock and in the nearby street. City officials let Lipton prowl all over their vessel while onlookers called out Lipton's name and cheered him. He responded by waving his cap and bowing.

"I never saw anything to beat you Americans," he told his police tour guide. "It seems as if everybody felt it his duty to do something to make me forget the beating you gave me."

If people were determined to console Lipton, it was because they had been primed by daily reports on the gallant man who cheerfully accepted defeat after spending huge amounts of money on his racers. His story, or at least the version of it they knew, offered hope for the little guy—he was born in a slum after all—and showed how a loss could be handled with grace. He was also a true sporting celebrity at a time when there were few in the world. Boxers John L. Sullivan and Gentleman Jim Corbett attracted big followings, but the modern Olympics had been held just twice and no true stars had emerged from the games. Professional baseball had yet to conduct a World Series, and international football (soccer to Americans) was in its infancy. In this moment no sporting event received the universal attention lavished on the America's Cup and as the spirit and force behind the challenge Lipton became its living symbol.

Blessed with charisma in an age before the word was widely used, Lipton always stood tall when he was in public. He smiled and glowed with self-confidence. Just being near when Lipton was "on" brought a person into a warm and happy light. No wonder thousands of people followed him from the police boat back to the Battery, where he climbed aboard a launch that would take him to the *Erin*. Lipton obliged them, standing at the rail on the stern of the boat and waving as they cheered.

In the crowd onshore, people said Lipton was "a brick" and "a true sport." He received more florid praise when a new Anglo-American friendship organization called the Pilgrims Society honored him at a lavish banquet. Many said they wished the challenger had won. General Joseph Wheeler called Lipton "the most prominent and conspicuous individual on the face of the globe" and added that he had "elevated the standard of Anglo-Saxon manhood."

The Pilgrims, who included men from the Astor, Schwab, and Gould branches of American aristocracy, represented a formal attempt to sort out the shifting relationship between America and Great Britain. With their emphasis on a shared cultural and even racial heritage, members drawn from both countries were especially eager to reassure themselves about the balance of power and security.

Although the future belonged to their country, the Americans still deferred to Britain in certain matters, and this was especially true when it came to questions of character and manners. Lipton was, in this light, a bridge between two nations, and two eras. Americans saw him as a friendly, admirable representative of the best Old World traditions. He reassured them that they were the rightful heirs to these traditions and shouldn't fear shouldering the leadership role long carried by the empire.

"You Americans are hard to beat in any line," said Lipton. ". . . I am a very disappointed man. Still it is a consolation to know that the conquerors belong to the same good old race, who are bound to us by the closest ties. The cup is still in the family and is simply held by a more go ahead branch."

From the Anglocentric point of view, Lipton got it about right. America was thought to be founded and populated by "go-ahead" emigrants from the British Isles (and just about every other corner of the world). He certainly believed this analysis and had done everything possible to adopt, translate, and exploit American-style business practices whenever and wherever possible. He was less accurate when he also claimed he had done nothing to earn the attention lavished upon him. In fact, he had shown more skill at cultivating the press and the public than anyone since Buffalo Bill, whose star was fading as Lipton's grew brighter.

Just about the only one who didn't seem interested in Lipton in the weeks after the cup races was one of the few men who could claim greater prominence—Theodore Roosevelt. Ten days after *Shamrock III* was finally defeated, the president declared he had seen and heard enough of Thomas Lipton. To be more precise, Roosevelt refused to appear at the annual dinner of his own Sewanhaka Corinthian Yacht Club if the members insisted on inviting Lipton. As one Washington official explained, Roosevelt had already socialized with Lipton at the White House and aboard the *Mayflower*. And even though the yacht club was located within sight of his home at Sagamore Hill, Roosevelt would not make the short trip to the banquet if he had to deal with Lipton again.

Coming as the rest of America serenaded the great loser Lipton, Roosevelt's objection to meeting him at the yacht club became a front-page controversy. As the press descended on the club's headquarters, members scattered and refused to answer questions. Soon the squabble was being called "The Lipton Episode" and the controversy was known nationwide.

In Buffalo, where he was stopped while on a trip to Chicago, Lipton denied having been invited to the dinner and in the process offered Roosevelt an out. The president seized the opening the next day, insisting that the kerfuffle had been a misunderstanding and adding that he would be delighted to see Lipton at the banquet if he could make it.

By the time the president had backtracked, the chance of Lipton actually appearing in Oyster Bay was nil. A slight stomachache he first reported on the train to Chicago had worsened and he was unable to leave his hotel. Doctors diagnosed appendicitis, but unlike his friend the king, Lipton was able to avoid surgery. While Sir Thomas lay in a hotel bed, the president stood and made a toast to his health at the yacht club banquet. Two weeks would pass before he felt well enough to leave his bed. Days later he summoned reporters so they could see him in good health and hear him claim he was eager to make another cup challenge.

The effort Lipton made to appear healthy and strong after his illness reassured the public that America's best friend was the same game and hearty fellow they always knew him to be. In fact his illness had been severe, requiring ample doses of morphine and a doctor's round-the-clock care. The experience left him chastened, and for the rest of his life Lipton would adhere to a very bland and health-conscious diet that included big servings of rice and limited spices. This serious turn in his habits was matched by growing evidence that he was not always a happy warrior, especially when it came to business.

For example, during his third cup challenge, reporters and yachting enthusiasts noted the glaring absence of Lipton's former promoter and American representative, David Barrie. In the previous year Lipton had sent an executive named H. H. Davies to audit his American operation and the man had reported there were too many employees in the firm. One of them, according to the visiting executive, was the head man,

Barrie. Lipton fired him. For a while Davies seemed the ideal promoter for Lipton, and he even practiced some of his own attention-getting stunts. (On an ocean crossing, Davies played chess by wireless with an opponent on a passing liner.) However, in less than two years H. H. Davies would meet the same fate as Barrie, Lipton accusing him of drawing too much salary. Things got worse for Davies when his fiancée, upon hearing he was suddenly jobless, broke their engagement.

Sudden dismissals became a habit for Lipton, one that would persist for the rest of his life. He also tried to avoid, for himself, any unpleasantness that might attach to these decisions. After a visit to New York, for example, he would reserve his judgments until he was traveling home and then send a wireless message directing his managers to dismiss one employee or another. The same process was followed when Lipton wanted to lodge criticisms or corrections. He preferred to write out his points and his orders rather than confront people face-to-face. But while he avoided conflict, Lipton also deprived himself of information that might have been gathered in direct conversations. Over time, he would grow ever more isolated and suspicious of his employees and subordinates. They, in turn, would come to dread not only his visits, but the days afterward, when painful orders might, or might not, come via telegraph or post.

Fiats issued by wireless and emissaries like H. H. Davies made it possible for Sir Thomas to attend to the job of running the Lipton business while maintaining his visibility as a devoted sportsman and beneficent social figure. As much as Sir Thomas wanted to be seen as an almost carefree man of limitless disposable wealth, the public offering that had made him an international figure also required that he answer to shareholders. In the previous year some had grumbled about the time he devoted to yachting, but business improved enough that such talk quickly subsided. When he returned to London his popularity was so great that some British intellectuals feared that the public obsession with the man and his yacht signaled the end of the empire.

"Which name, we would like to know, has been the more loudly sounded throughout the length and breadth of England, Thomas Lipton or [Boer campaign leader] Gen. Egerton? Was our failure to bring the Mad Mullah to brook in Somaliland to be mentioned in the same breath as the dismal shortcomings of *Shamrock*?"

In fact, Lipton and his racing yachts *were* far better known than Egerton and the British conflict with Dervish fighters led by Mohammed Abdullah Hassan in Somaliland, and this was what worried the editors of *Blackwood's Edinburgh Magazine*, who expressed their concern in a piece titled "A Nation at Play." *Blackwood's* put Lipton at the center of a Roman-style circus of sport that threatened the moral fiber of the empire. Distracted by frivolous pursuits, they wrote, the nation of shopkeepers risked assuming "the less enviable title of a nation of game players."

The call by *Blackwood's* for a more "Puritan" and "ascetic" Britain was more than just a bit of musing about Lipton, *Shamrock*, and the rise of frivolous pursuits. It was also a veiled challenge to the king, the Marlborough set, and the excesses of Edwardian society. More criticism of the king's bohemian taste would come, yet as a ruler he would prove serious and steady in reshaping the British military and the conduct of foreign affairs. Related by blood or marriage to most of the royals on the Continent, Edward was called "the Uncle of Europe," and he would use these relationships to build and strengthen alliances. This work, added to domestic social and education programs created in his reign, made Edward popular and blunted his critics' attacks.

Lipton also took a more serious turn in the Edwardian years. Experience with three *Shamrocks* had taught him that it was almost impossible to build a yacht that could cross the sea but also win against the light and powerful racers that Herreshoff could design with only the cup defense in mind. Although he talked about making another immediate challenge, he chose instead to open negotiations over the rules. The talk would go on for several years, which gave the New Yorkers who had to pay for defense of the cup the relief they had wanted. In the meantime Lipton would deal with more serious and controversial matters than *Blackwood's* editors would have ever anticipated.

TWELVE

Lots of Nerve, Lots of Cash

Convicted of treason, Arthur Lynch, member of Parliament, had escaped the executioner when his sentence was commuted from death by hanging to life in prison. The order to spare Lynch's life came as a relief to his wife, Annie, and his political allies, but they were not satisfied. As the first anniversary of his trial approached, they intensified their campaign for his release. Irish nationalist Michael Davitt, who led the fight, turned to his secret benefactor, Sir Thomas Lipton. In the days before Christmas, Davitt met with Lipton to review the Lynch case and beg him to intervene.

The life story of Arthur Lynch echoed with a scrappy ambition that would have been familiar to Sir Thomas. Born in Australia to an Irish father and Scottish mother, Lynch had gone abroad in his teens. He had worked as a London newspaper correspondent in Paris before *Le Journal* sent him to cover the Boer War. In a short time he joined a group of foreign volunteers called the Second Irish Brigade, who stood with the Boers against the British. A large, handsome man with a powerful command of language, Lynch was a natural leader and became a heroic figure in Irish communities worldwide. He also inspired hundreds of men from Australia, America, and other parts of the world to join the Boer fighters.

The Second Irish Brigade's combat record is to this day a matter for debate. The volunteers generally occupied rear-guard positions in battle, and Lynch served only for a brief time before leaving to write and speak on the Boers' behalf. In late 1901, the voters of Galway elected him their member of Parliament even though he was living in France. He was arrested when he and his wife landed at the English Channel port of New Haven on their way to London, where he intended to claim his seat.

Lynch might have languished in prison if the Boers' cause had attracted less support, but in fact press accounts had turned many world leaders against the British in this fight. The empire's "scorched-earth" tactics and the high death toll in the camps where they held Boer refugees appalled many, including loyal Britons. Against this background, Lynch's actions seemed to be, in part, a matter of conscience. In the United States, Lynch received wide support. Theodore Roosevelt, who met with Michael Davitt to discuss Lynch, expressed great interest in his welfare. Lynch was the one man, out of hundreds, convicted and held in prison for aiding the Boer cause.

In London, Thomas Lipton heard Davitt's review of the Lynch case, which included a report on Roosevelt's stance. Lipton then went directly to the king and argued for Lynch's release. Edward listened and then considered the wealth of opinion about Lynch along with the sentiment of his own people, including the Irish. In a matter of weeks he urged the government's Home Office to let the man go. Lynch was released, but not pardoned, on January 24, 1904. When Lipton and Davitt went to give his wife Annie the news, she fell speechless with joy and kissed Sir Thomas's hand.

As Arthur Lynch walked out of prison, Thomas J. Lipton shared the credit in the world press along with King Edward, President Roosevelt, and Michael Davitt. This event marked Lipton's first open involvement in such weighty public affairs, and the outcome would have a surprisingly positive effect in the long run. Lynch would be pardoned and reelected to Parliament. With the start of World War I, he would urge Irish nationalists to suspend their campaign against the Crown and fight Germany. Ultimately the firebrand would win respect across the political spectrum.

But while Lynch used his second chance to follow a new path, Lipton did not try to build on this one political success. Although his name was often mentioned when elections were called, he ignored every suggestion that he run for Parliament and refused to use his access to King Edward to promote more causes. Other men of great wealth, most notably his fellow Scot Andrew Carnegie, tried to use their money and influence to change the world. Perhaps because he lacked the background, education, or experience to promote a larger cause, Lipton was content to return his focus to the world he knew—business, society, and sport.

Thanks to the many silver Lipton cups he donated to serve as prizes for races, the Lipton name appeared in the papers year-round in connection with sailing regattas, canoe races, and contests between fishing boats. Lipton also kept up a frantic social life, hosting kings, queens, and emperors aboard the *Erin*. The king and Mrs. Keppel joined him aboard the yacht at Cowes. Empress Eugénie used the *Erin* as her personal cruise ship in the Mediterranean.

Service to the monarchs of Europe brought Lipton enough ribbons and medals to make a fine display on the uniforms he wore when required to appear in a ceremonial role as an honorary officer. When these events called for a parade, Lipton was a crowd favorite, as people who recalled his monster cheeses and elephant walks cheered their old friend. But he didn't always make the kind of dramatic impression he left with the citizens of Edinburgh who gathered for a military review at the end of the summer of 1905. As honorary colonel of Glasgow's Second Volunteer Battalion, Lipton was to lead them past the reviewing stand, where King Edward waited to inspect a total of forty thousand other soldiers and sailors.

An experienced rider, Lipton felt comfortable with his assignment. At the very least he knew that he could project the ramrod posture of a military officer and that his ruddy face, white mustache, and bright blue eyes would glow against the backdrop of a dark dress uniform splashed with medals. When a friend in Edinburgh offered him a "very good horse" for the day, Sir Thomas could imagine himself proudly passing in review at the head of a big column. Unfortunately, the horse didn't live up to his billing.

The trouble, as Lipton discovered the moment he climbed into the saddle, was that the horse was not ready for the stresses of parading. Once the men who were assigned to steady the horse and rider let go of the bridle, man and beast bolted. The horse may have been excited by the scene—thousands of people, flapping banners, drums and horns— or he may have been, as Lipton feared, simply never "broken in." Whatever the reason, the horse refused to be steered, stopped, or even slowed as he raced away from the mass of soldiers and into the line of march.

The record of what happened in Edinburgh that day was left by Lipton himself, in his memoir. He would recall bouncing and clattering out of control all the way to the grandstand, where "the king and his nobles and the generals and the admirals, together with the civic representative" were startled to see a fifty-six-year-old merchant, decked out like the very model of a modern major general, struggle to stay in the saddle.

It was at this moment, "as if to celebrate my advent under very peculiar circumstances," that a military marching band began to play, wrote

Lipton. The horse was startled and suddenly planted his feet and stood stock-still, his chest heaving. The steed then turned his head to examine his rider and, Lipton thought, "all the decorations on my chest, including the Grand Order bestowed on me by the King of Italy." Having determined the challenge, he then bucked furiously until Lipton flew into the air and down onto the pavement. He landed on his shoulder and arm. Then he was kicked in the face.

Lipton awakened in a nursing home to learn that he had suffered a concussion. Much improved after a few days of rest, he accepted the king's invitation to Balmoral Castle in the Highlands. (An expanded fifteenth-century estate house, Balmoral was an imposing but also fanciful place built of gray granite. It sported turrets topped with conical spires.) The usual friends were gathered at the royal family's Scottish retreat. As Lipton recalled it, Edward pulled him aside after dinner and said, as he tapped his shoulder, "And now Lipton I am going to bestow upon you a new honor. I promote you to the horse marines."

Although such a troop once existed, the Horse Marines were best known as the fictional and silly outfit described in a nursery rhyme about a "Captain Jenks" who fed his steed on "pork and beans." Always a good sport, Lipton would for the rest of his life tell the story about his accident and the king's appointing him to the Horse Marines. The tale amplified his image as a happy friend of royalty, but it also lent him an air of humility. What better way to connect with the public than a story that makes you the object of playful amusement for a king?

Whether he was dashing about in a ceremonial uniform or getting hauled into court for speeding in his car (he was arrested for knocking over a dog cart in France), Lipton all but roared through his middle years as a bachelor social figure and businessman-adventurer. He raised money for the victims of the *General Slocum* steamboat fire of 1904, and when Vesuvius erupted in 1905, he was there aboard *Erin* and made a sizable donation to the relief fund. He sent $5,000 to San Francisco after the terrible earthquake of 1906, which killed more than 3,000 and left more than 300,000 homeless.

Most of Lipton's donations were publicized, and this amounted to advertising for the Lipton businesses, which kept paying double-digit dividends. This success was due, in part, to ongoing improvements in the life of working-class Americans and Britons, who, except for farm-workers, saw steady growth in their incomes and thus had more money to spend on food and drink.

The American market was also blessed with continued immigration, which meant that a merely competent merchant would automatically do a greater volume of business every year. In Britain, where population growth was much more gradual, the Lipton tea business also benefited from greater per capita consumption—now over two pounds, or six hundred cups, per person annually—which was matched by an even sharper decline in the amount of alcohol people drank. Teetotaler campaigns had something to do with the switch from alcohol to tea, as did the rise in alternatives for discretionary spending. With more varied products and amusement competing for the spare shilling, beer and whiskey captured fewer of them.

Big technological and economic trends allowed Sir Thomas Lipton to lead the firm without devoting the kind of hours he logged when he was a sole proprietor. He kept in touch with the office by telephone, mail, and wire as he traveled frequently to America, where he often spoke of a new cup challenge. The talk kept Lipton in the public eye but failed to produce a formal challenge and a race. The main sticking point was Lipton's desire to compete on more equal terms. This could be accomplished if he were allowed to build his yacht in America or Canada, and thus be spared an ocean crossing, or if the defender were forced to comply with international rules that would favor a solidly built boat like those sent from Great Britain over fragile speed demons like the *Reliance*. The New Yorkers would not budge on these issues and stuck to their traditional standard, which seemed to guarantee that the cup would never leave America.

The impasse over the terms of the cup challenge continued for years but did nothing to diminish Lipton's popularity in the United States. Always eager to praise his hosts and play the role of rich British gentleman, Lipton was continually fêted by business clubs, sporting organizations, mayors, and governors. His mere arrival in a city such as Boston, Milwaukee, or Chicago was an occasion for celebration, and his hosts went to great lengths to outdo one another. For one "beefsteak dinner" in New York, where men ate slabs of meat with their bare hands, businessmen decorated the popular Reisenweber's Cafe on Columbus Circle to look like a garden in Ceylon. Waiters slid down a rope from a trapdoor dressed in sailor suits embroidered with shamrocks and served beer in mugs painted with Lipton's face.

At most of these dinners Sir Thomas entertained with a brief but charming talk full of praise for America and corny jokes. (One of his favorites was about a Scotsman who fights so hard against four muggers in London that they have to knock him out to rob him. When they discover just tuppence in his pocket, one says, "Thank God he didn't have a shilling. He might have killed us.") At more lavish events professional comics amused the crowd with Lipton as their affectionate target. A Broadway parody troupe called the Lambs, for example, roasted Lipton with a skit about his never-ending quest for the cup that ended with the launch of *Shamrock XXIII*. Photos of Lipton published in this period show he was still tall and square-shouldered. While others might look warily at the photographer, he would thrust his hands in his pockets and puff out his chest in a way that stretched the gold watch chain that ran from one vest pocket to another. In every picture he seemed to be enjoying himself more than anyone else.

As Lipton frolicked across America, the system of monopolies and trusts that had made so many of his friends almost incalculably rich came under attack by the Roosevelt administration and its allies. The president had the public on his side, and managed to break up syndicates that stifled competition in railroads, oil, and other industries, but his efforts had little immediate effect on the habits and styles of the rich who made Lipton a fixture at their parties and other events. When William K. Vanderbilt opened a private forty-mile-long auto racecourse on Long Island, Lipton was there. When the Gold Coast set gathered for private horse races in Great Neck, Lipton was there, too. The level of wealth he saw across the country amazed Sir Thomas, who returned to London to speak of a land where everyone seemed to be making piles of money.

Skeptics in Great Britain believed that the American wealth bubble was inflated by market manipulation and hype. Lipton insisted this was "a ridiculous theory. American prosperity," he preached, "is based upon the immense expansion of solid industries, the increased purchasing power of the people, and the legitimate development of agricultural and mining industries while the general confidence is such that nobody is afraid to spend lavishly."

Lipton became so bullish on America that he expanded his New York headquarters, signing a twenty-year lease on a six-story building that stretched along a short block of Hudson Street, not far from the West Side docks. This building would house Lipton's first complete tea-packing plant in America and serve as a base from which to expand his business across the United States. Unlike Lipton Ltd. in the United Kingdom, Thomas J. Lipton & Co. of America remained under his sole control. Every advance he made in the U.S. market added to his personal wealth, which may have had something to do with the amount of time he spent in the States. He was so much identified with the American scene that in 1910 the editorial writers of *The New York Times*, worried about King Edward's isolation, wrote with relief that at least he had regular contact with "Sir Tom Lipton," who "may be regarded as an American" in Britain.

In this period the States also exerted a strong pull on Lipton's friends Tommy Dewar and Harry Lauder. Dewar, like Lipton, focused on business, capturing a big slice of the high-end whiskey market. Lauder, a big vaudeville star in Great Britain, earned $2,250 per week ($52,000 per week in 2010) on his first American tour in 1905. Appearing in a kilt and tam-o'-shanter and carrying a cane made from a branch as crooked as a corkscrew, the round little Lauder offered songs, bits of acting, and jokes that packed every theater he played.

Lauder, like Dewar, would remain Lipton's friend and frequent companion for the rest of his life. Those relationships would help Sir Thomas fill the void that opened with the death of Edward VII on May 6, 1910. Long susceptible to bronchitis, the king came down with pneumonia and died at the age of sixty-eight. With him went the social prominence of the Marlborough set, including Thomas Lipton, and the kind of sporting life Edward adored. In its place, his heir, George V, brought a reserved and serious style to the throne. Less friendly toward Americans and more formal than his father, George would treat Edward's old friend with cordial respect, but they were not to be close.

Although Lipton's social visits to Buckingham Palace and weekends at the royal family's country estates were over, his fame, title, and wealth kept him circulating among lords, ladies, and leaders in business and finance. Kaiser Wilhelm II honored him and J. P. Morgan with a dinner aboard his yacht during the Kiel Regatta. (A Baltic city near the Danish border, Kiel was the home of the German navy.) While everyone else moved stiffly around the emperor, who was in a bad humor, Lipton got him to roar with laughter over some stories from his boyhood in the Gorbals. Years later, the Hapsburg archduke Leopold would write about this night on the Kaiser's yacht and describe diplomats who were stunned by Lipton's ability to make people "feel so much at home." Leopold said that Lipton's personality "could break down all barriers."

Lipton retained an uncanny knack for being present at major events or when news was made. Just two months after Edward's death, for example, Lipton attended a "flying tournament" at the south coastal city of Bournemouth. The main attraction at the event was auto manufacturer C. S. (Charles Stewart) Rolls, who flew a biplane based on a Wright brothers design and had recently made a record-breaking round-trip flight across the English Channel.

Seven years after the Wrights' breakthrough at Kitty Hawk, airplanes were still dangerous and experimental, but like the automobile they represented the future. Lipton, who had once crossed the English Channel by balloon, had been one of the first Britons ever to fly in an airplane. He had been taken aloft by Samuel F. Cody, an American who brought powered flight to the kingdom in 1908. (Cody, who changed his name from Cowdery, to capitalize on Wild Bill's fame, was a dramatic fellow who wore a goatee and a long, tightly twirled mustache that, when combined with his aviator helmet, made him look quite squirrelly.)

At Bournemouth, Lipton, an aero club member and "official observer," joined a grandstand packed with people who watched pilots attempting to land near a target marked on a field. The favorite among the competitors, Rolls thrilled the crowd as he flew past the grandstand, made a turn, and then approached at an angle that put the nose of the plane directly into the wind. A highly focused young man with neat dark hair and a sharply trimmed mustache, Rolls looked like a friendly workman in his blue overalls, not a daredevil. His appealing personality made the disaster that ended his flight all the more wrenching for the witnesses.

It began with a cracking sound as part of his airplane's frame split apart. With Rolls just eighty feet above them, everyone could see him desperately work the controls as the plane's rudders broke and its canvas began to rip. In a matter of seconds the plane was falling, nose first, to the ground, where it crumpled into a pile of wood, wires, cloth, and machinery. The engine exploded just after impact.

Pulled from the wreckage by a doctor, Rolls "showed but a quiver of life," according to one report of the accident, and he did not survive long. After he died, friends surrounded his body to protect it from press photographers.

Of all people, it was Sir Thomas Lipton who was sent to the Bournemouth train station to await Rolls's parents, who were traveling from London to attend the contest. A reporter who accompanied Lipton watched him approach John and Elizabeth Rolls (Lord and Lady Llangattock) when the two forty-five train arrived. "The grave face of Sir Thomas Lipton at once warned them that some serious accident had happened." Lipton broke the news in the privacy of the stationmaster's office.

The death of C. S. Rolls underscored the danger inherent in the hobbies of the dashing rich in the Gilded Age. Yachting, automobiling, and flying all required nerve along with cash, and Lipton possessed both. He was proud of the mishaps he had survived. He was proud, too, of his reputation as a host, and after Edward's death he continued to entertain the old crowd on summer cruises in the Mediterranean. Luxury and frivolity were combined in exquisite fashion on *Erin*, especially when Lipton conducted an elaborately (and ridiculously) costumed shipboard ceremony granting some voyager the freedom of the "borough" of *Erin*. In winter, Lipton's estate at Dambetenne, Ceylon, became a kind of pilgrim's destination for friends with the means to travel the world. There his friends could don pith helmets and watch elephants haul wooden crates with "Lipton" stenciled on their slats.

Dambetenne served as a refuge for Mrs. Keppel after the king's death. Although Alexandra had generously brought her to see Edward as he lay dying, once he passed, La Favorita was no longer welcome at Buckingham Palace. Isolated and overwhelmed with grief, she wrote at the time, "How people can do anything I do not know, for life with all its joys has come full stop, at least for me."

Arriving at Lipton's cottage in November, Mrs. Keppel's party of nine, including her daughter, Violet, stayed for three months. Most days were spent in quiet rest, with nothing more demanding than a picnic in the hills among the flowers and ferns. When they desired a little adventure they toured the tea plantation and famous sites like the ruins at Anuradhapura. A photo safari into the jungle, where they spotted big game, evoked memories of Kingy.

"Monkeys gamboled on a small precarious lawn. Parrots streaked from tree to tree, tiny hummingbirds skimmed huge greedy-looking flowers; I shared a room with a tame snake and a wild governess," wrote Violet, of her stay at Dambetenne.

Among the other visitors who met Lipton in Ceylon were the players, coaches, and managers of two major-league baseball teams who arrived in Colombo in January 1914.

Halfway through a world exhibition tour, the clubs were showing off both the American game itself and one of the first true celebrity athletes of the era, Jim Thorpe, who joined the New York Giants after winning both the pentathlon and decathlon competitions at the 1912 Olympics.

Thorpe's popularity had increased in 1913, when he was stripped of his medals after the press revealed he had once been paid to play minor-league baseball. (Olympic rules allowed amateurs only, but many thought Thorpe had been treated poorly.) Thorpe never excelled on the field with the Giants, but he was a great draw and proved, like Lipton in yacht racing, that a good story could attract fans as well as a good performance.

At the Colombo luncheon Thorpe was one of seventy men who gathered around Lipton at one of the city's grand old hotels and bathed in the aura of an even better-known entertainer and sportsman. Lipton joked about how the America's Cup was homesick for Britain, "where it has not been for sixty years," and he complained that he had to drink his tea from a saucer because he was unable to "lift the cup."

The most reliable record of the baseball banquet was made by John J. McGraw, the Giants' manager. Smart, tough, and demanding—his nickname was Little Napoleon—McGraw became the model of the feisty manager with a soft heart, which made him as much an American archetype as Lipton. In an article published by *The New York Times*, he painted a happy picture of events in Colombo, where, after lunch, five thousand curious onlookers watched the White Sox beat the Giants 4–1.

Given a platform, McGraw couldn't resist adding a dash of his personal politics to his report. As he saw it, many of the people the teams encountered on their tour showed snobby "European habits and social tastes." One of the worst was an American who wore a monocle and "handed out two or three snubs" to the ballplayers. But these effete types were inconsequential in McGraw's eyes, especially when bigger men, like Lipton, were "more sincere and democratic." By this measure, Lipton was admirable, modern, and practically an American.

If Lipton had been a little less American—or perhaps a little less de-tached from his British business responsibilities—he might have avoided the one scandal that ever tarnished his reputation. The crisis had begun to boil even before the baseball teams reached Ceylon, when eight Lipton employees and eight British officers were charged with bribery and corruption. Although it was gradually expanded, the main focus of the case was a garrison on the island of Malta, where the Lipton company supplied food and other items through mess officers and a regimental canteen. The bribes were small, but they were numerous, and the trial suggested a broad culture of corruption in which everyone from officers to cooks expected to be paid by agents for whatever com-pany might want a supply contract.

In the Lipton case, the head of the firm's "Naval and Military De-partment," Archibald Minto, apparently told his men in the field to offer bribes to military men, and to fund them from the commissions they earned on payments from the army. The Lipton representatives were not the first, and certainly not the only, businessmen to use this prac-tice. However, a recently enacted law had focused the legal system on the problem of corruption, and when a disgruntled former Lipton em-ployee named Edward Stratton Sawyer began spilling secrets, prosecu-tors were ready to make arrests. (Included in the evidence Sawyer presented were letters in which Lipton employees complained, "I have given away cash at barracks, when I was compelled to hand it over in a w.c., and once at Fermoy I had to give £5 in the corridors.")

Held on nine days spread out over five months, the trial put Lipton Ltd. in the center of the worst public scandal in many years. It also re-vealed how a corrupt system was reinforced by mutual blackmail. An unhappy cook or supply officer could threaten to make complaints that would end the company's business. Similarly, a Lipton man could with-hold bribes or hint at lodging a complaint with higher-ups. In general the system of mutual threats produced more cooperation than conflict, and the two sides usually worked together to preserve the lucrative status quo. In many cases army officials even helped the Lipton representatives manage their far-flung staff. As Sawyer noted, to the delight of the court-room, a quartermaster once sent him a telegram that said, "Your whole staff drunk. Send a new staff." As Stratton explained, "That was no part of the quartermaster's business, but the telegram was helpful."

The laughter at the Bow Street court betrayed a widely held but never stated assumption about the way the empire operated abroad. Stated most simply, this view held that once a man left the British Isles, he felt himself freed from many of the restraints that governed life at home. In business and play he might indulge almost any appetite as long as he was discreet. Of course the prosecution turned up evidence that the corruption had spread from Malta to posts in Great Britain, but even here the bad behavior was linked to maintaining imperial might and was therefore, somehow, less reprehensible.

This attitude of leniency when it came to foreign military affairs was at work even as the defendants were found guilty and sentenced. No civilian was required to serve any jail time and the maximum fine paid by a civilian was £500. The highest-ranking officer, a colonel, was sen-tenced to six months in prison and lost his pension, but lower-ranking military men were not even fined. In their cases the court found that bribes were traded at posts throughout the empire and the practice was so ingrained that they never even considered that they were committing a crime.

The court was also forgiving of Sir Thomas, who was considered for prosecution but eventually spared. One company director was charged and found guilty, but no evidence ever pointed to the top man's involve-

ment in the bribery scheme. Here again an "Everybody was doing it"
excuse was offered, and the court declared it would be wrong to as-
sume that anyone not charged in the conspiracy was involved. However,
Lipton did not escape unharmed. The criminal case was responsible for
declining revenues, excess legal costs, and an erosion of profits that
caused outrage at the company's annual meeting.

"Shame!" shouted some of the shareholders, as others rose to criticize Sir Thomas and the one member of the board—John Canfield—
who was among the guilty. When a stockholder demanded that the
company refrain from paying the cost of the defense against the charges
many cheered in agreement while Sir Thomas, presiding over the raucous event, called out, "Order! Order!" and insisted that Canfield had
tried to stop the bribery as soon as he learned of it.

Filled with complaints and demands for executives to be sacked, the
meeting, which took place at Winchester House, a fancy rented hall in
London, confronted Lipton with how far he had come from the days
when he ran the company as a dictator. Dividends had fallen into the
single digits in recent years, and the company's reserves were being de-
pleted. Now a scandal had led to noisy public protest, which Lipton was
required to both acknowledge and address. He earned a little calm when
he promised to find "new blood" for the board of directors, and the
crowd was also placated by the news that Canfield would pay his own
legal bills. But these concessions didn't end the complaints and questions related to the canteen case.

Standing before the crowd of unruly men, Thomas Lipton decided
he had endured enough. With several shareholders still on their feet
demanding to be heard, he called for a vote to close the meeting. Although hardly anyone responded, Lipton announced that his motion
had passed unanimously, declared the meeting over, and walked out.

Lipton Ltd. was so big, and its troubles so public, that the editors of the *Times* of London moved to calm the stock market with a soothing commentary on the company's reorganization, noting that the canteen scandal could turn out to be a "blessing in disguise" because it would require the company to reinvent itself. A well-respected accountant named Robertson Lawson became deputy chairman, and several directors were replaced. Lawson discovered big losses hidden in the firm's books, which were blamed mostly on the departed Mr. Canfield. When added to the loss of Lipton's military contracts, the shortfall exceeded £7 million ($25 million in 2010).

Confronted with this information at a meeting with several directors, Sir Thomas was first shocked and then moved to action. Although competing grocery chains had begun to make inroads in markets Lipton once dominated, he decided that the company would slow its drive for growth, opening far fewer new stores per year. Sir Thomas also pledged to make up for more than half of the shortfall out of his own pocket. This gesture quelled demands for further investigations into the company's finances and operations, but it did not end the firm's troubles. Real stability did not come until Lipton made a second payment, ten months later, which was even greater.

The cash that placed Lipton Ltd. back in the black came from Sir Thomas's personal fortune, which included his own stock—he had never sold a share—and revenues from foreign (mostly American) operations not offered when the company went public. Although his privately held businesses did not publicly report profits, his ability to make these payments offers one indication of their success. In this time he was also able to spend nearly a million dollars to build a new racing yacht, *Shamrock IV*, which he hoped would carry his fourth challenge for the America's Cup.

After more than ten years of stuttering negotiation, the Royal Ulster and the New York clubs had agreed to conditions and Lipton had hired designer/builder Charles E. Nicholson to create what he called "a cup lifter." The result was an odd-looking boat with a round nose and squared-off stern that even Nicholson described as ugly and others called "a nautical crime." Nicholson hoped the hull would perform like a hydroplane, skimming across the water, and in tests the yacht proved very fast. However, the challenge was postponed when the assassination of Archduke Franz Ferdinand in Sarajevo was followed by Austria-Hungary's declaration of war against Serbia, and Europe was quickly thrown into the First World War. In the next four years and four months ordinary life was suspended and war occupied much of the world. In the crisis, Lipton found opportunity both to serve and to restore his own reputation.

Big enough to be considered a small ship, the *Erin* was destined to go to war the moment Britain entered the conflict in August of 1914. In September, Lipton accompanied about one hundred doctors and nurses who sailed on the yacht from Southampton to Le Havre, where they would begin their mission to treat the wounded and dying. In early 1915 he arranged to convert the yacht into a hospital ship for the British Red Cross. Hundreds of thousands of people had been displaced by fighting in Serbia, and the sick and wounded overwhelmed local hospitals. Newspapers in Great Britain and the United States were filled with accounts of the suffering. Before spring, *Erin* was loaded with supplies and, with Sir Thomas aboard, set off for Belgrade.

Although big red crosses had been painted on *Erin*'s gleaming white hull, for much of the voyage the yacht seemed again like a floating palace for partygoers. After a stop at Monte Carlo, the ship went on to Piraeus, where Lipton entertained titled guests from Britain, Russia, and

Greece (King Constantine and Queen Sophie). Days later, however, Lipton was in Belgrade when it was bombarded and barely escaped injury when a shell landed near him. From there his group went overland to the small city of Nis, where they joined with American Red Cross teams treating the wounded and fighting a typhus epidemic fueled by the crush of refugees who had raised the city's population fourfold.

Spread by lice, which thrive in the crowded chaos of war, typhus could be endured by a healthy, well-nourished adult, but in a population weakened by shortages of food and water, it was often fatal. The Lipton group found hospitals overflowing, with three patients to a bed and others lying on piles of straw. Cemetery workers couldn't handle the flow of coffins and bodies that waited in carts to be buried.

While the Red Cross nurses, doctors, and orderlies struggled to stop the spread of lice and save patients strong enough to fight the disease, their sponsor traveled around the countryside in an effort to build Serbian morale. Incongruous as it may have seemed—an aging British raconteur in the ravaged Serbian countryside—Lipton's routine played so well that locals started calling him Tchika Toma (Uncle Thomas), and his jokes were repeated long after he departed. Cheer was one thing Lipton could always deliver.

Travel in the war zone gave Lipton material for letters, published in papers across Britain, in which he pleaded for more aid to Serbia. It also brought him in contact with Dr. James Donnelly, an American whom he had once met in New York. In the town of Gevgeli, Donnelly converted a factory into a hospital. Shells had landed nearby, and Donnelly wondered if his facility might be protected if he flew a large American flag over it. Lipton sent a telegram to the captain on the *Erin*, who promptly brought one to the doctor. When Sir Tea returned three weeks later, he discovered Donnelly had himself died of typhus. The flag covered his coffin when it was buried in a local grave, and Lipton carried out nine letters he had written to his family and friends.

While Lipton returned to London, *Erin* continued to ferry medical supplies from Marseilles to Salonika. When he went on his second personal visit in July, he was startled to see the typhus epidemic was almost extinguished thanks to a large corps of American public-health officers who had fought the spread of disease with mandatory baths for men, women, and children and with the distribution of sterile clothing. When fighting grew more intense, the medical teams Lipton had supported were forced to flee. *Erin* was then commandeered by the Royal Navy.

Equipped with guns and given the name she received when first launched—*Aegusa*—the yacht was manned mainly by Lipton's crew and patrolled the same Mediterranean waters she knew as a host for Europe's social elite. Allied navies and merchant ships were being terrorized by submarines, and on the last day of April 1916, *Aegusa* raced to recover the crew of a torpedoed ship, the *Nasturtium*. (A small, twin-stack minesweeper of the Flower class, the *Nasturtium* had been launched less than four months earlier.) Not long after *Aegusa* arrived in the area, Lipton's beautiful yacht was attacked and also sunk. Six of her veteran crewmen were killed.

Sir Thomas knew the sailors who died and was deeply affected by their loss. He also saw many of Lipton Ltd.'s best men march off to war, never to return. Among his friends, Harry Lauder suffered terribly when his son, an army captain, died in battle three days after Christmas 1916. Lipton, with his vast network of connections, heard of John Lauder's death even before the family had been notified. He figured this out when he telephoned Harry and was met with a cheerful, oblivious hello. Sir Thomas offered an impromptu New Year's greeting and hurried off the call. Later, after Lauder was informed, Lipton consoled him and urged him to get back to performing as soon as possible.

During the war years, Lauder had added a post-performance chat to his nights on stage. "It seemed presumptuous at first," he admitted, but audiences welcomed the chance to have a conversation about serious issues with a man who had seen much of the world. Lipton was present at Lauder's first show following his son's death and wept when Harry spoke to the audience about his loss after the final curtain. For the rest of the war Lauder managed his grief with work, taking a portable piano to the Continent and entertaining thousands of troops.

Lipton also turned to work during the war, spending long days at his City Road office. His attentions helped bring profits back to the point where shareholders once again received a double-digit dividend. (This was no easy feat, given wartime rationing.) He campaigned around the country for contributions to the war effort, including a so-called Tank Bank that funded construction of the new "landships" that were eventually deployed in the thousands and helped hasten the end of the war.

When the Armistice finally arrived on November 11, 1918, Lipton's reputation was restored and the world faced far more serious concerns than an old bribery scandal. Roughly 20 million people, more than half of them civilians, died as a result of fighting, disease, or related causes during World War I. Among them were nearly 1 million Britons and more than 113,000 Americans. Beyond the numbers, survivors were traumatized by the way people had been killed. Poison gas, flamethrowers, and modern machine guns had brought the practice of war to a horrifying new level in which a single battle, like the engagement at Verdun, could grind on for eight months and take 300,000 lives. The relentless and bloody conduct of the war, the longest in modern times, forced people to accept ghastly truths about human nature and the notion of "progress."

In the aftermath of the "war to end all wars," as President Wilson called it, a new order was clearly visible. The Russian, German, Ottoman, and Austro-Hungarian empires were gone, and kings, queens, and emperors were fast becoming obsolete. In America, a genuine Machine Age was at hand as the number of automobiles would exceed 9 million by 1920 (one for every eleven people). Telephones were in even wider use, with thirty-five percent of all households owning one. By comparison, fewer than one in a hundred Britons owned a car in 1920, and fewer than fifteen percent of British homes had a phone. (One commentator dubbed the development of telephone service in Great Britain "a comedy of errors.") With its leap forward in consumerism and technology, America represented the future of global business, and as soon as he could, Thomas J. Lipton returned. He sailed on the Cunard Line's *Aquitania*, which was still technically a troop ship and carried many American soldiers returning from war.

Lipton, who claimed to be sixty-eight but was actually almost seventy-one years old, was a grayer and more stooped figure than New Yorkers recalled. But still a showman and a publicity hound, he had refereed a boxing match on the ship, and he told reporters he had arrived carrying a photo of the martyred Dr. Donnelly's grave, which he intended to give to his widow.

Social obligations would occupy much of Lipton's time as he reacquainted himself with the United States, but he also intended to revive his cup challenge, and to direct the construction of a new headquarters for his American firm. In 1919 a fire had destroyed the Lipton factory and offices in Manhattan. In its place Lipton built an eleven-story office and factory complex across the Hudson River in Hoboken, New Jersey. A modern marvel, the Lipton building was topped by a large red sign—LIPTON—that was clearly visible from Manhattan, and from the deck of every ship that entered the harbor. The building was equipped with a heavy-duty elevator so large that the car carrying the boss to work could actually enter it and be lifted to the top floor. There Sir

Thomas would exit and occupy the only private space (every other office was partitioned with glass) and spend the day issuing orders, reviewing reports, and interrogating his managers.

The American business climate was so good in 1919 that Lipton also opened a second large packaging plant in San Francisco, which would help him dominate the tea business coast to coast. This expansion would be aided by a social development he found quite strange—Prohibition. Certified just two months before he arrived on the *Aquitania*, the Eighteenth Amendment to the U.S. Constitution would outlaw alcohol within a year. Lipton was astonished to find "that the freest people on Earth" had chosen to deny themselves a right that, in his mind, Britons would never give up. But as long as Americans were going to need an alternative beverage, he was happy to sell them his mildly stimulating brew.

Sir Tea was also happy to revive the yacht-racing challenge that had been postponed in 1914. The ungainly-looking *Shamrock IV*, snub-nosed and bulky, had spent the war years dry-docked at the Shewan and Sons shipyard in Brooklyn. When she was returned to the water in the fall of 1919, two hundred people gathered for the event and to show their support for Sir Thomas. An elegant reminder of a happier time before the great and terrible war, Lipton was embraced by New Yorkers who regarded him with nostalgic affection. They cheered the yacht's immersion and declared their heartfelt hope for a Lipton victory. Yes, it was the *America*'s Cup, and nationalism might argue loyalty to the New York Yacht Club, but Sir Thomas was such a charismatic figure that the more he lost, the more people hoped he would one day win.

In the warmth of the moment, a few of the people at the launch focused on the man instead of the boat. They noticed that Sir Thomas was recovering from a cold and asked how he was feeling.

"Oh, improving, thank you," he answered. "The American doctors know how to treat colds. They prescribe a pretty girl's arms around your neck."

"I'm sorry we cannot prescribe the remedy here, Sir Thomas."

"Ah, too many photographers around," he replied with a smile.

It was a playful, not predatory, quip and no one would have taken seriously the notion of an elderly Sir Thomas, with his white hair and old-fashioned floppy bow tie, pursuing romantic adventures. He was, in the public's eye, a happily confirmed bachelor, and his talk of beautiful women was softhearted and never serious. Ever since he left the house he had shared with his friend William Love, Lipton never lived with another soul, and never declared his love for anyone. Approaching the end of his life, Thomas Lipton had become, down to his marrow, Sir Thomas the international bachelor businessman celebrity. He was, if not a walking brand, the best product advertisement in the world. When you bought his wares you bought a bit of his story, and that included escapades with famous friends, adventures around the globe, and fabulously expensive and gallant campaigns for the most coveted trophy in the world.

With every defeat on the water, Lipton had won more American hearts. As his fourth challenge drew near, people across the country sent him letters of encouragement, mascots, and good-luck charms. Rabbit's feet and horseshoes arrived alongside boxes of lucky grasshoppers and tail-wagging Irish setters. People sent four-leaf clovers by the thousands, and a few were actually secreted aboard Lipton's racer before she left the usual mooring site inside Sandy Hook and headed for the starting line for the first race of the 1920 series.

Although thunderstorms were predicted, more than ten thousand people bought tickets and boarded ships that carried them to the course. Thousands more viewed the race from private boats and positions on-shore where they were lucky to catch sight of a sail. The press took advantage of technologies that were either developed or refined during the war. A Navy dirigible, dispatched from the Rockaway Naval Air Station, with a crew of eight and several reporters, hovered over the starting line. Airplanes dodged the clouds to give photographers a view of the scene, and radiomen aboard the U.S. Navy destroyer *Goldsborough* broadcast updates to points ashore, including Times Square, where hundreds of people, many pro-Lipton, gathered to hear the bulletins. The London *Daily Mirror* used the event to debut machines that could scan a picture, send it as a code across telegraph lines, and produce a picture at the other end. For the first time in history, pictures made in New York were published in London with the next day's paper. (Soon "wirephotos" would be commonplace.)

As the pictures showed, Lipton's challenger once again faced a Nathanael Herreshoff defender. Like *Shamrock IV*, the Bristol-built *Resolute* had been launched in 1914. And, like *Shamrock IV*, she measured seventy-five feet at the waterline. But unlike the challenger, *Resolute* was conventionally streamlined and rigged. The rules would require that *Shamrock IV*, equipped to show almost twenty percent more canvas, give *Resolute* extra time—approximately seven minutes—to compensate for the power differential.

The extra time would be a gift for *Resolute*'s skipper, Charles Francis Adams, who was a newcomer to the cup races. Adams replaced Charlie Barr, the legendary sailor who had beaten every other Lipton boat, who had died of a heart attack in 1911 while on a sailing trip in England. Adams's crew was entirely Scandinavian-American. They were challenged by a top British amateur captain named William Burton, whose white hair, mustache, and ramrod spine made him look like a younger Thomas Lipton. He brought with him a crew of his countrymen who had all sailed with him on the famous British racing yacht *Octavia*. Burton also brought his wife, an able sailor who would serve him as a

member of the so-called afterguard that would offer help with key decisions. (Her presence was considered unlucky by many of the crew.)

Burton, who had won fully five hundred races in his long career,
didn't need much of his skill or experience to give Lipton his first victory
off Sandy Hook. At the start of the first race of the series Burton actually
mistimed his approach and had to circle around and cross the line a
second time. *Shamrock IV* trailed *Resolute* by roughly one-third of a mile
as the racers fought through rain showers and approached the halfway
mark in the thirty-mile race. Aboard the steam yacht *Victoria*, which
Lipton had rented for the challenge, he seemed reconciled to another
defeat. Then suddenly disaster struck the *Resolute* as the halyard that
raised its mainsail broke. This break set off a cascade of events that left
the yacht unable to raise most of its canvas.

The disaster on *Resolute* all but stopped her in the water, and *Shamrock IV* quickly closed the distance and then passed. Captain Burton and
his men considered halting the race, as a show of sportsmanship, but
as one officer of the afterguard argued, the design, construction, and
maintenance of the yachts was part of the competition. The original
Shamrock had lost a race due to mechanical failure in 1899. There was
no shame in winning one now on the same basis. The challenger went
on to finish alone and notch the first British win since 1871. Sir Thomas,
who said, "I'd rather not accept a victory by accident," did not celebrate.

Though he won the first race, Lipton knew that Burton had been
out-sailed before *Resolute* broke down. (The skipper had been red-faced
after his false start and endured plenty of criticism.) When it came time
for the second race, Burton was accompanied by a local advisor—
Andrew Jackson Applegate—who would help him judge the wind and
tide. The Lipton yacht got an early advantage at the start and despite
ever-changing winds *Shamrock IV* reached the third leg of the race with
a lead. At a key moment when Burton needed more speed, the men he

assigned to handle a balloon jib tore it. When an attempt to use a spinnaker also failed, Burton improvised on the spot, sending a man up the mast to set a block and then throwing up a small sheet of canvas. This unorthodox rig—later dubbed "a fiddler's jib"—provided the extra energy the yacht needed.

The sight of *Shamrock IV* heeling through the water with her sails filled was exhilarating to see. On board the crew members scurried to heed the skipper's orders, getting soaked with spray and holding on for their lives when the bow broke the crest of a wave and then pounded into a trough. At the finish, *Shamrock IV* crossed the line more than nine minutes ahead of *Resolute*, which meant a victory even with the time penalty she carried. It was a clear win for Sir Thomas, unmarred by accident or breakdown, and he was thrilled.

On the course, most of the American spectators reacted as if they had won the race themselves. Great cheers erupted from the ships and boats gathered at the finish line and captains sounded horns, whistles, and bells. In Times Square, where hundreds gathered to watch bulletins posted by *The New York Times*, hope for Lipton had grown during the day. Interest in the race was so keen that people turned away from the bulletins about Babe Ruth's home-run crusade, which were posted on Seventh Avenue, to follow the yacht-race news as it went up on Broadway. When theater matinees ended, the sidewalk grew so crowded that police came to supervise; the finish was greeted by a huge cheer.

Aboard the *Victoria*, Thomas Lipton beamed with joy and accepted congratulations from Tom Dewar and a throng of friends that included Dr. James Donnelly's widow and son. Henry Ford led three cheers as he passed in his yacht, and Lipton asked his friends to keep secret the "fact" that Ford had rigged "a silent motor" on *Shamrock IV*. When reporters came aboard to ask questions he let himself imagine taking the America's Cup back home to Great Britain. "I have at home the greatest collection of sporting cups in the world," he said, referring to his many yachting victories in Europe. "The whole blooming lot of them I would give . . . if I could only win this tuppence ha'penny cup." Dewar told the press the victory was the "greatest thrill" of his life.

The next morning the headline that announced *Shamrock IV*'s second victory stretched across the width of *The New York Times*, just below the banner. An above-the-fold sidebar announced in large type "Sir Thomas Happy," and in the very center of the front page Lipton beamed from a photograph that showed him lifting a cup of tea. For the next few days the whole city, including many members of the New York Yacht Club, seemed delighted with the idea that Lipton, who needed just one more victory in three heats, might finally win.

Lipton didn't get to savor his victory for very long. On the day after his first and only untarnished win in twenty-one years of cup challenges, the yachts returned to the course. The Lipton team hoped for strong winds, which they believed would favor a boat designed to cross the Atlantic, but they were met in the morning by an ocean as still as a millpond and a sky covered by a blue-gray haze. Experienced locals saw the haze burning off and predicted that the heat of day would bring a modest southwest wind. The start of the race was delayed an hour and the predictions proved good. With sharp sailing Captain Burton brought *Shamrock IV* across the starting line first and seized a lead of about twenty seconds.

The spectators included a big crowd aboard the Holland-America Line's *Rotterdam* and three journalists in the cabin of the Navy dirigible C-10, which had been dispatched from its station at Rockaway Beach. Church Simpson of the Associated Press was delighted by the view from a thousand feet up: the boats looked like toys in a bathtub. Because of the haze, the highlands on the Jersey Shore appeared like mountains rising out of clouds, and Rockaway Beach, a barrier island, was just a yellow strip of sand. The two yachts with their towering sails moved more quickly than the AP correspondent expected, considering the light wind. From this perspective they were marvelously efficient machines, capturing all the power available in the breeze and cutting through the water.

When the starting gun sounded and *Shamrock IV* grabbed an early lead, the reporters in the blimp noted this in a radio message to shore. Moments later, as the yachts sliced toward a marker fifteen miles out to sea, the "great gas bag," as Simpson called it, began to leak and lose altitude. Commander A. W. Evans revved up the two propellers and called for his crew to dump weight. At first the men just dumped sand ballast into the ocean. Then they threw overboard equipment and furniture.

Evans managed to point the nose of the balloon upward and regain some altitude as he steered it toward the Rockaway base. The four crewmen and three reporters fell silent as Evans barked orders and kept them airborne until they crossed over Rockaway Beach and reached the airfield. By this time, however, Evans knew he didn't have enough control of the ship to land safely. He shifted his focus, aiming for Jamaica Bay, which was waiting on the other side of the Rockaway base. On his order the batteries for the radios and fuel for the motors were thrown overboard.

"Life preservers!" Evans shouted and all the men aboard strapped on their flotation vests. Minutes later the engines went dead and the nose of the dirigible hit the water. The bag was still buoyant enough that most of it floated, and the cabin was only partly submerged. The slow-motion crash-landing left the crew and passengers in shallow water just a hundred feet from shore. Navy launches quickly rescued them and they reached dry land wet but uninjured.

In the next day's papers, reports on the gas-bag crash matched the drama—and mild outcome—of the race that had continued on the course. *Shamrock IV* had maintained the lead she grabbed at the start and had even lengthened it on the homeward leg. She crossed the finish line first, which delighted those fans who were pulling for Lipton but didn't recall or understand the handicap system. Impressive as her performance was, the Lipton boat needed to win by about seven full minutes. Her margin was, in fact, less than half a minute, and as *Resolute* crossed the line, she captured the victory.

"If you went to a prize fight, you wouldn't want to see a knockout in the first round," said Lipton, after the race. *Resolute*'s victory did heighten interest in the race, and when she won again—evening the score at two races each—public interest soared. After poor conditions spoiled two attempted races, a sunny Sunday morning promised spectators a perfect view of what they hoped would be the decisive contest. The usual fleet of ships and boats left their docks, carrying thousands of passengers. At the same time, cars began streaming toward the New Jersey beach towns from Navesink to Asbury Park.

No cup race had ever attracted the number of day-trippers who flocked to the Jersey Shore that day. Traffic crawled along the oceanside avenues as drivers and passengers strained to look out onto the water. Picnickers jammed beaches and promontories and waved flags at every vessel that came into sight. Fluke conditions led both skippers to follow a course that brought them close to the beaches, and great shouts arose when the sails drew near the crowd. At Highland Beach many overly ambitious bathers thought they could swim close to the boats, but they tired in the swells.

Unfortunately, the conditions that made the day perfect for a record crowd—police guessed it exceeded seventy-five thousand—ruined the sailing. Time expired before either boat could finish. Many fewer were present the next day as the cup challenge was decided. By this time the men in charge of *Shamrock IV* had begun to bicker. Captain Applegate, the local advisor, fell into such a heated disagreement with the skipper, Burton—over proper tacking in the prevailing breeze—that he stayed onshore for the final race. When it was run, *Resolute* finally showed her superiority. In mild winds she managed to get more speed out of the air than *Shamrock IV* and crossed the line far ahead of the challenger. Applegate, for his part, blamed Burton and not the yacht for the loss.

Thomas Lipton's best-ever shot at lifting the cup fell one race short, and, as always, he applauded the winner and, despite his advanced age, promised another fight. He made this pledge even before the race was over, as he reminded reporters that no other British challenger had ever done as well as *Shamrock IV*. (Included in this record were four Lipton boats and ten previous British racers.)

The man's ability to find victory in defeat inspired the journalists who saw him fight deep feelings of disappointment with humor. The rumor that his yacht had been mistakenly dragging an anchor around the course "isn't true," he told them with a wink, "and you had better not print it." Three days after the race, in a cheerfully generous gesture, he invited all of New York to come aboard his yacht at a municipal pier at the Hudson River and West Ninety-seventh Street. While the owners of the winner *Resolute* refused tours and sent their yacht to Bristol, Lipton's boat was decorated with bunting and paraded smartly—with every vessel in sight tooting and honking approval—to the pier where Lipton welcomed the public himself. People responded by shouting, "Sorry you didn't win!"

Thirty-five thousand people toured *Shamrock IV* as Lipton kept her open for three days of public inspection. The city's mayor, John Francis Hyland, jumped ahead of the Lipton bandwagon to organize a Central Park concert in his honor, to be followed by a farewell banquet at the

Waldorf-Astoria. Ten thousand New Yorkers turned out for the music, and much of the city's elite attended the banquet, where the mayor himself wished Lipton "better luck next time."

So many Americans wanted to praise Lipton's sportsmanship that he had to delay his departure for London and mount a little farewell tour that included Boston, Toronto, Chicago, as well as some lesser settlements, including Sing Sing Prison, where he brought some cheer to a place that would soon set a record for executions: five in under an hour. (A few months later he sent the prisoners a silver cup to be used as a prize for their baseball league, accompanied by some cash to endow an annual gift for the winners.)

Even with all his travel, Sir Thomas failed to meet the demand for his presence. He couldn't, for example, attend a parade in Asbury Park, New Jersey, where the most popular float depicted him sipping tea aboard the *Shamrock IV*. When Lipton finally departed America, officials of the White Star Line in New York were so worried about public safety that they decided to bar visitors from the pier, and the ship *Baltic* actually left early. It's hard to imagine what precautions might have been required if he and his yacht had actually won the cup.

THIRTEEN

Sir Thomas Wins

When the triumphant loser Sir Thomas Lipton departed New York in late summer of 1920, one of America's leading political writers breathed a sigh of relief. As Charles Willis Thompson explained, the two men who sought to be the next president of the United States—Democrat James M. Cox and Republican Warren G. Harding—had barely made an impression with voters who knew "only of Sir Thomas Lipton, 'Mugsy' McGraw, Jack Dempsey and Charlie Chaplin." Perhaps with Lipton gone, he wrote, Cox and Harding would at last be heard, "if only through a megaphone afar off."

Considering all the love Lipton received during and after his cup challenge, Harding and Cox were lucky he didn't linger even longer. In 1920, Sir Thomas was a bigger attraction than all but a few actors and professional athletes, and none of the world's businessmen commanded more public admiration. People liked Lipton because, as writer P. W. Wilson said, he knew that "the aim of trade is life, not that the aim of life is trade." The man seemed to have fun with every step he took, and few could resist joining in. Wherever he went, he was met by welcoming committees and police escorts.

At home, in Great Britain, Glasgow showed its appreciation for Lipton's charitable works—he made frequent donations to aid the local poor—by giving him the Freedom of the City, the highest municipal honor. The affection shown by his hometown was real, but in Britain Sir Thomas didn't enjoy quite the same status as an icon of empire and eccentricity that he held in the States. Many British cities claimed a colorful old character who had invented something or become rich against the odds, like Lord Lever. In this context, Lipton was one of many.

Similarly, Lipton Ltd. was no longer the only chain grocer serving the British public. The firm faced rising competition from Sainsbury and from a company called Home and Colonial, which operated shops under its own name as well as Maypole and Meadow Dairy. With house brands, pleasant stores, and efficient systems for purchasing and distributing goods, these firms copied many of Lipton's original innovations and matched his prices and service. None of them, however, possessed a human billboard the likes of Sir Thomas, who continued to promote the company by simply being himself.

Lipton could always get his name in the paper with a comment about another challenge for the America's Cup, and he did this regularly. He got still more attention by keeping up a torrent of correspondence with famous and important people. When Thomas Edison turned seventy-five, Lipton's name appeared in the second paragraph of the *New York Times* article about the event, because he had sent a greeting. With a cable of condolence marking the death of Warren G. Harding, Lipton moved up to the first paragraph in the report about the president's widow.

When no milestones were at hand, Lipton could always rely on friends and colleagues to involve him in a publicity stunt like the experiment in transatlantic radio conducted by two department stores in

1922. On a Sunday evening in October he went to Louis Bamberger's department store in Newark, New Jersey, where a radio station—WOR—occupied the sixth floor. He began talking at 8:10 p.m. and soon a telegram came from Selfridges, the department store in London, where "experts agree that the voice of Sir Thomas Lipton was heard momentarily." The broadcast, which made front-page news in both countries, marked the first time a voice had been carried from America to Europe by radio waves.

Men like Bamberger and H. Gordon Selfridge chose Lipton for escapades like the radio experiment because he was so well-known and so well liked. Sophie Tucker, the great singer and comedian, used Lipton for the same reason, substituting his name for the Prince of Wales when she discovered that no one on a London stage ever used the heir apparent as the butt of a joke. (The joke had something to do with her turning Lipton away even though he offered to give her all of his tea.) Lipton was also a convenient choice for Harry Lauder, who used him as a foil when entertaining the press.

During the visit that included his Bamberger's radio address, Lipton told reporters that Lauder had dropped three pence overboard during his recent crossing aboard the *Mauretania*. The next day Lauder pretended to be angry as he corrected Sir Thomas. As he explained it, Lipton had departed for New York aboard the *Baltic* on the day Lauder sailed on the *Mauretania*. The two men had made a shilling bet on who would arrive in New York first. Lauder, worried that his ship was going too slowly, went to the engine room to investigate. It was there that he misplaced the three pence. He never found the coins and wound up paying the engineers five pounds to pour on some speed. In the end the *Mauretania* won the race and Lauder got his shilling from Lipton, although, as he admitted, "it cost me five pounds."

With the aid of men like Lauder, who was twenty years his junior,

Lipton was able to continue his boyish ways even in his mid-seventies. When heavyweight Jack Dempsey defeated Luis Firpo before ninety thousand at the Polo Grounds, Lipton was ringside with Babe Ruth, George M. Cohan, and Florenz Ziegfeld. At Coney Island, Lipton performed the honors of crowning a Mardi Gras king and queen. Others, like old friend William Love, who actually married at age seventy, changed in dramatic ways as they matured, but Lipton remained essentially the same whether at play or at work. In London, long days at the office were followed by a bite at his favorite restaurant, the Ivy, or perhaps a gathering of friends or colleagues at home. At Osidge, which now overflowed with exotic decorations—yachting trophies, ship models, and souvenirs of his travels around the world—he still lived alone, except for his Sinhalese "house-boys," who catered to his every need.

Although he continued to cultivate the public image of a strong, energetic, and fearless sportsman, in this time Lipton became privately obsessed with his own health and safety. According to one account, he had a doctor give him a thorough physical checkup every day. He fitted the house with an extensive burglar-alarm system and paid a watchman to patrol the house and grounds every night. It was about this time that Lipton also wired his house with a secret system of microphones so he could listen to his guests—mainly colleagues brought for working dinners—when he left them alone.

If Sir Thomas did feel vulnerable, it should have been mainly in his role as chairman of Lipton Ltd., which faced new challenges in the years after the war. Wages were rising steadily and prices for most foodstuffs increased as well. (One exception to the trend was the "empire tea" produced in India and Ceylon, which enjoyed favorable tariff rates.) The company suffered a ten-percent drop in profits in 1924 but was nevertheless able to pay a dividend. The next year, the balance sheet was even worse and the dividend disappeared entirely. When Sir Thomas was unable to restore it in 1926, shareholder grumbling grew into angry complaints.

The July annual meeting of Lipton Ltd. became a trial for the aging founder of the company. One stockholder claimed the company was overdrawn at its main bank and demanded to know exactly how much was owed. Others recommended he take a yearlong sabbatical on his yacht or resign altogether. When it was his turn to speak, Lipton didn't deign to defend himself. Instead, he just introduced a new deputy—a former British defense official, John Ferguson—who would lead a management committee to investigate the firm's condition. Ferguson tried to calm the raucous crowd by admitting that the outrage was justified considering that "the company's competitors continue to flourish."

The once powerful Lipton Ltd. seemed ripe for a takeover and rumors of a sale spread among financiers. Investors who circled the firm saw that the tea business was strong and that the company's six different food processing and packaging complexes were well run. The trouble was in the management of the retail shops themselves. Half of the outlets in England were actually losing money in the face of competition from cooperatives and new chains. At least one potential investor, the Dutch-based Van den Bergh organization, blamed Sir Thomas himself. He was too mercurial, too autocratic, and too old-fashioned. He had also failed to develop competent, modern-minded managers. This was true. Sir Thomas preferred to hire men who were, like him, mostly self-taught and a bit rough around the edges. The trouble was, these fellows weren't always the best-suited to work in a complex and sprawling organization of well over six hundred properties and fifteen thousand employees.

In his old age Lipton's impatience and other quirks had grown more acute. Although he spent lavishly on yachts and his own travel, he questioned the smallest expenses accrued by his men in the field and demanded that nothing of potential value—including worn-out machinery—ever be thrown away. Fear of corporate spies led him to communicate via coded telegrams, and the code, which reduced words to single letters, was changed regularly. Because of this practice, managers at his shops, factories, depots, and warehouses often had to labor over his frequent messages, which, upon translation, said something like "Sales were terrible last month. What are you going to do about it?"

The men who received the chairman's notes knew to respond quickly because the boss found it easy to fire anyone, from a clerk to a department head, on the basis of a single negative impression. Lipton's tendency to judge others harshly was applied to every rank in the company. He had so much trouble getting along with his board of directors that seven out of seven departed in a span of six years. People around Lipton became so defensive that they had trouble working together. Those who feared that the boss dispatched spies to his distant colonies were right to be suspicious. Lipton *did* ask his employees to report on each other and often based decisions concerning promotions, pay, and even dismissals on what they told him.

As chairman, and the single largest shareholder, Sir Thomas could have continued to run the company in any way he chose, and he did resist the calls for his retirement for more than six months. But while the other shareholders lacked the power to oust him, the banks that held Lipton Ltd.'s debt loans could force his hand. As the lenders lost confidence it became clear that the firm's survival would involve the founder's retirement and the sale of his stock, which would bring a new dominant owner into control.

Obvious as the case seemed to others, Lipton struggled to accept the inevitable. He still loved his work, and still believed he was the best and only man to run the company. Near the end of 1926, his friend William

Blackwood (a descendant of the founder of *Blackwood's* magazine) went to City Road for a visit. Blackwood admired Lipton because he "put on no airs whatsoever," but he also considered him "the most self-centered and self-sufficient individual I have ever met in my life." For years Sir Thomas had shown little interest in anything outside his own experiences in business, sport, and society, recalled Blackwood, and rarely much enthusiasm for learning anything new. "It was quite enough for him," noted Blackwood, "that he was Tom Lipton." But now that his realm was being reduced, Blackwood encountered a raging Lipton, who believed that his closest allies had betrayed him. Blackwood tried to cheer him up, but to no avail. As he left he saw tears in his old friend's eyes.

Soon after Blackwood's visit, the clerks and executives at the City Road headquarters noticed that Sir Thomas had stopped coming to work. At the same time, the members of a formal Committee of Inquiry, composed of outside examiners, roamed the offices, conducting interviews and checking ledgers. Anxiety reigned on every floor of the office building as every man or woman who occupied a desk feared the end of the company, or at least the end of his or her job. For a time the chairman's absence was ascribed to illness, but then his inner sanctum was invaded and all of his books, papers, and belongings were removed. On the last day of January, the very day the investigation was completed, came the announcement that Thomas Lipton had resigned "to avail himself of an immediate and well-earned rest." Given a lifetime honorary position, he might consult with Ferguson or attend a board meeting at some future date, but he no longer held any authority. Lipton Ltd. would go on without him.

By the summer, John Ferguson would identify parts of the company that were failing and beyond rescue—this included about twenty

shops—and put them up for sale. He hired many new managers, established a reserve fund, and began to put some order to a salary system that
had been governed mainly by Sir Thomas's preferences and prejudices.
Ferguson spelled out these moves at the first stockholder meeting after
Lipton's departure, and his announcement was met by cheers, applause,
and cries of "Hear, hear!" A roar of laughter concluded the meeting as
Ferguson predicted that within a year or two the stockholders would feel
the urge to shake his hand rather than throw bricks at his head.

The turnaround came much sooner than Ferguson suggested. On
Thursday, September 8, the Van den Bergh group bought Lipton's shares
and in a single stroke took control of the firm. Every stockholder saw the
value of his or her shares rise with the deal, which suddenly assured that
Lipton Ltd. had the capital to rebuild and prosper.

Approaching age seventy-nine, Sir Thomas Lipton had been dismissed from the British-based commercial empire he had begun
in his parents' tiny shop in Glasgow and built into a renowned institution. However, he still controlled his business in the United States, and
he still owned, outright, his most valuable creation—himself. Of all his
achievements, the construction of the personality called Thomas Lipton
was his most artful and enduring.

After six decades, the persona that was Sir Thomas was set and
hardened. Of course he tended to repeat his stories. And his gestures,
manners, and dress now suggested a period piece. But if he had ever
consciously played the "part" of Sir Thomas in the past, this was no
longer the case. The sailing cap and bow tie were not elements of a costume. They were his clothes. The banter and big smiles were not expressions of a role. They had become essential and authentic expressions of
a real man and they would see him through the rest of his life.

After he was banished from City Road, Thomas Lipton set up an office at Osidge, which would remain his home. But his attention turned to the place where he first tested himself and refined both his ambition and his methods—the United States. Over time Lipton had become so involved in so many aspects of life in the States that he was as much an American as a person could be without taking the oath of citizenship. Likewise, Americans were so familiar with Lipton that his name came readily to mind whenever they wanted to celebrate. When the city of Buffalo got international "radiophone" service in 1927, a local newspaper publisher placed the first call to Sir Thomas. (The event marked the transformation of an experimental marvel—instant voice communication across the sea—into a useful technology for those able to pay the $75 minimum charge. A transatlantic phone cable would not arrive until 1956.) Lipton also received the first international wireless call placed from Yonkers. The man who made it eagerly told the press that he had learned that Sir Thomas would soon depart London for New York.

As he sailed in first-class splendor aboard the SS *Leviathan*, Sir Thomas recalled crossing the Atlantic in 1866 in the wretched steerage compartment of the SS *Caledonia*. He thought about Mike McCauligan's boardinghouse in New York and Sam Clay's farm in Virginia. He also leafed through a collection of letters he had brought along for inspiration. Among them were notes from Andrew Carnegie and Herbert Hoover. Two of the letters came from Theodore Roosevelt. One was sent from the White House during his presidency. The other was written when he was a U.S. Army officer in charge of the Rough Riders. Like the logbook from the *Erin*, which had been signed by hundreds, if not thousands, of the world's most important people, the letters proved that he was fully part of a society most people couldn't imagine. For a man about to celebrate his seventy-ninth birthday with no wife or romantic partner, no children and no extended family, these talismans held extra importance. They proved that he mattered.

In New York, Sir Thomas embarked on a furious publicity campaign that began when he knotted his floppy bow tie, donned a soft fedora, and headed for Yankee Stadium and the civil ritual called Opening Day. A crowd of more than seventy-two thousand people set an attendance record and cheered the raising of the pennant won in the previous season. Mayor Jimmy Walker threw out the first pitch and then presented Babe Ruth with a loving cup. Sir Thomas took everything in from the seat next to Yankees owner Jacob Ruppert and got his picture in the next day's paper.

Everywhere he went, whether it was back to Sing Sing to visit death-row inmates or to the theater for a Will Rogers benefit show to aid victims of a recent Mississippi River flood, Lipton got the best seat, heard applause from the crowd, and received a mention in the press. (One social critic called him a champion "space getter" in a league with Bobby Jones and Knute Rockne.) At the Democratic Party's annual Jefferson Dinner, Lipton was the only foreigner to get a mention, and he applauded Governor Al Smith's presidential aspirations like a loyal Tammany man. And no matter the occasion—Mother's Day, or Lindbergh's flight across the Atlantic—Sir Thomas was sought for a comment. Mothers should be honored every day, he said, and "Lindy" was "a grand boy!"

If Lipton needed any more reassurance about his status after his setback in London, he got it on the day when the most famous flier in history returned to the United States. After watching the welcome ceremony from a favored spot on the grandstand at City Hall, Sir Thomas was one of a few dozen invited to a private dinner for Lindbergh, which took place at Harbor Hill, one of the grandest estates on Long Island.

Designed by Stanford White and built of light gray stone, Harbor Hill looked like a French château and was surrounded by several hundred acres of gardens and woods. On this night, seven thousand Japanese lanterns—red, white, and blue—hung in the trees that lined the driveway of the estate, turning the setting into a patriotic fantasy land. Floodlights illuminated the front of the enormous house, where two doormen in blue velvet suits guarded the entry. Inside, Lipton met, along with the "grand boy," some of the richest and most powerful people in the country.

No one fit more naturally into a purely social function like the Lindbergh party than Sir Thomas. He was practically allergic to talk about politics, or any other subject that might lead to discomfort, and he possessed hundreds of pleasant anecdotes, which he deployed with the same skill an actor might use to make his lines sound fresh during his hundredth performance of a play. In 1927 one of his favorites involved a performer at Coney Island who dressed like a devil, growled in some unknown language, but at an opportune moment whispered, "I worked for you at Greenock, Sir Thomas."

The stories worked whether he was chatting with millionaires on Long Island or laying a wreath at the grave of the last living Boston Tea Party "Indian" in Chicago, which was a duty he fulfilled after meeting Lindbergh. But if conversation ever lagged, Lipton could always talk about the America's Cup and his next challenge. Without fail Lipton would say that he expected to race again soon, but given the traditional negotiations and delays that were part of the process, no one really held him to these promises. The difference now was the old man's mortality. Two years beyond his admitted age of seventy-eight, Sir Thomas brought up the issue himself, promising another bid "if I am alive."

In the year after his involuntary retirement from Lipton Ltd. in London, Sir Thomas spent twice as much time in the United States as he did in Great Britain. New York was his base, and in the Roaring Twenties it was one of the most exciting cities in the world. Prohibition, hand in hand with a great expansion of both real and speculative wealth, had helped to create an atmosphere of rebellion and stylish revelry. Sir Thomas was seen about town but limited himself to admiring comments about the beautiful women he saw.

When winter settled on New York at the end of 1927, Lipton traveled across the country to California. He had been there once before, in 1914, and was stunned by the development that had taken place since. He toured Hollywood, befriended the movie mogul Louis B. Mayer, and visited the famous Breakfast Club, where members met one another with the greetings "Hello, Ham" and "Hello, Egg." Like most first-timers at the club, Sir Thomas had his photo taken astride a hobbyhorse. He was flanked by the boxer Jack Dempsey and the actor Tom Mix. In his brief talk to club members he promoted his next challenge for the America's Cup.

Years of negotiation had produced a new format for the cup races, which would feature a relatively new type of yacht called the J-class, which was designed to satisfy standards set by maritime insurers at Lloyd's of London. This agreement meant that the American boat could not be constructed with a hull that was dramatically lighter or flimsier than a *Shamrock* that had to cross the ocean. Once again Lipton turned to the designer/builder Charles Nicholson, and once again he said he hoped to win. This time he added that he believed "the Americans . . . would be just as pleased as anyone else to see me win."

Lipton was correct. The American public had watched him mount four challenges costing $10 million over thirty years' time, and he had become their sentimental favorite. In the fall of 1929 the nation's broadcasters chose him to open the Radio World's Fair at Madison Square Garden, where a glass room had been constructed to serve as a studio. Standing before the microphone, with hundreds of people gathered on the other side of the glass, Lipton addressed "my millions of friends" and imagined a day when news of *Shamrock V*'s victory would be "flashed throughout the world."

A few weeks later, Lipton was honored by a thousand members of the New York Athletic Club, where he was introduced as "the greatest sportsman in the world." As he stood to address the black-tie gathering, Sir Thomas didn't protest the honor. Rather, he returned the compliment, declaring the NYAC the greatest athletic club in the world, and held up one of Dewar's postcards bearing his likeness—and no address other than "New York City, U.S.A."—which he claimed to have received at his hotel.

It was an old gambit and from a distance could be seen as an unabashed display of self-promotion. He might as well have said, "Look how famous I am!" But coming from Sir Thomas, this bit of bragging wasn't offensive. People had long ago embraced Lipton's rise from poverty to international renown as proof of something good and optimistic. Lipton was a living symbol of hope, and as they honored, and perhaps even humored, him, people also honored their own belief in a world that rewarded talent, effort, and fair play. It didn't matter whether Lipton lived up to these ideals, although he mostly did. What mattered was that this smiling old fellow with the twinkling blue eyes and leathery brogue fit perfectly into a common fantasy of happiness and success.

Ten days after the banquet, months of bad economic news finally sparked panic selling on the New York Stock Exchange. On October 24 a record 13 million shares were sold and the market lost more than six

percent of its value. Black Thursday was followed by even worse de-
clines on Black Tuesday and a cascade of losses that heralded the Great
Depression. Many months would pass before investors, politicians, and
the public grasped the depth of the crisis. In this time, hundreds of
banks would close their doors, and unemployment rose steadily. But
amid the growing hardship, boat builders reported a surge in demand
for yachts. Super-wealthy members of the New York Yacht Club backed
a record number of boats—four in all—to compete for the honor of
defending the cup. The only other time four contenders underwent trials was in 1893.

Named *Enterprise, Weetamoe, Yankee,* and *Whirlwind,* the contenders raced through much of July and August to determine which one
would mount the defense against Sir Thomas's challenge. The trials
were held off Newport, Rhode Island, where the cup races would also
be conducted. The change from Sandy Hook was made to take advantage of the more consistent breezes. The tight competition produced a
winner—*Enterprise*—that promised almost certain victory in a series
that had been expanded to a best-of-seven.

Managed and skippered by Harold S. "Mike" Vanderbilt, *Enterprise*
was the first cup defender in thirty-seven years that had not been designed by Nat Herreshoff. Though built at the Bristol yard, she had been
drawn by architect W. Starling Burgess, who incorporated elements of
aircraft technology in his design. His most obvious innovations were a
twelve-sided aluminum mast and a triangular boom—so wide it was
nicknamed a "Park Avenue"—that was fitted with color-coded pegs and
holes to guide the crew as they attached the sail in different configura-
tions. Most of the winches used to trim the sails were located below,
leaving the deck clear of excess equipment and men. *Enterprise* and
her crew were variously described as a "robust robot" and a "box of
clockwork" that operated with astounding precision. The twenty-six

members of the crew were uniformed with different-colored sweaters and given numbers, which Vanderbilt used instead of names when he barked his commands. Whenever men switched assignments, they also exchanged their sweaters and numbers. It was a bit of a bother for the crew but spared Vanderbilt the chore of learning their names.

Against the obsessively organized and efficient *Enterprise*, Lipton offered a truly graceful and fast yacht, and a crew that included some of the best sailors in Great Britain. But although each man possessed great skill and experience, the crew was, in effect, a collection of individual stars rather than a well-coordinated team. The men of the *Enterprise*, by contrast, were so well bonded by their long battle against the other American contenders that they practically moved as a single organism. Under Vanderbilt's command they were favored by bettors two to one.

In the gloom that came with the spread of the Great Depression, widespread layoffs, factory shutdowns, and daily bank failures, Americans in the summer of 1930 turned to sport. Fans flocked to baseball parks in record numbers, and with his grand slam of victories in the four major American tournaments, Bobby Jones led a surge in the number of people playing and watching golf. Whether viewed live, or reported in the media, sports provided a kind of communal relief from the anxiety of the era. When the world's greatest yachtsman came to New York, the city sent the police boat *Macom* and the fire department band to meet him as he arrived in New York Harbor aboard the liner *Leviathan*.

While newsreel crews and print reporters recorded every moment, Lipton was greeted by the police commissioner, Grover Whalen, as well as by Boston mayor James M. Curley, who just happened to be meeting his sons, who had also sailed on the *Leviathan*. People who lined the decks of the ocean liner shouted, "We hope you win!" and applauded as Lipton waved his sailing cap. Later Lipton told Curley's daughter that the colonists dumped tea in Boston Harbor because "they found it wasn't Lipton's." He then quipped that his first challenge for the cup had been made "shortly after the great flood."

City officials had allowed two national radio networks to rig a transmitter on the *Macom*, and as the police boat pulled away from the *Leviathan*, Commissioner Whalen and Sir Thomas stepped up to the microphones. Across the nation people heard Whalen confess that his boss, Mayor Jimmy Walker, hoped that the challenger would finally win and take the cup back to Britain. "This is a different reception than when I landed here as an immigrant seventeen years old," said Lipton. "Now I'm getting to be a devil of a fellow."

The fellow, who admitted to being eighty, was actually eighty-two years old, and weary. After waving to a crowd of a thousand who greeted him at Pier 1, Lipton was taken by police motorcade to the Hotel Biltmore, where he retired early. Though overwhelmed with invitations, he would remain inside the hotel for several days, accepting well-wishers but going out only to visit his factory and office in Hoboken. People who saw him in person noticed that age had finally slowed Sir Thomas. Those looking for a signal about the man's condition also noticed that for the first time a personal physician was included in the official party that came for the races.

In Newport, Lipton would live aboard a steam yacht he had purchased at the start of the year to support the cup challenge. Originally named *Albion III*, the ship was renovated and renamed *Erin*. She flew the same green-and-gold shamrock flag that had decorated the old yacht, and the same pennant from the Royal Ulster Yacht Club. The yacht club flag featured a red hand, recalling the legend of a sailor who had won a race that required a crewman to touch the shore by cutting off his own hand and throwing it on the beach. Sir Thomas, it seemed, wasn't the only man ever to become fanatical about a boat race.

But while the original *Erin* had been a sort of floating banquet hall, where hundreds were entertained at a time, the new *Erin* was a refuge for a man who needed more rest than company. Rumors that Lipton was sick circulated around Newport and made it into the press. Sir Thomas's aides offered denials, but the quiet on the yacht and his absence from parties onshore signaled that he was no longer the man Americans thought they knew.

When the first race day finally arrived, three hundred vessels appeared, carrying spectators from New York, Boston, and other eastern ports. Although it was the largest fleet ever assembled for an America's Cup event, the actual number of people who turned out to see the race fell below the record floating crowd of fifty thousand who saw *Shamrock III* battle *Reliance* in 1903. The new location, far from New York City, had something to do with the turnout, but the smaller figure was also a result of the rising popularity of other sports. The America's Cup remained the most valuable trophy in the world, but baseball championships and boxing titles had a much broader public appeal and were more accessible. These sports were easier for the casual fan to grasp, and attracted huge radio audiences. They also presented the kinds of stories that appealed to working-class Americans in a moment of economic crisis.

From the perspective of a typical listener tuning in to the national broadcast of the 1930 America's Cup races, the only story that mattered belonged to Thomas Lipton. Everyone else involved, except for the anonymous crewmen, seemed to come from the kind of background—family money, or stock-market wealth—that made people either suspicious or resentful. Under the clouds of the Great Depression the sport itself was just too fancy and expensive to suit the average person. If not for Lipton, they might not have cared about it at all.

The public's interest in the races peaked when *Enterprise* won an easy victory in the first heat and demonstrated to the world that *Shamrock V* had no real chance of capturing the cup. The difference between the yachts was painfully clear to Lipton who put up a good front but knew what the next few contests held for him. He lost the second race by an even bigger margin and showed his temper when some British sailors came aboard the *Erin* for a visit and were too shy to speak. "What's the matter with you?" he barked. "Don't you speak English?" Such a public display of temper was uncharacteristic, and Lipton quickly apologized. However, he couldn't mask his disappointment over the prospect of yet another failed campaign.

Thanks to perfect sailing, *Shamrock V* stole the lead at the start of the third race and Sir Thomas's spirits rose. *Enterprise* caught up before they reached the halfway point of the race, and the contest seemed to be very close. Then, suddenly, the main cord securing *Shamrock V*'s sail snapped. The canvas started flapping, and some of it fell into the water. Vanderbilt noticed the breakdown and circled back to make sure no one had been injured or knocked overboard. When he was assured that everyone on the challenger was safe, he sailed on to an easy victory. As a black tugboat came to retrieve *Shamrock V*, her owner tried to encourage his friends aboard *Erin* with a few jokes and brave talk, but at least one of his guests was so disappointed she went belowdecks to cry.

Will Rogers was also disappointed. After *Shamrock V* was whipped in the third race, the great humorist used his nationally syndicated column, "Daily Telegram," to beg the American side to let Lipton win. "If Vanderbilt wants to make himself America's latest hero," wrote Rogers, "he will break a rudder or hit an iceberg with that boat of his and let that old man win. Then we will start a Vanderbilt-for-President club."

Vanderbilt didn't want to be America's hero, and he didn't want to be president. All he wanted was to win. He reached his goal with the very next race. The outcome was clear shortly after the halfway point, as *Enterprise* built a lead of more than five minutes. Lipton, who was clearly worn-out by the challenge, recognized the defeat, bowed his head, and admitted, "I will not challenge again. It's no use. We cannot win." After three decades of effort and defeat, he was through.

Minutes later, Sir Thomas managed a smile as he congratulated the winners. He knew that many people were disappointed by the outcome of the races. New Yorkers would be described in the press as "despondent," and the feeling was shared beyond the city limits. Speaking for many, a woman named Elsie Brown, in South Orange, New Jersey, wrote that she was "quite as heartbroken as Sir Thomas." But as much as he appreciated these feelings, said Lipton, "you cannot blame them [Vanderbilt and crew] for doing their very best to win."

In fact, Lipton was right. The men of the *Enterprise* were supposed to try their best, and their victory was earned fair and square. Still, many people weren't happy with the end of the story. They wanted a different conclusion. They were offered one by Will Rogers. Writing again in his daily column, Rogers called on readers to donate to a fund to buy a loving cup for Lipton "bigger than the one he would have got if he had won." Rogers volunteered New York mayor Jimmy Walker to accept the donations and present the prize. He also suggested an inscription:

> To possibly the world's worst yacht builder, but absolutely the world's most cheerful loser. You have been a benefit to mankind Sir Thomas. You have made losing worthwhile.

Across America, people who were enduring seemingly endless bad news about events and problems beyond their control—unemployment, collapsing markets, bank failures—found in Rogers's proposal a way to turn one bit of bad news around. Within days, letters arrived at Mayor Walker's office from every state in the nation. Governor Franklin D. Roosevelt sent a donation with a note that explained that Sir Thomas "and his good sportsmanship are a lesson to every American." An association of miners in Utah offered fifty pounds of silver for the cup. Former presidential candidate James Cox, whom Lipton pushed off the front page in 1920, sent five dollars, and the pastor of New York's Church of St. John the Evangelist called for a cup so big "Thomas Lipton will not be able to lift it." Not to be outdone, John R. Voorhis, the 101-year-old Grand Sachem of the Tammany Hall political club, offered the kind of gesture one might expect from an organization that seemed to operate under its own special rules.

"Why wouldn't it be a good thing to give him the real cup he wants?" asked Voorhis. As he saw it, Lipton had "earned it" through his many challenges and graceful response to defeat. Making the America's Cup a gift to him would spare New Yorkers "the expense of defending it" and reward the man's valor. Besides, added Voorhis, "wouldn't it be a shame if someone else came along and actually did win it?"

The idea of simply giving Lipton the actual America's Cup as a reward for trying never attracted much support, but the outpouring of kindness revived Thomas Lipton's flagging optimism. As he prepared to go home, he started to talk about another challenge. In a letter to Mayor Walker he said he hoped to make "another try," and promised to return within weeks to accept the loser's cup, which was already being fashioned by Tiffany's.

The Utah silver found its way into the base of the Lipton trophy, but the loving cup itself was made of eighteen-carat gold. The lid was decorated with carved shamrocks and a finial shaped like a seashell. Around the rim were inscribed the words: "In the name of hundreds of thousands of Americans and well-wishers of Sir Thomas Johnstone Lipton Bart., K.C.V.O." Below the inscription Tiffany's had decorated the face of the trophy with an image of the America's Cup.

When Lipton returned to receive his honor, he was escorted by the police to New York's City Hall, where several thousand people—those who had been unable to get tickets for the ceremony inside—cheered for him from the sidewalk. Elsewhere in New York, soup kitchens served growing numbers of hungry people and formerly employed men sold apples on street corners. Walker's administration faced complaints of corruption and soon the famous Seabury Commission would force him to testify in public. But for a moment the mayor and the people could forget their problems and the troubles that loomed on the horizon. They could focus on a man who stood for the ambition, courage, and glamour of the fast-fading past. Sir Thomas represented a happy ideal that was worth celebrating one last time.

Inside, the balcony of the ornate old city council chamber was draped in American flags. Every seat and inch of standing room was occupied, and radio reporters clustered on one side of the room, waiting to describe the event to a national network. (Four New York stations would broadcast the proceedings live.) The police department band played loud military marches.

At noon the music stopped and the crowd burst into cheers and applause as Mayor Walker and the chairman of the council led Sir Thomas to the dais. Seemingly recovered from his defeat, Sir Thomas towered over the diminutive Walker, and appeared far younger than his eighty-two years. A showman and a microphone hog, Walker recalled Lipton's valiant defeats, the suggestion made by Will Rogers (who could not attend the event), and his belief that the cup represented "the finest enthusiastic outburst of affection, admiration and esteem that any man has ever received from any people." Of course Lipton deserved it all, added Walker, because he was "the greatest sportsman of our time, and the greatest loser throughout the history of mankind."

For the first time anyone in America had ever seen, Thomas Lipton lost his composure. He stood and tried to speak. "Although I have lost," he said with his voice trembling, "you make me feel as if I had won." After a few more words, The Great Lipton turned to Walker, signaled his distress and sat down. Walker went right to the microphone.

"I'm not surprised that Sir Thomas finds it hard to speak. I sometimes do myself, though for other reasons."

Walker asked the city council chairman to finish reading Lipton's prepared remarks, which included more thanks and a bit about his determination to race again for the America's Cup. Lipton seemed to recover and when the ceremony ended and the band began to play "The Star-Spangled Banner," he started to rise. Walker urged him to remain seated. Lipton complied, but when the band then played "God Save the King," he took to his feet. When the last bars were sounded, the hall was filled with applause, which followed him outside. There the crowd of thousands cheered.

In his final public moment in New York City, Lipton had his great American victory. Two days later he boarded the *Leviathan* and crossed the ocean for the last time. In roughly seventy full years of travel on the sea—beginning with his first sailing from the Broomielaw as a cabin boy—he had seen as much of the world as any man in his generation. Along the way he had made himself into the most recognized businessman in the world and one of the great sportsmen of all time. In all of his life he had missed just two of the targets he had pursued with real vigor. One was the America's Cup, and the prize he brought home at the end of 1930 went far toward making up for this failure. The other was admission to the Royal Yacht Squadron.

Five concerted campaigns for the America's Cup on behalf of the United Kingdom, great works of charity, and invaluable service to the relationship between the Crown and the United States finally earned Sir Thomas entry to the RYS on the day he turned eighty-three years old. The honor came with the support of King George V, son of Lipton's departed friends Edward and Alexandra, as well as the British public. The decision to bring him into the club may have been helped by the passing of some of the old snobs who had blackballed Lipton in the past. It definitely signaled the start of an era when even the king's grocer could be admitted to the most exclusive club in the world. In the subsequent season at Cowes, *Shamrock V* entered all the big races. The season was a strange one. King George was aboard *Britannia* when Second Mate Ernest Friend was swept overboard and drowned. On another day three people, including a vice admiral and Lady Hulton of Lancashire, were badly burned when a motor yacht caught fire. The most important race of the regatta, the King's Cup, was won by Lipton's *Shamrock V*, which had been fitted with an aluminum mast like the one used on *Enterprise*.

Although he watched some of the racing at Cowes in the summer of 1931, Lipton was mostly absent from the social scene. Many of his friends, including Lord Dewar, had died, and others were living more quietly. Sir Thomas busied himself with work on an autobiography and the pleasant chore of giving away much of his wealth. He wrote big checks to charities serving the poor in Glasgow and other cities and gave his home in Cambuslang (Johnstone Villa) to house nurses for a local hospital. Continuing a practice begun decades earlier, he donated "Lipton Cups" to serve as prizes all over the world. Before he was done, people around the globe were racing sailboats, canoes, motorboats, and even fishing trawlers for a Lipton trophy. The prizes would keep the Lipton name alive in sport the way that his tea and grocery companies would keep it going in business.

After falling in love with the sea, and a life of adventure, Lipton had lived on a scale he could not have imagined as a boy on the Broomielaw quay. He succeeded mainly because of his intelligence, toughness, and uncanny ability to read other people. He didn't apply this talent in the pursuit of intimate relationships. Perhaps that was impossible for someone who had seen so much death and suffering in childhood. However, he did use his personal talents to understand and then meet the material needs of everyone from the women who shopped for butter and eggs on Crown Street to the kings and queens of Europe.

Lipton also benefited from both the technology and the economic climate of his time. He made his fortune in an age when the most aggressive merchants and industrialists were respected and rewarded at levels that would not be seen again until the end of the twentieth century. Wealth and great displays of wealth were regarded as Darwinian proofs of a man's natural superiority. This notion would finally recede with the Great Depression, but for as long as he lived, Thomas Lipton enjoyed almost universal admiration and avoided such "unpleasantness" as high tax rates, unions, and powerful antitrust laws.

The technologies that allowed Lipton to become a public sensation were all related to mass communications. The rise of the daily newspaper, the telegraph, photography, and, finally, radio, meant that for the first time in history, tens of millions of people who lived in far-flung places could receive the same information about the same people and events at roughly the same time. With an ever growing appetite for stories, the new media sought reports and, later, pictures that entertained and informed an increasingly literate public. And for the first time ever, a man (or woman) with the right story and the right look could use the press to become someone new.

Because the era marked the beginning of mass media, those who staked their claims in this time became archetypes. William "Buffalo Bill" Cody made long flowing hair and fringed leather synonymous with the Old West. Thomas Edison, plain and serious, set the template for inventors. And Thomas Lipton, with his athletic bearing, bright eyes, and bushy mustache taught the world what a successful British raconteur and sportsman should look like. His image, like his many stories, became so widely known that the merest sketch of a mustachioed chap in a yachting cap made people think of a cup of tea, and graceful yachts, their sails filled with the breeze, knifing through the waves.

Racing yachts occupied Lipton's imagination through the summer of 1931 as he negotiated the terms for his sixth America's Cup challenge. This time the New Yorkers offered a series of concessions that made it look as if they were trying to give Lipton better odds. They agreed to ban the aluminum mast and below-deck winches that had afforded *Enterprise* some advantage. They also planned to require that the defender be built with accommodations for a crew. For the first time, the Americans wouldn't be able to race with a vessel that would be fast in competition but useless as a practical oceangoing vessel.

The new rules would have allowed Lipton to challenge again with an updated *Shamrock V*, while the New Yorkers could have defended without necessarily building an expensive new racing freak. These changes would be good for Lipton and might reduce the cost of the great competition. But as the world descended more deeply into the worst economic crisis of modern times, the idea of conducting such a display of upper-class wealth and privilege seemed vulgar and insensitive. In the summer of 1931, as unemployment in the United States reached sixteen percent and Great Britain severed its currency from the gold standard, the challenge was set aside.

On the last day of summer, Thomas Lipton caught a cold. Unaccustomed to illness, he held to his usual schedule of work in his office at Osidge and dinner with friends in the evening. On September 30, a Wednesday, he followed up this routine with a game of billiards; the stuffed head of an elephant—tusks, trunk, and all—gazed down at the table from high on the wall. After his guests had left and the house grew quiet, Lipton retired to his bedroom. Later that night his staff found him there unconscious.

Four physicians, including the prominent Scottish surgeon Sir John Thomson-Walker, tended The Great Lipton over the next three days. He regained consciousness and for a while they hoped that his body was strong enough to recover. One of Lipton's aides told the press that the crisis had passed and, barring complications, he should recover. He died the next day, overwhelmed by a respiratory infection that could not be stopped in the age before antibiotics. He was eighty-three years old, and held a ticket to sail again to America a few days later.

Although he didn't have the comfort of family, at his death Thomas Lipton was attended by friends and received the care of doctors and servants whom he had long trusted as part of his inner circle. For a man who lived so much of his life in the public view, the response to his death was everything Lipton could have hoped for. Regrets came from mayors, governors, leaders of industry, royals, and even the president of the United States, Herbert Hoover.

Front pages around the world carried the news of Lipton's death. Although he never learned just how a big boat was sailed, and only took the wheel to have his photo taken, he was hailed as a great yachtsman as well as a philanthropist, goodwill ambassador, and self-made man. St. George's Church in Glasgow was filled with floral arrangements made to look like shamrocks, anchors, life preservers, and Irish harps. The United States Lines sent an arrangement of roses, lilies, and chrysanthemums shaped to look like the liner *Leviathan*. During the service, the minister described Lipton as an inspiring example of the Scottish virtues of determination, industry, and service. He didn't say that Sir Thomas was also a man who managed to make self-promotion and self-indulgence socially acceptable, and even admirable.

As much as any man, Thomas Lipton had lived the story of the Gilded Age. The truth of this could be seen in the crowd of nobles, wealthy men, and political leaders who filled St. George's for his memorial service, and in the throngs that waited in the rain for his cortege to pass on the way to the cemetery. A week earlier, Glasgow had been rocked by violence as unemployed workers marched to call attention to their plight. When police tried to break up the parade, a riot broke out. Cobblestones and beer bottles flew when officers with batons tried to make arrests. At the height of the battle people dropped old furniture and flowerpots from open windows, and heads were bloodied by sticks and bottles. More violent protests lay ahead for Glasgow as the Great Depression brought even more hardship. But when Sir Thomas died, the anger and resentment were set aside; people from all walks of life paid their respects. On Crown Street, poor and working-class men and women filled the sidewalk and stared from every window in a show of respect. They saw, as the hearse rolled by, the passing of a man and of an era.

Lipton's death marked the end of a time when getting rich and living with sunny extravagance made a man into a romantic hero worthy of fame and public adoration. Hard years of economic retrenchment, resentment, and recrimination were at hand. Sir Thomas Lipton would face none of it. Often blessed with good timing and good luck—except when challenging for the America's Cup—Lipton departed before the worst arrived. In his death, the great optimist had been rewarded once again.

Postscript

At the time of Sir Thomas J. Lipton's death, his friend William Blackwood described the old fellow as a soul isolated in a world of his own making. His business interests circled the globe, from London to Ceylon to America. His hobby brought him public notoriety and contact with the social elite. But these interests revealed no warm or sentimental attachments to other people. For evidence of this part of the man, of his heart, one must turn to his last will and testament.

In these documents Lipton mentions nothing about the sport he loved, the powerful people he had known, or his commercial concerns. Instead he focuses on the people he knew as a boy and served with his first shop. The poor and sick, mainly in his home city of Glasgow, received the money realized from the sale of his corporate assets. Osidge, like Johnstone Villa in Cambuslang, was turned into a charitable retirement home for nurses. The People's Palace, a cultural center for all the citizens of Glasgow, received his huge collection of trophies. His papers went to the city's other great public institution, the Mitchell Library. Lipton may have spent his entire life becoming a globe-straddling

figure, but in his death he returned to the very spot on earth where he
had begun.

L ipton's London-based grocery firm would be bought and sold several times and disappear entirely in a merger in the mid-1980s. His
tea business would be purchased by Unilever, a conglomerate founded
in 1929 with the merger of the British firm begun by William Lever and
the Dutch company Margarine Unie. Under this firm's management,
Lipton Tea would spread to more than 180 countries and become the
largest-selling tea in the world. By 2010, the brand would include scores
of products with more than $3.5 billion in annual sales, which was ten
percent of the global tea market. This business was aided by a joint
venture with PepsiCo (which marketed cold drinks such as Sparkling
Green Tea) and Starbucks for the sale of its tea in grocery stores.

With its own plantations in East Africa and a worldwide manufacturing and distribution network, Lipton is one of very few brands involved in every aspect of the tea business. (In 2010 company officials
estimated that two million people earned at least part of their income
from Lipton Tea.) This global presence invites the attention of groups
that monitor corporate environmental trade policies. Unilever, which
has been assertive in its pursuit of eco-friendly practices, pledged that
by 2015 all of its source farms for tea would qualify for certification by
the Rainforest Alliance.

Unilever's drive to make Lipton a "green" brand was matched by efforts to establish the health benefits of tea drinking. The company's
Institute of Tea is a world leader in research on the effects and possible
uses for *Camellia sinensis*. Through its sponsorship, researchers have
identified psychological, neurological, and even immune-system benefits from tea drinking.

In sport, the Lipton name survives on dozens of trophies. Yacht clubs from Sri Lanka to South Africa and British Columbia present Lipton cups to regatta winners. Among the most prestigious of the Lipton races are the contests held by the Royal Singapore Yacht Club and the San Diego Yacht Club.

The first two America's Cup challenges after Lipton's death were mounted by the famous British aviator and airplane manufacturer Thomas Sopwith. His *Endeavor* won two heats in 1934 but was then swept four in a row by the American yacht *Ranger*. Sopwith had worse luck with *Endeavor II*, which didn't win a single heat in 1937. With Sopwith's withdrawal from the competition, twenty years passed with no British yachtsman coming forward with either the desire or the money to send a big boat to Newport. Finally the hosts rewrote the rules to admit smaller and presumably less costly boats, and the series was resumed in 1958.

The new cup format produced the same old results—American victories—until 1983. In that year a swaggering Australian businessman named Alan Bond, who had already been beaten three times in a row, showed Lipton-like persistence with a fourth challenge. Bond came to America with a yacht called *Australia II*—and a golden wrench, which he promised to use to unbolt the trophy. He wrested the cup from the New Yorkers in a four-to-three series and set off decades of technological and legal controversies over the construction of cup racers and the rules of competition. Although American boats won three times after the Australian coup, since 1995 the cup has been held by winners from New Zealand (twice) and Switzerland (twice).

At the start of 2010, the Swiss defender, a team called Alinghi, faced a challenge from the BMW/Oracle team led by Larry Ellison, an American software mogul believed to be one of the richest men in the world. The races are expected to cost more than $50 million per team.

Acknowledgments

Without the kindness of friends, family, editors, agents, archivists, and other guides, no book is possible. In this case, I received above-the-call-of-duty assistance from Gordon Finlay of Bangor, Northern Ireland, who led me to archival materials and welcomed me at the Royal Ulster Yacht Club, Sir Thomas's original sailing sponsor. In Glasgow, I was fortunate to meet Fiona Hayes, Hazel McLatchie, and Irene O'Brien, who helped me understand the great city where Lipton made his start. At the Unilever corporate archive in Port Sunlight, England, Emma Burgham and Lesley Owen made it easy for me to navigate the Lipton papers. John Cooper, expert on the Anderston district of Glasgow, answered my questions with patience and good humor.

In North America, Sir Thomas found adventure and success in many regions and arenas. I was able to follow his tracks with the aid of historians Ron Seagrave and Terry Botts in Virginia, and John Palmieri and Norene Rickson at the Herreshoff Marine Museum in Rhode Island. Further aid came from the library staff of the New York Yacht Club. Unilever's Mary Pfeil (USA) and Michiel Leijnse (France) helped me understand the Lipton legacy in more than one hundred countries and offered me access to valuable historical records, photographs, and artifacts.

Copy editor Ed Cohen kindly saved me from myself without hurting my feelings, and at Riverhead Books, I received just the right amounts of encouragement, support, and prodding from Geoffrey Kloske and Laura Perciasepe, who would not be my allies but for the wisdom of my agent, David McCormick. I will always be grateful to him for putting me in such capable hands. As Sir Thomas said, "A good start is half the battle." With Geoff and Laura, I got a very good start.

Sources

The most complete record of Thomas Lipton's life, attitudes, and feelings can be found in his autobiography. The edition consulted for this book is Sir Thomas J. Lipton and William Blackwood, *Lipton's Autobiography*, New York: Duffield and Green, 1932 (cited below as *Lipton's Autobiography*).

Other comprehensive biographies used as references for this book include:

Charles T. Bateman, *Sir Thomas Lipton and the America Cup*, Edinburgh: Oliphant Anderson and Ferrier, 1903.

Robert A. Crampsey, *The King's Grocer: The Life of Sir Thomas Lipton*, Glasgow: Glasgow City Libraries, 1995.

James Mackay, *The Man Who Invented Himself*, Edinburgh: Mainstream, 1998.

Alec Waugh, *The Lipton Story*, New York: Doubleday, 1950.

ONE. GLASGOW (PAGES 1–12)

Throughout this book, details on races and the dimensions of yachts have been drawn from contemporary newspaper accounts, as well as from two authoritative sources: www.America'sCup.com, and Ian Dear, *The America's Cup*, New York: Dodd, Mead, 1980.

For diet and living conditions in Great Britain: John Burnett, *Plenty and Want: A Social History of Food in England from 1815 to the Present Day*, Hampshire, England, 1989; and "Lipton Gifts for Children," *Scotsman*, July 5, 1930.

Lipton's reference to himself as The Great Lipton noted in Mackay, *The Man Who Invented Himself*, p. 14.

For "industrial hell": http://www.glasgowmerchantcity.net/history.

Lipton's love for publicity noted in: "Sir Thomas Lipton, an International Figure," *Times* (London), October 3, 1931.

Conditions in the slums of Glasgow in 1930 are described in this classic novel of the day, A. McArthur and H. Kingsley Long, *No Mean City*, London: Transworld, 1989; also: R. H. Cage, "The Standard of Living Debate," *Journal of the Economic History Association*, March 1983, pp. 175–83; and Andrew Gibb, *Glasgow: The Making of a City*, Kent, England: Croom Helm, 1983.

For a comprehensive consideration of the Scottish intellectual tradition and its effect on America: Arthur Herman, *How the Scots Invented the Modern World*, New York: Crown, 2001; Craig Smith, "Great Reformation in the Manners of Mankind; Utopian Thought in the Scottish Reformation and Enlightenment," *Utopian Studies*, Spring 2005; and Bernard Aspinwall, *Portable Utopia: Glasgow and the United States, 1820–1920*, Aberdeen: Aberdeen University Press, 1984.

For American attitudes about Europe: Mark Rennella and Whitney Walton, "Planned Serendipity: American Travelers and the Transatlantic Voyage in the Nineteenth and Twentieth Centuries," *Journal of Social History*, Winter 2004; also: http://www.glasgowmerchantcity.net/home.htm.

For Sinclair and Speck: Mackay, *The Man Who Invented Himself*, pp. 48–50.

For the American Civil War in British eyes: Lorraine Peters, "Impact of the American Civil War on the Local Communities of Southern Scotland," *Journal of Civil War History*, vol. 49, no. 2 (2003).

For observations on conditions in nineteenth-century slums: Karl Marx, *Capital: A Critique of Political Economy*, New York: The Modern Library, 1906, p. 519; and William Logan, *The Great Social Evil: Its Causes, Extent, Results, and Remedies*, London: Hodder and Stoughton, 1871.

Ireland at the time of the famine is depicted in Thomas Keneally, *The Great Shame*, New York: Doubleday, 1999.

Two. America (pages 13–36)

Henry Fry, *The History of North Atlantic Steam Navigation: With Some Accounts of Early Ships and Shipowners*, New York: S. Low, Marston, 1896.

Robert Louis Stevenson, *The Amateur Immigrant*, Chicago: Stone and Kimball, 1895.

Paul Gottheil, "Historical Development of Steamship Agreement," *Annals of the*

American Academy of Political and Social Science, vol. 55 (September 1914), pp. 48–74.

For statistics on Castle Garden steamships and immigration: "How Steamers Are Drawn to New York," *New York Times*, February 28, 1874, p. 4.

Description of Castle Garden from "Marine Intelligence" column, *New York Times*, December 23, 1866.

For labor trends: Robert J. Steinfeld, *Coercion, Contract, and Free Labor in the Nineteenth Century*, Cambridge, England: Cambridge University Press, 2001.

For ships lost at sea: http://www.globalsecurity.org/military/systems/ship/passenger 19.htm.

For a description of lower Manhattan in the mid-1860s: "Our Dirty Streets," *New York Times*, June 5, 1865, p. 8; also: "Local Intelligence," *New York Times*, January 18, 1866, p. 8.

For sanitary conditions in nineteenth-century New York: James Joseph Walsh, *History of Medicine in New York*, New York: National Americana Society, 1919.

"New York the Unclean" is a chapter title in *The City That Was*, a study issued by the Sanitary Association in 1864.

For comprehensive information on the rise of New York in the nineteenth century: Edwin Burrows and Mike Wallace, *Gotham: A History of New York City*, New York: Oxford University Press, 1999. For a more contemporary view: Matthew Hale Smith, *Sunshine and Shadows of New York*, Hartford: J. B. Burr, 1868; also: M. H. Dunlop, *The Gilded City*, New York: William Morrow, 2000.

For a view of the South as Lipton saw it on his first visit to America: Roger L. Ransom et al., *One Kind of Freedom: The Civil War and Reconstruction*, New York: W. W. Norton, 2001.

For a biography of A. T. Stewart: "Death of A.T. Stewart," *New York Times*, April 11, 1876, p. 1.

For New York scenes throughout the nineteenth century: Allan Schoener, *New York: An Illustrated History of the People*, New York: W. W. Norton, 1998; Ralph Howar, *History of Macy's in New York*, Cambridge, Massachusetts: Harvard University Press, 1943; "Riots in Gretna," *New York Times*, October 24, 1868, p. 3; Kevin Boyle, "White Terrorists," *New York Times Book Review*, May 18, 2008, p. 24; Smith, *Sunshine and Shadow in New York*, p. 52; "The City Department Store, The Evolution of 75 Years," *New York Times*, February 12, 1933, p. 130; and "The Art Gallery," *New York Times*, April 12, 1876.

THREE. HOMECOMING (PAGES 37–57)

John McKean Thomson, *City Places*, vol. 9, no. 1, Berkeley: University of California, 1994.

A. K. Cairncross, "The Glasgow Building Industry," *Review of Economic Studies*, vol. 2, no. 1 (October 1934), pp. 1–17.

David Hounshell, *From the American System to Mass Production, 1800–1932: The Development of Manufacturing Technology in the United States* (Studies in Industry and Society), Baltimore: Johns Hopkins University Press, 1985.

Thomas P. Hughes, *American Genesis: A Century of Invention and Technological Enthusiasm, 1870–1970*, Chicago: University of Chicago Press, 2004.

Mira Wilkins, *The Free-Standing Company, 1870–1914: An Important Type of British Foreign Direct Investment*, Oxford, England: Oxford University Press, 1998.

Krishnendu Ray, "The Migrant's Table," *Economic and Political Weekly*, vol. 29, no. 31 (July 30, 1994), pp. PE86–104.

Stephen J. Nicholas, "The Overseas Marketing Performance of British Industry, 1870–1914," *The Economic History Review*, New Series, vol. 37, no. 4 (November 1984), pp. 489–506.

Charles H. Feinstein, "Pessimism Perpetuated: Real Wages and the Standard of Living in Britain During and After the Industrial Revolution," *Journal of Economic History*, vol. 58, no. 3 (September 1998), pp. 625–58.

Peter H. Lindert, "English Population, Prices, and Wages, 1541–1913," *Journal of Interdisciplinary History*, vol. 15, no. 4 (Spring 1985), pp. 609–34.

Edward Tyas Cook and Alexander Wedderburn, *The Works of John Ruskin*, Whitefish, Montana: Kessinger, 2007.

"Market System in Glasgow," *Special Consular Reports: Cottonseed Products in Foreign Countries*, U.S. Bureau of Foreign Commerce, 1908.

For "radical coffee" and other aspects of the Glaswegian diet: T. Ferguson, "Public Health in Britain in the Climate of the Nineteenth Century," *Population Studies*, vol. 17, no. 3 (March 1964), pp. 213–24.

For an understanding of cartoons in the Victorian era: David Kunzle, "The First Ally Sloper: The Earliest Popular Cartoon Character as a Satire on the Victorian Work Ethic," *Oxford Art Journal*, vol. 8, no. 1 (1985).

Telegraph/telephone information: from Francis H. Groome, *Ordnance Gazetteer of Scotland*, Glasgow: Grange, 1885.

William Alan, *The Industrial Archaeology of Northern Ireland*, Madison, New Jersey: Fairleigh Dickinson University Press, 1983.

Four. P. T. Lipton (pages 59–76)

For the stories of the Lipton name and the turkey import: Mackay, *The Man Who Invented Himself*, p. 82.

S. N. Broadberry et al., *Britain in the International Economy: 1870–1939*, Cambridge, England: Cambridge University Press, 1992.

Mary Welch, ed., *Economic Effects of Technological Advances in Agriculture*, West Lafayette, Indiana: Purdue University Press, 1990.

Michael Anderson and Donald J. Mores, "High Fertility, High Emigration, Low Nuptiality: Adjustment Processes in Scotland's Demographic Experience 1861–1914," *Population Studies*, vol. 47, no. 1 (March 1993), pp. 5–25.

Enterprise in the Provision Trade, Glasgow: Larkhall Press, May 11, 1878.

T. Ferguson, "Public Health in Britain in the Climate of the Nineteenth Century," *Population Studies*, vol. 17, no. 3 (March 1964), pp. 213–24.

For British eccentrics: Catherine Caufield, *The Emperor of the United States of America, and Other Magnificent British Eccentrics*, London: Transworld, 1982.

For Lipton's fake currency: "The Bank Note Advertisements," *The Scotsman*, April 24, 1877; "The Lipton Note," *The Scotsman*, June 21, 1877; and "At the Western Police Court," *The Scotsman*, September 15, 1877.

Lipton's poem and other promotions are noted throughout Mckay, *The Man Who Invented Himself*.

Lipton's "fairy cave" described in Waugh, *The Lipton Story*, p. 35.

Daniel Pool, *What Jane Austen Ate and Charles Dickens Knew: From Fox Hunting to Whist—The Facts of Daily Life in Nineteenth-Century England*, New York: Touchstone, 1994.

Susan Strasser, *Satisfaction Guaranteed: The Making of the American Mass Market*, Washington, D.C.: Smithsonian, 1989.

Five. The Big Cheese (pages 77–99)

The *Devonia* was described in detail in the press when she arrived in New York on her maiden voyage: "The New Steam-Ship Devonia," *New York Times*, June 20, 1877, p. 8.

"Speeding Little Yachts," *New York Times*, July 27, 1880, p. 8.

For public health and Dr. Elisha Harris: James Joseph Walsh, *History of Medicine in New York*, New York: National Americana Society, 1919.

Winifred Eva Howe, *A History of the Metropolitan Museum of Art*, New York: The Metropolitan Museum of Art, 1913.

"A Large Increase in Immigration," *New York Times*, July 1, 1880, p. 8.

"A New Batch of Mormons," *New York Times*, July 22, 1880, p. 3.

For Kelvin's telephones: Norman Lockyer, "Famous Scientific Workshops: Lord Kelvin's Laboratory," *Nature* (London), March 25, 1897, pp. 486–92.

For New York in this era: Robert A. M. Stern, Thomas Mellins, and David Fishman, *New York 1880: Architecture and Urbanism in the Gilded Age*, New York: Monacelli, 1999.

Jane Mushabac and Angela Wigan, *A Short and Remarkable History of New York City*, New York: Fordham University Press, 1999.

"A Desperate Bull Fight," *New York Times*, August 1, 1880, p. 1.

Cincinnati: A Guide to the Queen City, Washington, D.C.: Writers Program of the Works Progress Administration, 1943.

Charles Morris, *The Tycoons*, New York: Henry Holt, 2005, pp. 113–20.

Ray Stannard Barker, "Railroads on Trial," *McClure's*, November 1905–April 1906, pp. 398–400.

For Chicago and its development in the nineteenth century: Donald Miller, *City of the Century*, New York: Simon & Schuster, 1996.

Sarah Bernhardt, *My Double Life*, London: Heinemann, 1907.

For a chart showing British per capita consumption of various foods from 1860 to 1913: Roderick Flid and Donald McCloskey, *The Economic History of Britain Since 1700*, Cambridge, England: Cambridge University Press, 1994, vol. 2, p. 279.

Anna Davin, "Loaves and Fishes: Food in Poor Households in Late-Nineteenth Century London," *London History Workshop Journal*, Spring 1996, pp. 167–92.

Details of cheese making in Whitesboro, New York, are provided in the state's annual reports on agriculture, and in a letter written to the *Deseret News* of Salt Lake City by the wife of Dr. Wight's partner, found in the *Deseret Weekly* bound volume for December 1889, p. 670.

The great cheeses bestowed on presidents are noted in William Walsh, *A Handy Book of Curious Information*, Philadelphia: Lippincott, 1913, pp. 198–200.

"Fifteen Huge Cheeses," *New York Times*, October 30, 1886, p. 3.

Lipton meatpacking noted in James Savage, *History of the City of Omaha, Nebraska, and South Omaha*, Chicago: Munsel, 1894.

Lawrence H. Larson, *Upstream Metropolis*, Lincoln: University of Nebraska Press, 2007, pp. 112–18.

"The Cattle Industry," *New York Times*, September 3, 1889, p. 5.

"Armour's Beef Business," *New York Times*, December 1, 1889, p. 2.

Lipton's purchase of the Myer Packing House reported in: "Chicago Hog Business," *New York Times*, September 7, 1890, p. 13.

Charles Bushnell, "Some Social Aspects of the Chicago Stock Yards," *American Journal of Sociology*, September 1901, pp. 145–70.

SIX. TEA TOM (PAGES 101–127)

James MacAulay, *Speeches and Addresses of H. R. H. the Prince of Wales: 1863–1888*, London: John Murray, 1889.

T. Raffles Davison, *Pen-and-Ink Notes at the Glasgow Exhibition*, London: J. S. Virtue, 1888.

Anandi Ramamurthy, *Imperial Persuaders*, Manchester, England: Manchester University Press, 2003, pp. 92–100.

Manorama Savur, "Labour and Productivity in the Tea Industry," *Economic and Political Weekly*, vol. 8, no. 11 (March 17, 1973), pp. 551–59.

Facts on tea and tea history from United Kingdom Tea Council: www.tea.co.uk.

Cynthia Brandimarte, "To Make the Whole World Homelike: Gender, Space, and America's Tea Room Movement," *Winterthur Portfolio*, Spring 1995.

Anna Blair, *Tea at Miss Cranston's*, London: Shepheard-Walwyn, 1985.

Joseph M. Walsh, *Tea-Blending as a Fine Art*, Philadelphia: Henry Coats, 1894.

Brian R. Mitchell, *British Historical Statistics*, Cambridge, England: Cambridge University Press, 1988.

C. H. Denyer, "The Consumption of Tea and Other Staple Drinks," *Economic Journal*, March 1893, pp. 33–55.

Derek S. Miller, *The Making of the British Diet*, Totowa, New Jersey: Roman and Littlefield, 1976.

Robert Fortune, *Two Visits to the Tea Countries of China*, London: John Murray, 1853.

Lenox A. Mills, "Ceylon Under British Rule," *Far Eastern Survey*, October 1942, pp. 218–21.

Yasmine Gooneratne, "The Two Societies: A Study of Town Life in Nineteenth-Century Ceylon," *Historical Journal*, vol. 9, no. 3 (1966), pp. 338–59.

Sarath C. Jayawardna, "The Lipton Legacy," *Sunday Observer* (Colombo, Sri Lanka), May 27, 2001.

Bhubanes Misra, "Quality Investment and International Competitiveness: Indian Tea Industry, 1880–1910," *Economic and Political Weekly*, vol. 22, no. 6 (February 7, 1987), pp. 230–38.

George Barker, *A Tea Planter's Life in Assam*, London: Thacker, Spink, 1884.

George S. Low and Ronald A. Fullerton, "Brands, Brand Management, and the Modern Brand Manager System," *Journal of Marketing Research*, May 1994.

M. E. Chamberlain, "The Alexandria Massacre of 11 June 1882 and the British Occupation of Egypt," *Middle Eastern Studies*, vol. 13, no. 1 (January 1977), pp. 14–39.

For background on the British plantation model: L. C. A. Knowles, *The Economic Development of the British Overseas*, London: Routledge, 1924.

The Ceylon tea plantations and their development are described in John Ferguson, *Ceylon in the Jubilee Year*, London: John Haddon and Son, 1887.

Seven. Astride the World (pages 129–154)

For Indian and Ceylon tea: George Watt, *A Dictionary of the Economic Products of India*, London: W. H. Allen, 1893; Reports from the Consuls of the United States, Washington, D.C., United States Bureau of Foreign Commerce, 1892, p. 661; and Bhubanes Misra, "Quality Investment and International Competitiveness: Indian Tea Industry, 1880–1910," *Economic and Political Weekly*, February 7, 1987.

Tea quip in *American Grocer* reprinted in: "Pickings," *New York Times*, March 15, 1890, p. 4.

James Morone, "One Side to Every Story," *New York Times*, February 17, 2009, p. 33.

Mira Wilkins, *The History of Foreign Investment in the United States to 1914*, Cambridge, Massachusetts: Harvard University Press, 1989.

"Tea for Millionaires Only," *New York Times*, March 12, 1891, p. 3.

Sherrie A. Inness, *Cooking Lessons: The Politics of Gender and Food*, Lanham, Maryland: Roman and Littlefield, 2001.

Report of the Committee on Awards, World's Columbian Exhibition, Washington, D.C.: U.S. Government Printing Office, 1901.

Report of the Canadian Department of Agriculture Dairy Commissioner, 1894, Ottawa, 1895.

Anandi Ramamurthy, *Imperial Persuaders*, Manchester, England: Manchester University Press, 2003, pp. 92–100.

The Mammoth Cheese of Perth: www.urbanmarket.com/all-about-perth/past/mammoth.html.

For background on the British plantation model: L. C. A. Knowles, *The Economic Development of the British Overseas*, London: Routledge, 1924.

For Haputale's development: C. F. Gordon Cumming, *Two Happy Years in Ceylon*, Edinburgh: Blackwood, 1892, p. 328.

John Ferguson, *Ceylon in 1903*, Colombo: John Ferguson, 1903.

For Lipton's golden-tip tea sale: C. H. Denyer, "The Consumption of Tea and Other Staple Drinks," *Economic Journal*, March 1893.

Arnold Wright, *Twentieth Century Impressions of Ceylon*, London, 1907 (available in reprint from Indus Books of New Delhi).

For Sambar deer: Harry Storey et al., *Hunting and Shooting in Ceylon*, London: Longmans, Green, 1907, p. 365.

For Lipton's house at Osidge and tree house: Pamela Taylor and Joanna Corden, *A Pictorial History of Barnet, Edgware, Hadley and Totteridge*, London: Phillimore, 1994.

A. N. Wilson, *The Victorians*, New York: W. W. Norton, 2003, pp. 572–96.

Adrienne Munich, *Queen Victoria's Secrets*, New York: Columbia University Press, 1996, pp. 214–18.

"Royal Appeal for the Poor," *New York Times*, May 1, 1897, p. 9.

"£25,000 to Dine London's Poor," *New York Times*, May 18, 1897, p 7.

Elizabeth Hammerton and David Cannadine, "Conflict and Consensus on a Ceremonial Occasion: The Diamond Jubilee in Cambridge in 1897," *Historical Journal*, vol. 24, no. 1 (March 1981), pp. 111–46.

Greg King, *Twilight of Splendor*, New York: John Wiley & Sons, 2007.

"He Fed London's Poor," *New York Times*, July 11, 1897, p. 9.

For dog party and horseback banquet: *Andrew Carnegie: Gilded Age*, PBS, *The American Experience*, www.pbs.org.

"British New Year's Honors," *New York Times*, January 1, 1898, p. 3.

Eight. A Real Shamrock (pages 155–187)

"Cheap Meals for London Poor," *Public Opinion*, March 9, 1900, p. 399.

Anna Davin, "Loaves and Fishes: Food in Poor Households in Late-Nineteenth Century," *London History Workshop Journal*, Spring 1996.

For the loneliness of Princess Alexandra: Joyce Marlow, *The Oak and the Ivy*, New York: Doubleday, 1977.

Anthony Dalton and Gregory O. Jones, *Herreshoff Sailboats*, Osceola, Wisconsin: MBI, 2004.

Doug Riggs, *Keelhauled*, Newport, Rhode Island: Seven Seas Press, 1986.

Samuel Carter III, *The Boatbuilders of Bristol*, New York: Doubleday, 1970.

John H. Illingworth, *Twenty Challenges for the America's Cup*, New York: St. Martin's Press, 1968.

John Young, *Two Tall Masts*, London: Stanley Paul, 1965.

Ian Dear, *The Early Challenges of the America's Cup*, Topsfield, Massachusetts: Salem House, 1986.

For *Corsair II*: Ron Chernow, *The House of Morgan*, New York: Touchstone, 1990, p. 60.

The Herreshoffs are on vivid display in Samuel Carter III, *The Boatbuilders of Bristol*, New York: Doubleday, 1970; and in Christopher Pastore, *Temple to the Wind*, Guilford, Connecticut: Lyons Press, 2005.

The story of Howard W. Ream is from M. H. Dunlop, *Gilded City*, New York: William Morrow, 2000, pp. 127–28.

"Lord Dunraven Gives Up the Contest," *New York Times*, September 13, 1895, p. 1.

"Dunraven's Case Stated," *New York Times*, December 28, 1895, p. 6.

"Lord Dunraven's Charges Fully Disproved," *New York Times*, February 1, 1896, p. 1.

Lipton's sale and the disruption of markets noted in "Round About Europe," *New York Times*, March 13, 1898, p. 19.

"What the English Say," *New York Times*, February 1, 1896, p. 1.

For London, poverty, and the Alexandra Trust dining rooms: Arthur Henry Beavan, *Imperial London*, London: Dent, 1901.

Letters to the editor critical of Lipton's charity appeared in the *Times* (London), September 27 and October 4, 1898.

"The Prince Advises Dunraven," *New York Times*, February 5, 1896.

For Lipton coffee plantation: *Bulletin of the Pan American Union*, Washington, D.C.: Pan American Union, November 1898, p. 802.

Details concening the destruction of the *Maine* and the Spanish-American War generally: U.S. Navy, Naval Historical Center, http://www.history.navy.mil/faqs/faq71-1.htm.

The sexual content of New York media at the turn of the century is described in M. H. Dunlop, *The Gilded City*, New York: William Morrow, 2000, pp. 160–87.

"Flag for Sir Thomas Lipton," *New York Times*, July 3, 1898, p. 3.

"Wireless Telegraphy," *New York Times*, March 29, 1899, p. 1.

"The Columbia Launched," *New York Times*, June 11, 1899, p. 1.

Tom Bell, "The U.S. Boat Won the 1985 America's Cup, but Deer Isle Boys Sailed Her," *Portland Press Herald*, June 24, 2007.

"Charlie Barr, Premier of the Yachting Skippers," *New York Times*, June 4, 1905, p. 5.

"Columbia a Wonder," *New York Times*, June 26, 1899, p. 1.

"Prince Sees the Shamrock," *New York Times*, June 25, 1899, p. 3.

"Shamrock Launched," *New York Times*, June 27, 1899, p. 3.

"Cup Challengers Speed," *New York Times*, July 10, 1899, p. 1.

NINE. NEVER FEAR! (PAGES 189–225)

"Shamrock in Port After Quick Trip," *New York Times*, Aug 18, 1899, p. 1.

"Thousands See Shamrock," *New York Times*, August 20, 1899, p. 3.

"Sunday on the Shamrock," *New York Times*, September 4, 1899, p. 2.

"Shamrock's Wash Day," *New York Times*, August 21, 1899, p. 3.

"Dewey Tells His Plans," *New York Times*, July 25, 1899, p. 4.

"Sir Thomas Lipton Here," *New York Times*, September 2, 1899, p. 1.

For Lipton quotation on women: Ian Dear, *The America's Cup*, New York: Dodd, Mead, 1980, p. 82.

For Victorian attitudes on sex and romance: M. H. Dunlop, *Gilded City*, New York: William Morrow, 2000, chap. 5.

For J. P. Morgan: Ron Chernow, *The House of Morgan*, New York: Simon & Schuster, 1990, pp. 48–49; for *Corsair III*, see p. 80.

Charles B. Spahr, *An Essay on the Present Distribution of Wealth in the United States*, New York: Crowell, 1896.

"Expect Columbia to Win," *New York Times*, September 4, 1899, p. 2.

"Shamrock and Columbia" (editorial), *New York Times*, September 7, 1899, p. 6.

For recollections of *Valkyrie II*: Letter to the editor by Henry Romeike, *New York Times*, September 10, 1899, p. 9.

"Praise for Sir Thomas Lipton," *New York Times*, September 10, 1899, p. 9.

For the import of Admiral Dewey's victory: "The Meaning of the Celebration," *New York Times*, October 1, 1899, p. 20.

For Lipton's encounter with Dewey: *Lipton's Autobiography*, New York: Duffield and Green, 1932, pp. 244–45; and many other sources, most notably Waugh, *The Lipton Story*, New York: Doubleday, 1950, pp. 109–12; also "Dewey Arrives Ahead of Time," *New York Times*, September 27, 1899, p. 1.

"On the Programme Today," *New York Times*, September 29, 1899, p. 2.

For a complete account of New York's Dewey celebrations: Lewis Stanley Young, *The Life and Heroic Deeds of Admiral Dewey*, Boston: James Earl, 1899.

"Millions Welcome Him," *New York Times*, September 30, 1899, p. 4.

"Warships in Fairy Scene," *New York Times*, September 30, 1899, p. 3.

"Dewey's Tars Made Happy," *New York Times*, October 1, 1899, p. 7.

"Want Lipton in Parliament," *New York Times*, October 1, 1899, p. 11.

The quotation from the banquet is noted in Mackay, *The Man Who Invented Himself*, p. 179.

"Lipton's Is a Double Stake," *New York Times*, October 7, 1899, p. 2.

"How London Will Get the News," *New York Times*, October 4, 1899, p. 2.

"Great Excitement in London," *New York Times*, October 4, 1899, p. 3.

"First Yacht Race for Neither Boat," *New York Times*, October 4, 1899, p. 1.

"Shamrock Pleases England," *New York Times*, October 4, 1899, p. 2.

"Sermon on the Yacht Race," *New York Times*, October 16, 1899, p. 3.

Estimate of Lipton's popularity reported in "Excitement in London," *New York Times*, October 8, 1899, p. 2.

"Gambler's Boat a Trap," *New York Times*, October 8, 1899, p. 1.

"Yachts Again in a Fizzle," *New York Times*, October 13, 1899, p. 3.

"Shamrock Disabled, Loses Second Race," *New York Times*, October 19, 1899, p. 1.

"A Possible Challenger," *New York Times*, October 20, 1899, p. 3.

"The America's Cup Will Remain Here," *New York Times*, October 21, 1899, p. 1.

Some details of the final race between *Shamrock II* and *Columbia* from Christopher Pastore, *Temple to the Wind*, Guilford, Connecticut: Lyons Press, 2005, pp. 102–4.

Thomas Lipton, *Leaves from the Lipton Logs*, London: Hutchinson, 1932, pp. 243–46.

"Many See Thomas Lipton Off," *New York Times*, November 2, 1899, p. 12.

Ten. Celebrity (pages 227–255)

"British Premier's Speech," *New York Times*, November 10, 1900, p. 7.

Charles Ponce de Leon, *Self-Exposure: Human-Interest Journalism and the Emergence of Celebrity in America, 1890–1940*, Chapel Hill: University of North Carolina Press, 2002, p. 106.

"Sir Thomas Lipton's Offer Declined," *New York Times*, November 19, 1899, p. 3.

"British War Fund Increases," *New York Times*, November 28, 1899, p. 2.

For the story of Edward VII, especially his lifestyle: Theo Aronson, *The King in Love*, New York: Harper & Row, 1988; Philip Magnus, *King Edward the Seventh*, New York: E. P. Dutton, 1964; Richard Hough, *Edward and Alexandra*, New York: St. Martin's Press, 1992; and John Pearson, *Edward the Rake*, New York: Harcourt Brace Jovanovich, 1975. Also: Gordon Brooke-Shepherd, *The Uncle of Europe*, New York: Harcourt Brace Jovanovich, 1975.

For Lipton's relationship with royalty: Waugh, *The Lipton Story*, pp. 121–35.

Also: Lillie Langtry, *The Days I Knew*, North Hollywood, California: Panoply, 2005; and Paul Thompson, *The Edwardians*, New York: Routledge, 2004.

For history of the Royal Yacht Squadron: http://www.rys.org.uk/da/11662.

For Lipton's exclusion from the RYS: "Foreign News: Private Pants," *Time*, August 16, 1937.

For details on *Britannia*: *Outing, an Illustrated Magazine of Sport*, April 1901.

Lipton's letter of February 9, 1901: Public Record Office of Northern Ireland.

"New Cup Challenger Shamrock II Afloat," *New York Times*, April 21, 1901, p. 1.

For helicopter development and experiments: J. Gordon Leishman, *Principles of Helicopter Aerodynamics*, Cambridge, England: Cambridge University Press, 2006, p. 12.

"Shamrock II Defeated," *New York Times*, May 14, 1901, p. 3.

"To Remodel Shamrock II," *New York Times*, May 16, 1901, p. 6.

"Shamrock II Won Trial," *New York Times*, May 21, 1901, p. 10.

The Churchill quotation: Theo Aronson, *The King in Love*, New York: Harper & Row, 1998, p. 205.

"Shamrock II Wrecked, King Edward Aboard," *New York Times*, May 23, 1901, p. 1.

"Constitution Wrecked While on Trial Spin," *New York Times*, June 5, 1901, p. 1.

"English Are Pleased," *New York Times*, June 5, 1901, p. 2.

The "some years" quotation: Christopher Pastore, *Temple to the Wind*, Guilford, Connecticut: Lyons Press, 2005, p. 8.

"Appraisers List Lawson's Treasure," *New York Times*, October 3, 1922, p. 39.

"Lipton Starts for America," *New York Times*, August 15, 1901, p. 5.

For American reaction to Mrs. Keppel: "The Man on the Street," *New York Times*, September 8, 1901, p. 1.

"Arctic Traveler Returns," *New York Times*, September 18, 1901, p. 7.

For McKinley's assassin: website of the PBS series *The American Experience*: http://www.pbs.org/wgbh/amex/1900/peopleevents/pande16.html.

"An Anarchist Hotbed in London," *Times* (London), cable published in *New York Times*, September 11, 1901, p. 1.

"Interest in Germany Keen," *New York Times*, September 11, 1901, p. 2.

"Closing Hours at the President's Bedside," *New York Times*, September 14, 1901, p. 1.

"Hunt over Mountains for Mr. Roosevelt," *New York Times*, September 14, 1901, p. 1.

"Yacht Races Unsettled," *New York Times*, September 15, 1901, p. 9.

"Sir Thomas Is Hopeful," *New York Times*, September 27, 1901, p. 3.

"Columbia Wins by Narrow Margin," *New York Times*, September 29, 1901, p. 1.

"Erin's Narrow Escape," *New York Times*, September 29, 1901, p. 3.

"Sir Thomas Wants Wind," *New York Times*, September, 29, 1901, p. 2.

"Columbia Wins a Decisive Victory," *New York Times*, October 4, 1901, p. 1.

"The Race in Detail," *New York Times*, October 5, 1901, p. 1.

"Sir Thomas Lipton Keenly Disappointed," *New York Times*, October 5, 1901, p. 2.

Eleven. Injured by a Tea Rose (pages 257–285)

Adolph Klauber, "Of People and Things Theatrical," *New York Times*, July 20, 1902, p. 5.

"Entertainment Prepared for Summer Visitors," *New York Times*, June 29, 1902, p. 10.

"Summer Amusement Season Underway," *New York Times*, July 6, 1902, p. 9.

"Sir Thomas Lipton," *The Windsor Magazine*, November 1901, pp. 411–18.

The columnist's comments and the story of Christopher Sykes: Waugh, *The Lipton Story*, pp. 126–27.

The description of King Edward VII's attitudes, as well as the "red ink" anecdote: numerous sources, but chiefly Donald Spoto, *The Decline and Fall of the House of Windsor*, New York: Simon & Schuster, 1995.

Richard Hough, *Edward and Alexandra: Their Private and Public Lives*, New York: St. Martin's Press, 1991, pp. 226–27.

"Lipton's Automobile Wrecked," *New York Times*, August 23, 1902, p. 9.

For the development of automobile racing and its effects: Tom McCarthy, *Auto Mania*, New Haven, Connecticut: Yale University Press, pp. 8–15.

"Insane New Yorker Arrested in London," *New York Times*, August 11, 1902, p. 1.

The "unduly covetous" quotation is from Waugh, *The Lipton Story*, p. 140.

For C. Oliver Iselin: "Men and Women of the Outdoor World," *Outing* annual, 1903, p. 623.

"The Postponed Festivities," *New York Times*, June 26, 1902, p. 2.

"Coronation Honors Are Made Public," *New York Times*, June 26, 1902, p. 2.

For additional details concerning the coronation: Philip Magnus, *King Edward the Seventh*, New York: E. P. Dutton, 1964, pp. 293–99.

For Lipton's challenge, and especially the response from Iselin, Herreshoff, and others: Christopher Pastore, *Temple to the Wind*, Guilford, Connecticut: Lyons Press, 2005, pp. 1–7 and 135–44.

"Sir Thomas Lipton's *Shamrock II* Launched," *New York Times*, March 18, 1903, p. 6.

"*Shamrock*'s Defeat a Fluke?" *New York Times*, April 13, 1903, p. 3.

"Serious Accident to Shamrock III," *New York Times*, April 18, 1903, p. 9.

"The Bart's Progress," *Punch*, July 29, 1903, p. 62.

"Welcome Again to Sir Thomas," *New York Times*, June 25, 1903, p. 6.

"Mr. Morgan Home Again," *New York Times*, June 25, 1903, p. 6.

"Sir Thomas at White House," *New York Times*, June 27, 1903, p. 2.

"All Kissed Sir Thomas," *New York Times*, August 16, 1903, p. 2.

"Destroyers Crash at Naval Review," *New York Times*, August 18, 1903, p. 1.

"Storm Spreads Terror on Land and Water," *New York Times*, August 26, 1904, p. 1.

"Excursion Fleet at Race," *New York Times*, August 23, 1903, p. 3.

Wringe's quotation about Barr and *Reliance*: Pastore, *Temple to the Wind*, p. 223.

"Swift Reliance Keeps Cup Here," *New York Times*, September 4, 1903 p. 1.

"Sir Thomas Toasted at Pilgrims' Banquet," *New York Times*, September 5, 1903, p. 3.

"Sir Thomas Lipton Discharges Mr. Barrie," *New York Times*, July 2, 1902, p. 16.

"Train Kills David Barrie," *New York Times*, February 3, 1908, p. 1.

Lipton's capriciousness noted in Waugh, *The Lipton Story*, p. 230, and Mackay, *The Man Who Invented Himself*, p. 289.

Mark Twain, "Mark Twain, Able Yachtsman, on Why Lipton Failed to Lift the Cup," *New York Herald*, August 30, 1903, section II, p. 3.

"Sir Thomas Has a Happy Day Off," *New York Times*, September 7, 1903, p. 3.

"A Nation at Play," *Blackwood's Edinburgh Magazine*, January 1904, p. 21.

Twelve. Lots of Nerve, Lots of Cash (pages 287–318)

For the Irish Brigade and Arthur Lynch: Michael Davitt, *The Boer Fight for Freedom*, New York: Funk & Wagnalls, 1902, pp. 321–25.

"Boer Colonel Wins Kentucky," *Irish American*, November 30, 1901.

For Roosevelt and Arthur Lynch: Mackay, *The Man Who Invented Himself*, pp. 222–23.

For more on Lynch, see his entry in Australian Dictionary of Biography Online: http://adbonline.anu.edu.au/biogs/A100173b.htm.

"King Sees Lipton Hurt," *New York Times*, September 19, 1905, p. 5.

For Lipton's horse problem: Mackay, *The Man Who Invented Himself*, pp. 218–19.

"Horse Marines Do Exist," *New York Times*, April 27, 1913, p. F1.

Roderick Floud and Deirdre McCloskey, eds., *The Economic History of Britain Since 1700*, Cambridge, England: Cambridge University Press, 1994, pp. 275–88.

Jack S. Blocker, David M. Fahey, and Ian R. Tyrrell, *Alcohol and Temperance in Modern History*, Santa Barbara, California: ABC-Clio, 2003, p. 17.

"America's Cup Races Under the New Rules," *New York Times*, October 31, 1905, p. 10.

"Sir Thomas Guest at Beefsteak Dinner," *New York Times*, November 11, 1906, p. 6.

"Lambs Gayly Gambol for Sir Thomas Lipton," *New York Times*, November 5, 1906, p. 7.

"We Startled Lipton," *New York Times*, December 1, 1906, p. 1.

For Lipton's business growth in America: chronology provided by Unilever archive, Port Sunlight, England.

"London Smart Set Likely to Suffer," *New York Times*, May 8, 1910, p. 3.

Flight, the publication of the Aeroclub of the United Kingdom, June 12, 1909, and July 16, 1910.

"Aeroplane Accident," *Times* (London), July 13, 1910, p. 12.

"C. S. Rolls Killed by Fall of Biplane," *New York Times*, July 13, 1910, p. 1.

For Mrs. Keppel's visit to Dambetenne: Diana Souhami, *Mrs. Keppel and Her Daughter*, New York: St. Martin's Press, 1996, pp. 97–101.

For Violet's remembrance: Mitchell A. Leaska and John Philips, *Violet to Vita*, New York: Viking, 1990, p. 12.

John J. McGraw, "Giants and White Sox Praise Lipton as an Entertainer in Colombo," *New York Times*, February 22, 1914, p. S3.

The "canteen trial" was the subject of numerous articles published in the *Times* (London) between January and August 1914.

For Lipton in World War I: Thomas Lipton, *Leaves from the Lipton Log*, New York: Duffield and Green, 1932, pp. 253–58.

"Lipton Idolized by Serbs," *New York Times*, March 11, 1915, p. 3.

"Typhus in Serbia Effectively Checked," *New York Times*, June 29, 1915, p. 4.

"Americans Saved Serbia, Says Lipton," *New York Times*, July 18, 1915, p. 5.

Waugh, *The Lipton Story*, pp. 182–86.

"Sunk Either by Mine or Submarine," *Rudder*, annual, December 1919, p. 551.

"Yacht Sunk by Mine Was Lipton's Erin," *New York Times*, May 3, 1916, p. 1.

For Lauder and Lipton at the time of John Lauder's death: Mackay, *The Man Who Invented Himself*, pp. 258–59.

For Lauder during the war years: Aviel Roshwald and Richard Stites, *European Culture in the Great War: The Arts, Entertainment and Propaganda*, Cambridge, England: Cambridge University Press, 1999, p. 340; and Harry Lauder, *Between You and Me*, New York: James A. McCann, 1919, pp. 256–60.

For telephone statistics: William Gifford, *Quarterly Review*, annual, 1921, pp. 308–16.

For discussion of Lipton's cold: "*Shamrock IV* Takes Water in Brooklyn," *New York Times*, November 13, 1919, p. 15.

"Great Throng Watched Times Square Board," *New York Times*, July 21, 1920, p. 4.

"Sir Thomas Happy: Now Sees Victory," *New York Times*, July 21, 1920, p. 1.

"Reporter Describes His 3000 Foot Fall," *New York Times*, July 22, 1920, p. 2.

For Applegate's criticisms: "Applegate Tells How It Happened," *New York Times*, July 28, 1920, p. 3.

For conduct of the race, also: Jerome Brooks, *The $30,000,000 Cup*, New York: Simon & Schuster, 1958, pp. 193–205.

"*Shamrock* Skipper Discusses Defeat," *New York Times*, September 19, 1920, p. 21.

THIRTEEN. SIR THOMAS WINS (PAGES 319–346)

Charles Willis Thompson, "Paid Spellbinders and Others," *New York Times*, August 29, 1920, p. BRM6.

P. W. Wilson, "Must Old John Bill Go," *New York Times*, October 19, 1924, p. 5.

Peter Mathias, "Manufacturers and Retailing in the Food Trades," in Barry Supple, ed., *Essays in British Business History*, Oxford, England: Oxford University Press, 2001.

"Lipton's Voice by Radio from Newark," *New York Times*, October 8, 1922.

Lipton's life in his later years is described in Waugh, *The Lipton Story*, pp. 207–15.

For Lipton's frequent medical checkups, and for further recollections of Lipton's later life: Mackay, *The Man Who Invented Himself*, pp. 270–80.

R. J. Hammond, "British Food Supplies, 1914–1939," *Economic History Review*, vol. 16, no. 1 (1946), pp. 1–14.

Barry Supple, *Essays in British Business History, Economic History Society*, Oxford, England: Oxford University Press, 2001, pp. 147–160.

"Lipton Under Fire at Company Meeting," *New York Times*, July 13, 1926, p. 23.

Lipton's final years as chairman of Lipton Ltd. are described in bright detail in Waugh, *The Lipton Story*, pp. 215–23.

For Lipton's management style, see also: Robert Smallwood, *Sir Thomas Lipton, England's Great Merchant Sportsman*, monograph of The Newcomen Society, New York (undated).

William Blackwood offers his assessments and remembrances of his friend Lipton at the end of *Lipton's Autobiography*.

"The Lipton Inquiry," *Times* (London), February 1, 1927, p. 19.

"Lipton Limited Trading and Financial Position," *Times* (London), July 12, 1927, p. 21.

For Meadow Dairy purchase: "Bank Advances and Investments," *Times* (London), September 9, 1927, p. 15.

The letters Lipton carried and his desire to see the Clay farm are noted in: "Lipton Gives Order for Fifth Shamrock," *New York Times*, April 1, 1927, p. 14.

James R. Harrison, "72,000 Pack Park, Set Crowd Record As Yanks Triumph," *New York Times*, April 13, 1927, p. 20.

"Lipton, If Alive, to Challenge Again," *New York Times*, October 18, 1927, p. 24.

Clair Price, "Again Sir Thomas Launches a Shamrock," *New York Times*, April 13, 1930, p. 80.

For details on the yachts and the 1930 races: Ian Dear, *The America's Cup*, New York: Dodd, Mead, 1980, pp. 100–10; also: Laurence Brady, *The Man Who Challenged America*, Edinburgh: Birlinn, 2007, pp 207–13.

"The Business Slump and the Sports Boom," *New York Times*, September 2, 1930, p. 28.

"City Hails Lipton Here for Cup Race," *New York Times*, August 17, 1930, p. 1.

Henry R. Ilsley, "Sir Thomas Mourns Failure as Final," *New York Times*, September 19, 1930, p. 30.

Will Rogers's columns on Lipton are included in: James M. Smallwood and Steven K. Gragert, eds., *Will Rogers' Daily Telegrams*, Stillwater: Oklahoma State University Press, 1978, vol. 2, pp. 190–94, 219.

For the Voorhis proposal: "Pier Crowds Cheer as Lipton Departs," *New York Times*, September 28, 1930, p. 3.

For details of Lipton's final year and death: "Sir Thomas Lipton," *Times* (London), October 3, 1931, p. 15.

"Sir Thomas Lipton Dies at 81 in London," *New York Times*, October 3, 1931, p. 1.

"Sir Thomas Lipton Obituary," *Times* (London), October 8, 1931, p. 15.

POSTSCRIPT (PAGES 347–349)

Crystal F. Haskell et al., "The Effects of l-theanine, Caffeine and Their Combination on Cognition and Mood," *Biological Psychology*, February 2008, pp. 113–22.

Arati Kamath et al., "Antigens in Tea Beverage," *Proceedings of the National Academy of Sciences*, vol. 100, no. 10 (May 13, 2003), pp. 6009–14.

Profile of Unilever operations from the company's public affairs office.

Index

Index

ABOUT THE AUTHOR

Michael D'Antonio is the author of many acclaimed books, including *Atomic Harvest*, *Tin Cup Dreams*, *Mosquito*, *The State Boys Rebellion*, *Hershey*, and *Forever Blue*. His work has also appeared in *Esquire*, *The New York Times Magazine*, *Los Angeles Times Magazine*, *Discover*, *Sports Illustrated*, and many other publications. Among his many awards is the Pulitzer Prize, which he shared with a team of reporters for *Newsday*.

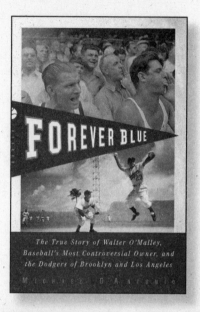

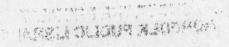